AICT 2016

The Twelfth Advanced International Conference on Telecommunications

May 22 - 26, 2016

Valencia, Spain

AICT 2016 Editors

Eugen Borcoci, University Politehncia Bucharest, Romania

Kevin Daimi, University of Detroit Mercy, USA

Tulin Atmaca, Telecom SudParis, France

Printed from e-media with permission by:

Curran Associates, Inc.
57 Morehouse Lane
Red Hook, NY 12571

Some format issues inherent in the e-media version may also appear in this print version.

Printed by Curran Associates, Inc. (2016)

International Academy, Research, and Industry Association (IARIA)
412 Derby Way
Wilmington, DE 19810

Phone: (408) 893-6407
Fax: (408) 527-6351

petre@iaria.org

Additional copies of this publication are available from:

Curran Associates, Inc.
57 Morehouse Lane
Red Hook, NY 12571 USA
Phone: 845-758-0400
Fax: 845-758-2633
Email: curran@proceedings.com
Web: www.proceedings.com

TABLE OF CONTENTS

AICT 5: ARCHITECTURES AND COMMUNICATION TECHNOLOGIES

AICT 2016

Foreword

The Twelfth Advanced International Conference on Telecommunications (AICT 2016), held between May 22-26, 2016, in Valencia, Spain, covered a variety of challenging telecommunication topics ranging from background fields like signals, traffic, coding, communication basics up to large communication systems and networks, fixed, mobile and integrated, etc. Applications, services, system and network management issues also received significant attention.

The spectrum of 21st Century telecommunications is marked by the arrival of new business models, new platforms, new architectures and new customer profiles. Next generation networks, IP multimedia systems, IPTV, and converging network and services are new telecommunications paradigms. Technology achievements in terms of co-existence of IPv4 and IPv6, multiple access technologies, IP-MPLS network design driven methods, multicast and high speed require innovative approaches to design and develop large scale telecommunications networks.

Mobile and wireless communications add profit to large spectrum of technologies and services. We witness the evolution 2G, 2.5G, 3G and beyond, personal communications, cellular and ad hoc networks, as well as multimedia communications.

Web Services add a new dimension to telecommunications, where aspects of speed, security, trust, performance, resilience, and robustness are particularly salient. This requires new service delivery platforms, intelligent network theory, new telecommunications software tools, new communications protocols and standards.

We are witnessing many technological paradigm shifts imposed by the complexity induced by the notions of fully shared resources, cooperative work, and resource availability. P2P, GRID, Clusters, Web Services, Delay Tolerant Networks, Service/Resource identification and localization illustrate aspects where some components and/or services expose features that are neither stable nor fully guaranteed. Examples of technologies exposing similar behavior are WiFi, WiMax, WideBand, UWB, ZigBee, MBWA and others.

Management aspects related to autonomic and adaptive management includes the entire arsenal of self-ilities. Autonomic Computing, On-Demand Networks and Utility Computing together with Adaptive Management and Self-Management Applications collocating with classical networks management represent other categories of behavior dealing with the paradigm of partial and intermittent resources.

We take here the opportunity to warmly thank all the members of the AICT 2016 Technical Program Committee, as well as the numerous reviewers. The creation of such a broad and high quality conference program would not have been possible without their involvement. We also kindly thank all the authors who dedicated much of their time and efforts to contribute to AICT 2016. We truly believe that, thanks to all these efforts, the final conference program consisted of top quality contributions.

Also, this event could not have been a reality without the support of many individuals, organizations, and sponsors. We are grateful to the members of the AICT 2016 organizing committee for their help in handling the logistics and for their work to make this professional meeting a success.

We hope that AICT 2016 was a successful international forum for the exchange of ideas and results between academia and industry and for the promotion of progress in the field of telecommunications.

We are convinced that the participants found the event useful and communications very open. We hope that Valencia provided a pleasant environment during the conference and everyone saved some time to enjoy the charm of the city.

AICT 2016 Chairs:

AICT General Chair
Jaime Lloret Mauri, Polytechnic University of Valencia, Spain

AICT Advisory Committee
Tulin Atmaca, Telecom SudParis, France
Eugen Borcoci, University Politehncia Bucharest, Romania
Michael D. Logothetis, University of Patras, Greece
Go Hasegawa, Osaka University, Japan
Michael Massoth, University of Applied Sciences - Darmstadt, Germany
Mariusz Glabowski, Poznan University of Technology, Poland
Djafar K. Mynbaev, New York City College of Technology - Brooklyn, USA
Dragana Krstic, Faculty of Electronic Engineering, University of Nis, Serbia
Mohammed Al-Olofi, Duisburg-Essen University, Germany
Kevin Daimi, University of Detroit Mercy, USA

4G and 5G Wireless Networks
Naceur Malouch, Sorbonne Universités, UPMC Univ Paris 06, France

AICT Industry/Research Chairs
Andres Arjona, Nokia Siemens Networks, Japan
Michael Atighetchi, Raytheon BBN Technologies-Cambridge, USA
Kazuya Tsukamoto, Kyushu Institute of Technology-Fukuoka, Japan
Guillaume Valadon, French Network and Information Security Agency, France
Sergei Semenov, Broadcom, Finland
Abheek Saha, Hughes Systique Corporation, USA
John Vardakas, Iquadrat Barcelona, Spain
Sladjana Zoric, Deutsche Telekom AG, Bonn, Germany
Hussein Kdouh, IETR, France
Yasunori Iwanami, Nagoya Institute of Technology, Japan

AICT 2016

COMMITTEE

AICT General Chair

Jaime Lloret Mauri, Polytechnic University of Valencia, Spain

AICT Advisory Committee

Tulin Atmaca, Telecom SudParis, France
Eugen Borcoci, University Politehncia Bucharest, Romania
Michael D. Logothetis, University of Patras, Greece
Go Hasegawa, Osaka University, Japan
Michael Massoth, University of Applied Sciences - Darmstadt, Germany
Mariusz Glabowski, Poznan University of Technology, Poland
Dragana Krstic, Faculty of Electronic Engineering, University of Nis, Serbia
Mohammed Al-Olofi, Duisburg-Essen University, Germany
Kevin Daimi, University of Detroit Mercy, USA

AICT Special Area Chairs

4G and 5G Wireless Networks

Naceur Malouch, Sorbonne Universités, UPMC Univ Paris 06, France

AICT Industry/Research Chairs

Andres Arjona, Nokia, Japan
Michael Atighetchi, Raytheon BBN Technologies-Cambridge, USA
Kazuya Tsukamoto, Kyushu Institute of Technology-Fukuoka, Japan
Guillaume Valadon, French Network and Information Security Agency, France
Sergei Semenov, Broadcom, Finland
Abheek Saha, Hughes Systique Corporation, USA
John Vardakas, Iquadrat Barcelona, Spain
Sladjana Zoric, Deutsche Telekom AG, Bonn, Germany
Hussein Kdouh, IETR, France
Yasunori Iwanami, Nagoya Institute of Technology, Japan

AICT 2016 Technical Program Committee

Fatma Abdelkefi, High School of Communications of Tunis - SUPCOM, Tunisia
Sachin Kumar Agrawal, Delhi Technological University (DTU), India
Mahdi Aiash, Middlesex University - London, UK
Anwer Al-Dulaimi, Brunel University - Middlesex, UK
Tiago Alves, Instituto de Telecomunicações - Instituto Superior Técnico, Portugal
Sabapathy Ananthi, University of Madras, India
Josephina Antoniou, University of Central Lancashire, Cyprus
Pedro A. Aranda Gutiérrez, University of Paderborn, Germany

Jerzy Domżał, AGH University of Science and Technology, Krakow, Poland
Roman Dunaytsev, Saint-Petersburg State University of Telecommunications, Russia
Sourav Dutta, Max-Planck Institute for Informatics, Germany
Zbigniew Dziong, École de Technologie Supérieure - Montreal, Canada
Ghais El Zein, IETR - INSA Rennes, France
Mohamed El-Tarhuni, American University of Sharjah , UAE
Anna Esposito, Second University of Naples, Italy
Mário Ezequiel Augusto, Santa Catarina State University, Brazil
Mário F. S. Ferreira, University of Aveiro, Portugal
Bruno Filipe Marques, Polytechnic Institute of Viseu, Portugal
Claudio Forlivesi, Bell Labs - IoT, Belgium
Pedro Fortuna, University of Porto, Porutgal
Paraskevi Fragopoulou, TEI of Crete, Greece
François Gagnon, Cégep de Sainte-Foy, Canada
Alex Galis, University College London, UK
Ivan Ganchev, Telecommunications Research Centre (TRC) - University of Limerick, Ireland
Seema Garg, Nokia Networks, India
Rung-Hung Gau, National Chiao Tung University, Taiwan
Bezalel Gavish, Southern Methodist University Dallas, USA
Christos K. Georgiadis, University of Macedonia - Thessaloniki, Greece
Mircea Giurgiu, Technical University of Cluj-Napoca, Romania
Mariusz Glabowski, Poznan University of Technology, Poland
Savo Glisic, University of Oulu, Finland
Claire Goursaud, INSA de Lyon - Villeurbanne, France
Roger J. Green, University of Warwick, UK
Stefanos Gritzalis, University of the Aegean, Greece
Carlos Guerrero, University of the Balearic Islands, Spain
Lei Guo, Northeastern University, China
Jan Haase, University of the Federal Armed Forces Hamburg, Germany
Ibrahim Habib, City University of New York, USA
Go Hasegawa, Osaka University, Japan
Mannaert Herwig, University of Antwerp, Belgium
Ilias Iliadis, IBM Zurich Research Laboratory, Switzerland
Muhammad Ali Imran, University of Surrey - Guildford, UK
Lucian Ioan, University: "Politehnica" of Bucharest (UPB), Romania
Jose M. Jimenez, Universidad Politécnica de Valencia, Spain
Henric Johnson, Blekinge Institute of Technology, Sweden
Branislav Jovic, Defence Technology Agency (DTA) | New Zealand Defence Force (NZDF), Auckland, New Zealand
Peter Jung, University Duisburg, Germany
Michail Kalogiannakis, University of Crete, Greece
Georgios Kambourakis, University of the Aegean - Samos, Greece
Dimitris Kanellopoulos, University of Patras, Greece
Charalampos Karagiannidis, University of Thessaly - Volos, Greece
Kashif Kifayat, Liverpool John Moores University, UK
Insoo Koo, University of Ulsan, Korea
Francine Krief, LaBRI, France
Robert Koch, University of the Federal Armed Forces / German Navy, Germany

Dragana Krstic, University of Nis, Serbia
Hadi Larijani, Glasgow Caledonian University, UK
Lazaros Gkatzikis, Huawei France Research Center, France
Hoang Le, Sandia National Laboratories, USA
Bertrand Le Gal, Institut Polytechnique de Bordeaux (IPB), France
Brian Lee, Software Research Institute, Ireland
Isaac Lera, Universitat de les Illes Balears, Spain
Keqin Li, State University of New York - New Paltz, USA
Wenzhong Li, Nanjing University, China
Jia-Chin Lin, National Central University, Taiwan, ROC
Diogo Lobato Acatauassú Nunes, Federal University of Pará - Belém, Brazil
Michael Logothetis, University of Patras, Greece
Renata Lopes Rosa, University of São Paulo, Brazil
Malamati Louta, University of Western Macedonia, Greece
Pavel Mach, Czech Technical University in Prague, Czech Republic
Juraj Machaj, University of Zilina, Slovakia
Naceur Malouch, University Pierre et Marie Curie, France
Lefteris Mamatas, University of Macedonia, Greece
Zoubir Mammeri, IRIT - Toulouse, France
Michel Marot, Telecom SudParis, France
Alexandru Martian, Politehnica University of Bucharest, Romania
Michael Massoth, Darmstadt University of Applied Sciences, Germany
Martin May, Techniclor, France
Natarajan Meghanathan, Jackson State University, USA
Jean-Marc Menaud, École des Mines de Nantes / INRIA, LINA, France
Amalia Miliou, Aristotle University of Thessaloniki, Greece
Werner Mohr, NOKIA, Munich, Germany
Lynda Mokdad, Université Paris-Est-Créteil, France
Miklós Molnár, LIRMM/University of Montpellier II, France
Philip Morrow, University of Ulster-Coleraine, Northern Ireland, UK
Ioannis Moscholios, University of Peloponnese, Greece
Petr Münster, Brno University of Technology, Czech Republic
Juan Pedro Muñoz-Gea, Universidad Politécnica de Cartagena, Spain
Masayuki Murata, Osaka University, Japan
David Naccache, Université Paris II/Ecole normale supérieure, France
Amor Nafkha, SUPELEC, France
Katsuhiro Naito, AIT Aichi Institute of Technology, Japan
Antonio Navarro Martín, Universidad Complutense de Madrid, Spain
Nikolai Nefedov, ETH Zürich, Switzerland
Petros Nicopolitidis, Aristotle University of Thessaloniki, Greece
Vladimir Nikolikj, VIP Operator, Macedonia
Serban Obreja, University "Politehnica" Bucharest, Romania
Niyazi Odabasioglu, Istanbul University, Turkey
Masaya Okada, Shizuoka University, Japan
Minoru Okada, Nara Institute of Science and Technology, Japan
Sema Oktug, Istanbul Technical University, Turkey
Edgard Luciano Oliveira da Silva, Universidade do Estado do Amazonas (UEA), Brazil
Cristina Oprea, Politehnica University of Bucharest, Romania

Further Throughput Optimization of IEEE 802.11 Networks based on Successive Interference Cancellation

Ho Chun Leung Sammy Chan

Department of Electronic Engineering
City University of Hong Kong
Hong Kong SAR
P.R. China
Email: {hcleung35-c@my. eeschan@}cityu.edu.hk

Masaki Bandai

Department of Information and Communication Sciences
Sophia University
Tokyo
Japan
Email: bandai@sophia.ac.jp

***Abstract*—Successive interference cancellation (SIC) is a physical layer mechanism, which eases packet collisions. It can decode simultaneously transmitted packets from multiple stations with different transmitting power levels, and hence raises the throughput of wireless networks. In an earlier work, the optimal throughput of an IEEE 802.11 network with SIC for a given initial contention window (W) is investigated. In this paper, we suggest that an optimal W can be chosen to further improve the optimal throughput. We re-visit the throughput optimization problem with W being another degree of freedom, and propose an efficient way to obtain the optimal W and the corresponding probability mass function of power levels. Numerical results have verified that the optimal throughput can be further increased by allowing W to be an optimal variable.**

***Keywords*—multiple-packet reception; successive interference cancellation; power randomization; 802.11.**

I. Introduction

An IEEE 802.11 wireless local area networks (WLAN) is a shared medium network. When operated in the infrastructure mode, it comprises an access point (AP) and a number of stations. Each station communicates with each other or external networks via the AP. When stations transmit packets to the AP, they need to contend for the channel. How each station accesses the channel is governed by the contention-based distributed coordinated function (DCF) [1]. Because of the shared medium, if more than one station transmits packets at the same time, a collision happens and no packet can get through the channel. It results in packet retransmissions and hence throughput degradation.

To improve such a situation, multiple packet reception (MPR) techniques can be used at the physical layer. They enable an AP to resolve collisions and successfully decode multiple packets. Early MPR techniques are based on single-user-detection approaches [2], which can only achieve low information rate. On the other hand, various multi-user-detection approaches [3] have been proposed, including zero-forcing, maximum likelihood, parallel interference cancellation and successive interference cancellation (SIC). These approaches can support high information rate.

Recently, an in-depth study of using SIC for MPR is reported in [4]. The authors propose that, when transmitting a packet, each station randomly chooses a power level so that the probability of recovering the signals during a collision can be increased. Hereafter, this scheme is referred to as SIC with power randomization (SPR). More importantly, they derive a discrete set of *optimal* power levels which only depends on the target information rate. In other words, the set of optimal power levels is applicable to any shared-medium wireless networks, irrespective of their medium access control (MAC) protocols. On the other hand, the MAC layer throughput depends on the probability mass function of the optimal power levels and the MAC protocols.

In [5], the throughput performance of an IEEE 802.11 WLAN using SPR is evaluated. Analytical expressions relating the probability mass function and throughput are obtained. Furthermore, an optimization problem is formulated to determine the probability mass function which maximizes the throughput. When solving the optimization problem, the authors of [5] assume that the initial contention window, W, is fixed and given. This limits the achievable optimal throughput. In this paper, we relax this assumption and treat W as one of the optimizing variables. As will be shown in the results, this allows an IEEE 802.11 WLAN based on SPR to achieve a higher optimal throughput.

The remainder of the paper is organized as follow. Section II briefly reviews SPR. Section III summarizes the throughput model developed in [5] for DCF with SPR. The formulation of throughput optimization is given in Section IV. Then, Section V presents our solution approach and Section VI provides some numerical results. Finally, conclusions are given in Section VII.

II. Review of SPR

First, let us consider the case of Gaussian channel. Assume that the mean and variance of the channel noise power are 0 and N_0, respectively. Let E_i be a positive real value recursively defined below,

$$E_i = \begin{cases} 0 & i = 0, \\ (2^R - 1)(E_{i-1} + N_0) & i = 1, 2, 3, \dots \end{cases} \quad (1)$$

A set $\mathcal{E}$ of discrete power levels can be formed as follows,

$$\mathcal{E} = \begin{cases} \{E_1, \cdots, E_Q\} & R < 1, \\ \{E_1, \cdots, E_i, \cdots\} & R \geq 1, \end{cases} \quad (2)$$

where R is the target information rate, and E_Q is the solution of the equation $E_Q = (2^R - 1)(E_Q + N_0)$.

Consider that two stations are transmitting packets simultaneously, with randomly chosen power E_i and E_j from $\mathcal{E}$, respectively. When receiving the combined signal due to the two packets, the AP can first decode the stronger signal while treating the weaker signal as noise. Subsequently, the AP can subtract the stronger signal from the combined signal, and then decode the weaker signal. In other words, as long as $E_i \neq E_j$, both packets can always be decoded successfully. This is because, for any E_i and E_j where $E_i \neq E_j$, (1) guarantees that the following conditions for reliable communication [6] are always satisfied:

Condition for first decoding step:

$$\log_2 \left(1 + \frac{E_i}{E_j + N_0}\right) \geq R. \quad (3)$$

Condition for second decoding step:

$$\log_2 \left(1 + \frac{E_j}{N_0}\right) \geq R. \quad (4)$$

It has been proved in [4] that (2) gives an optimal set of power levels in that sense that the achieved throughput is not worse than any other power profiles while less average power is consumed.

For the case of fading channel, each station only needs to ensure that the power levels received by the AP fall into $\mathcal{E}$. Assuming that the instantaneous channel gain g is known and that the channel is reciprocal. Then, the optimal power levels for each station are $\{E_1/g, E_2/g, \dots E_i/g, \dots,\}$.

III. Throughput of DCF with SPR

Consider an IEEE 802.11 WLAN with N stations deploying SPR with M available power levels. When transmitting a packet, each station chooses power level E_i, $i = 1, \dots, M$, with probability p_i. Assuming that, for each station, packets arrive at the MAC layer from the upper layer with rate λ (packet/second), and that each station has an infinite buffer. Let τ be the attempt rate per slot of each station. In [5], a fixed point equation relating τ to λ, W, $\{p_i, i = 1, \dots, M\}$ is derived, and is denoted in here as

$$\tau = \mathcal{F}(\tau, \lambda, W, \{p_i\}) \quad (5)$$

In other words, τ is determined by a given λ, W and $\{p_i\}$.

Packets can be successfully received by the AP if no more than two stations are transmitting simultaneously. Therefore, the average throughput T is given by

$$T = \frac{LP_1 + 2LP_2}{T_v}, \quad (6)$$

where L is the payload size of a packet, P_1 is the probability that only one station transmits, P_2 is the probability that two stations are transmitting simultaneously, and T_v is the mean slot duration after taking into account the deferment process in DCF.

Clearly, we have

$$P_1 = \binom{N}{1}\tau(1-\tau)^{N-1}, \quad (7)$$

and

$$P_2 = \binom{N}{2}\tau^2(1-\tau)^{N-2}(1 - \sum_{i=1}^{M} p_i^2), \quad (8)$$

where $1 - \sum_{i=1}^{M} p_i^2$ is the probability that the power levels of the two simultaneously transmitted packets are different.

From [1], T_v is given by

$$T_v = (1 - P_b)\sigma + P_b P_s (T_s + \sigma) + P_b(1 - P_s)(T_s + \sigma), \quad (9)$$

where $P_b = 1 - (1-\tau)^N$, $P_s = \frac{P_1 + P_2}{P_b}$, and both T_s and σ are system parameters. Since T_v is effectively a function of τ, it is thus denoted as $T_v(\tau)$. Then, overall, T is given by

$$T = LN \frac{\tau(1-\tau)^{N-1} + (N-1)\tau^2(1-\tau)^{N-2}(1 - \sum_{i=1}^{M} p_i^2)}{T_v(\tau)}. \quad (10)$$

This analytical model for throughput of IEEE 802.11 networks operating in DCF mode with SPR has been extensively validated by simulations. Its accuracy is demonstrated by the results reported in [5]. In this paper, this model is used to evaluate the throughput for a given set of network parameters.

IV. Formulation of Throughput Optimization

To optimize the throughput, the following formulations are given in [5].

A. Gaussian Channel

$$\begin{aligned} \max \quad & T \\ \text{subject to} \quad & \sum_{i=1}^{M} p_i = 1 \\ & \sum_{i=1}^{M} p_i \tau E_i \leq E_{av} \\ & 0 \leq p_i \leq 1, \quad i = 1, \dots, M. \end{aligned} \quad (11)$$

where E_{av} is the average power limit.

B. Fading Channel

For the case of fading channels, a channel gain g is associated with $\{p_i(g), i = 1, 2, \dots, M\}$, where $p_i(g)$ denotes the probability that a station transmits with power $\frac{E_i}{g}$. In order to optimize the throughput, the optimal $\{p_i(g)\}$ for each channel gain g need to be found. Since, in general, g is continuously distributed, this makes finding the exact optimal solution extremely difficult. To simplify the problem, the continuous distribution is approximated by a discrete distribution as follows. The range of g, $[0, \infty)$, is divided into H intervals according to $H+1$ thresholds $\{g^h | h = 0, \ldots, H\}$, and uniform distribution within each interval is assumed. That is

$$p_i(g) = p_i^h, g \in [g^{h-1}, g^h), h = 1, 2, \ldots, H \quad i = 1, 2, \ldots M. \tag{12}$$

Clearly, $\sum_{i=1}^{M} p_i^h = 1$, $\forall h$. Let $\Psi(g)$ is the probability density function of g. Then,

$$p_i = \sum_{h=1}^{H} p_i^h q^h, \tag{13}$$

where $q^h = \int_{g \in [g^{h-1}, g^h)} \Psi(g) dg$.

When the received power is E_i, and the channel gain is $g \in [g^{h-1}, g^h)$, the corresponding transmitted power is E_i/g with probability density $p_i^h \tau \Psi(g)$. The average transmitted power is thus given by

$$\sum_{h=1}^{H} \sum_{i=1}^{M} \int_{g \in [g^{h-1}, g^h)} (E_i/g) p_i^h \tau \Psi(g) dg = \sum_{h=1}^{H} \sum_{i=1}^{M} p_i^h \tau E_i / \bar{g}^h, \tag{14}$$

where $1/\bar{g}^h = \int_{g \in [g^{h-1}, g^h)} \frac{1}{g} \Psi(g) dg$.

Then, the throughput optimization problem can be formulated as follows,

$$\begin{aligned} \max \quad & T \\ \text{subject to} \quad & 0 \le p_i^h \le 1, \quad i = 1, \ldots, M, h = 1, \ldots, H \\ & p_i = \sum_{h=1}^{H} p_i^h q^h, \quad i = 1, \ldots, M \\ & \sum_{i=1}^{M} p_i^h \tau \le 1, \quad h = 1, \ldots, H \\ & \sum_{i=1}^{M} \sum_{h=1}^{H} p_i^h q^h = 1 \\ & \sum_{i=1}^{M} \sum_{h=1}^{H} p_i^h \tau \frac{E_i}{\bar{g}^h} \le E_{av} \end{aligned} \tag{15}$$

V. Optimal Solutions

Referring to the optimization problems given in (11) and (15), it can be seen that both are non-convex. In [5], these problems are simplified by assuming W is fixed and given. When W is given, from (5), τ is effectively a function of $\{p_i\}$. Thus, the optimal variables in (11) and (15) are $\{p_i\}$ only. As a result, the optimization problems become as follows.

Gaussian Channel:

$$\begin{aligned} \min \quad & \sum_{i=1}^{M} p_i^2 \\ \text{subject to} \quad & \sum_{i=1}^{M} p_i = 1 \\ & \sum_{i=1}^{M} p_i \tau E_i \le E_{av} \\ & 0 \le p_i \le 1, \quad i = 1, \ldots, M. \end{aligned} \tag{16}$$

Fading Channel:

$$\begin{aligned} \min \quad & \sum_{i=1}^{M} p_i^2 \\ \text{subject to} \quad & 0 \le p_i^h \le 1, \quad i = 1, \ldots, M, h = 1, \ldots, H \\ & p_i = \sum_{h=1}^{H} p_i^h q^h, \quad i = 1, \ldots, M \\ & \sum_{i=1}^{M} p_i^h \tau \le 1, \quad h = 1, \ldots, H \\ & \sum_{i=1}^{M} \sum_{h=1}^{H} p_i^h q^h = 1 \\ & \sum_{i=1}^{M} \sum_{h=1}^{H} p_i^h \tau \frac{E_i}{\bar{g}^h} \le E_{av} \end{aligned} \tag{17}$$

The problems specified by (16) and (17) are convex and can be solved readily by standard techniques. However, fixing W limits the search space and thus the achievable optimal throughput. We believe optimizing τ and $\{p_i\}$ concurrently would further enhance the optimal throughput. By allowing τ to be an optimal variable, it just means that W is not fixed anymore. Instead, W is determined by the resulting optimal τ. To this end, we propose to solve (11) and (15) exactly and efficiently in the following two-step approach. In the first step, for a fixed τ, we find $\{p_i^*\}$ and $\{p_i^{h*}\}$, which are the solutions of (16) and (17), respectively. In the second step, the optimal τ, τ^*, is obtained by a full search over the range $(0, 1)$.

Once τ^* is obtained, the corresponding W can be obtained by the following algorithm:

Algorithm 1 Finding W from τ^*

Require: $\tau^*, \lambda, \{p_i\}$
1: Let W=8
2: **repeat**
3: solve $\tau = \mathcal{F}(\tau^*, \lambda, W, \{p_i\})$
4: Set W=$W+1$
5: **until** $(\frac{\tau - \tau^*}{\tau^*} < 0.001)$
6: Obtain optimal W

Initializing $W = 8$ can reduce the computation time of Algorithm 1. Since an extremely small value for W results in many collisions, the resultant throughput would be far from optimal. Thus, $W = 8$ is sufficiently large to initialize the algorithm.

VI. Numerical Results

In this section, we compare the performance of our proposed solution approach with that of [5]. We solve the optimization problems using Matlab with the CVX optimization toolbox for various E_{av}. The fixed system parameters used are listed in Table I.

First, we consider the case of Gaussian channel. The results are shown in Figures 2-3. With $R = 1, M = 5, N = 5$, Figure 2 plots the resulting optimal throughput (normalized) versus E_{av} when the optimal W and $W = 32$ (an arbitrary

TABLE I. SYSTEM PARAMETERS

Slot Time	20 us
SIFS	10 us
DIFS	50 us
Retransmission limit	7
Data rate	11 Mbps
Control bit rate	1 Mbps
Header	576 bits
ACK	272 bits
No. of nodes	5
No. of discrete power levels	5
Packet arrival rate	250
R	2
N_0	1

chosen value) are used, respectively. Obviously, the optimal throughput corresponding to the optimal W is higher than that corresponding to an arbitrary chosen W. Since the optimal W corresponds to the most suitable back-off time, the collisions are resolved in a better manner. This results in a higher optimal throughput. Note that when E_{av} is small, the optimal throughput corresponding to optimal W and $W = 32$ are similar. According to [5], when E_{av} is small, stations are forced to use low power levels with higher probabilities so as to fulfil the constraint of average consumed power. SPR is not effective to resolve collisions under small number of power levels. Therefore, it is reasonable for the low optimal throughput occurring at small E_{av}. Apparently, this phenomenon also happens in the case of optimal W.

Figure 2 shows a similar difference between optimal W and $W = 32$ when R is increased to 2. This demonstrates that SPR is applicable when the network is operated at high information rate. Comparing with Figures 2 and 3, it can be seen that the improvement becomes less. This is due to two reasons. First, it should be recalled that the throughput under $W = 32$ is already sub-optimal; it is obtained by solving the optimization problem given by (11). Second, as explained below, the optimal W increases with N, and $W = 32$ happens to be close to the optimal W. Thus, the improvement that can possibly be made becomes smaller. However, our approach guarantees that the optimal throughput is obtained.

Table II provides more comparison results for various M and N. It can be seen that the optimal throughput is further enhanced by our approach. Note that the optimal W increases with N. As the collision probability increases with N, a larger back-off time is required to reduce the collision probability. This leads to a larger W. Therefore, a network with larger N needs a larger W to achieve the optimal throughput. As a whole, we notice that more discrete power levels provided by SPR is the ultimate key to increase the optimal throughput.

TABLE II. Comparison of optimal throughput under different network configurations for Gaussian Channel and $R = 2$

Config	Throughput (W=32)	Throughput (Variable W)	%	Optimal W
M=5, N=5	0.372	0.403	+8.49	14
M=3, N=5	0.362	0.378	+4.3	14
M=5, N=10	0.3912	0.3967	+1.4	17
M=3, N=10	0.372	0.374	+0.53	24

Then, we consider the case of Rayleigh fading channel with averaged power gain equal to 1. The whole range of

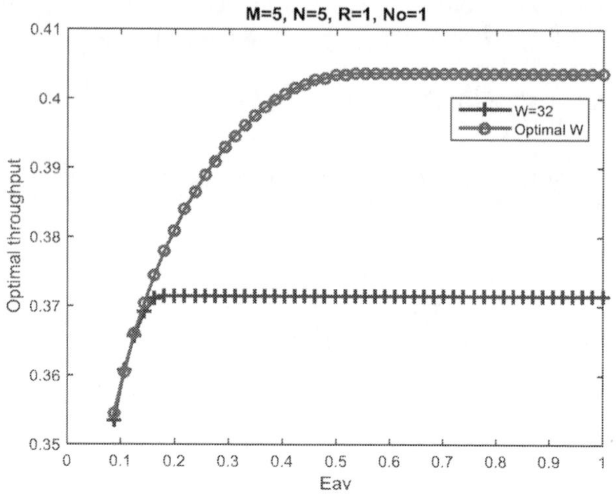

Fig. 1. Optimal throughput comparison in Gaussian channel, $R = 1, M = 5, N = 5$.

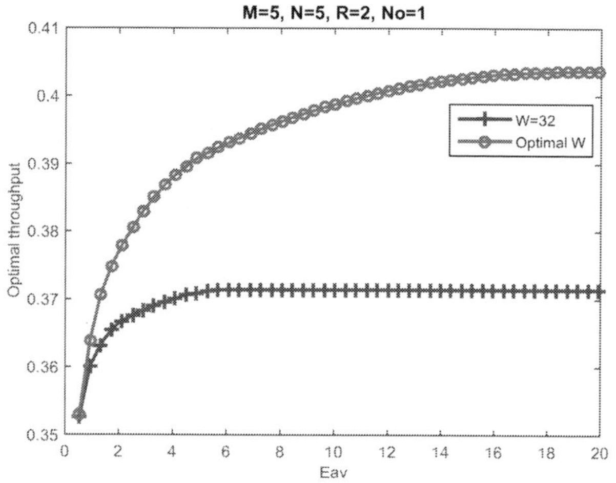

Fig. 2. Optimal throughput comparison in Gaussian channel, $R = 2, M = 5, N = 5$.

g, i.e., $[0, \infty)$, is divided into 20 intervals. Figures 4-6 plot the resulting optimal throughput versus E_{av} for both solution approaches under various system parameters. The observations are similar to that of Figures 2-3. It demonstrates the efficacy of our solution approach for the case of fading channels.

Table III provides more comparison results for various M and N. Again, similar observations as the case of Gaussian channel can be made.

TABLE III. Comparison of optimal throughput under different network configurations in fading channel with R=2

Config	Throughput (W=32)	Throughput (Variable W)	%	Optimal W
M=5, N=5	0.372	0.404	+8.6	14
M=3, N=5	0.362	0.3779	+4.4	14
M=5, N=10	0.3912	0.397	+1.5	17
M=3, N=10	0.372	0.373	+0.26	24

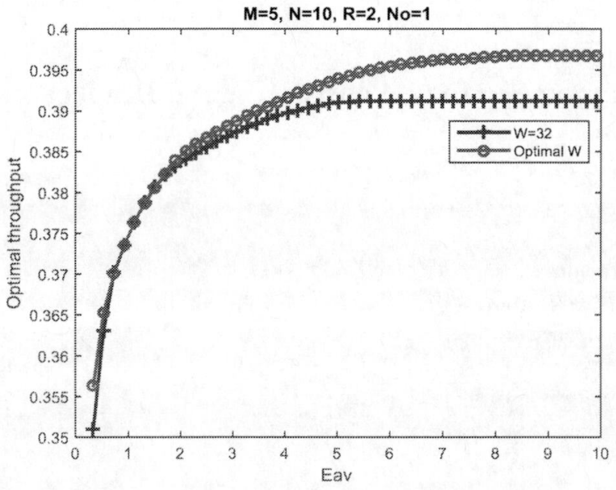

Fig. 3. Optimal throughput comparison in Gaussian channel, $R = 2, M = 5, N = 10$.

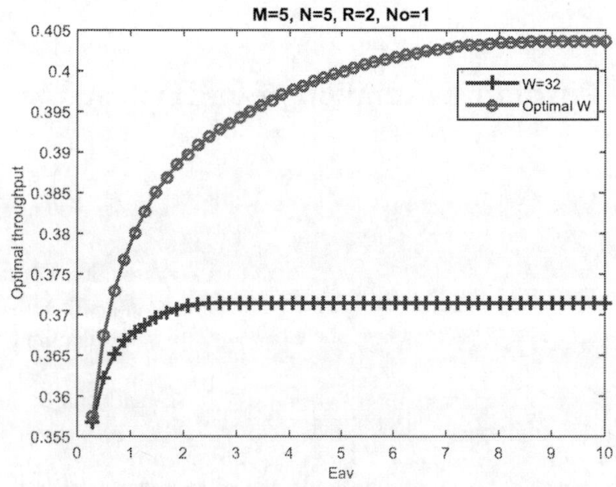

Fig. 5. Optimal throughput comparison in fading channel, $R = 2, M = 5, N = 5$.

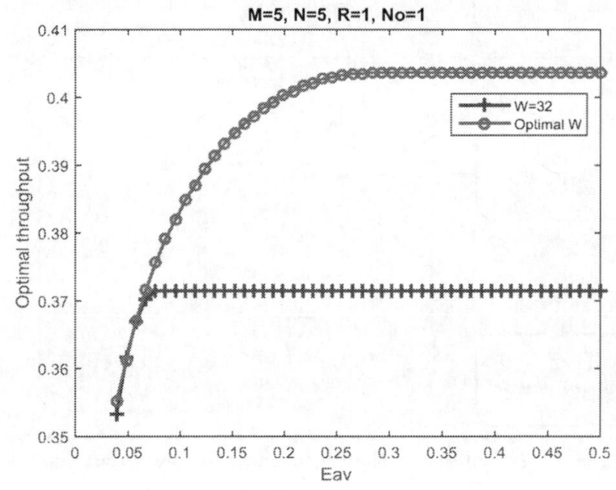

Fig. 4. Optimal throughput comparison in fading channel, $R = 1, M = 5, N = 5$.

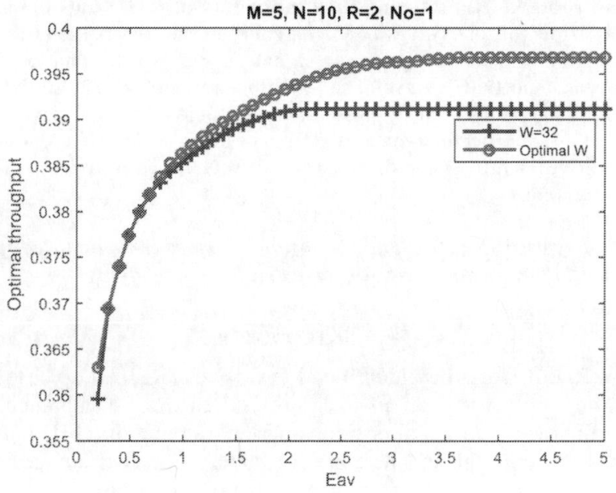

Fig. 6. Optimal throughput comparison in fading channel, $R = 2, M = 5, N = 10$.

VII. CONCLUSION

In this paper, we have suggested that the initial contention window can be suitably chosen to further optimize the throughput of IEEE 802.11 network based on successive interference cancellation with power randomization. To this end, we have formulated the optimization problem and proposed an efficient way to obtain the optimal initial contention window. We have compared the resultant optimal throughput with the approach of arbitrarily chosen window size for both Gaussian and Rayleigh fading channels. Numerical results have shown that, by allowing the initial window size to be suitably chosen, a higher optimal throughput can be achieved.

REFERENCES

[1] G. Bianchi, "Performance Analysis of the IEEE 802.11 Distributed Coordination Function," *IEEE J. Selected Area in Comm.*, vol. 18, no. 3, March 2000, pp. 535-547.

[2] J. Luo and A. Ephremides, "Power Levels and Packet Lengths in Random Multiple Access with Multiple-packet Reception Capability," *IEEE Trans. on Inf. Theory*, vol. 52, no. 2, February 2006, pp. 414-420.

[3] S. Verdu, *Multiuser Detection*, Cambridge Univ. Press, 1998.

[4] C. Xu, Li Ping, P. Wang, S. Chan, and X. Lin,"Decentralized Power Control for Random Access with Successive Interference Cancellation," *IEEE J. Selected Areas in Comm.*, vol. 31, no. 11, November 2013, pp. 2387-2396.

[5] M. Zou, S. Chan, H. Vu, and Li Ping, "Throughput Improvement of 802.11 Networks via Randomization of Transmission Power Levels", *To appear in IEEE Trans. on Vehicular Technology*, DOI: 10.1109/TVT.2015.2427845.

[6] D. Tse and P. Viswanath, *Fundamentals of Wireless Communication*, Cambridge University Press, 2005.

Position Estimation of RFID based Sensors using Surface Acoustic Wave Devices

M. Brandl, K. Kellner
Center for Integrated Sensor Systems
Danube University Krems
Krems. Austria
e-mail: martin.brandl@donau-uni.ac.at

***Abstract*—A lot of all-day products are equipped with radio frequency identification (RFID) tags to enable a wireless identification, payment etc. For a lot of applications, especially for sensor based applications, location information of the RFID based sensor tag would be helpful. In this paper an accurate and robust method for position estimation of RFID tags based on time of arrival (ToA) calculation of a transmitted broadband spread spectrum signal is described. The used spread spectrum waveforms are broadband chirp signals which are generated by passive surface acoustic wave devices (SAW). The performance of RFID position estimation under additive white Gaussian noise (AWGN) conditions was simulated.**

Keywords-RFID tags; position measurement; chirp modulation; surface acoustic wave devices; correlation.

I. INTRODUCTION

Radio frequency identification devices (RFIDs) are used in numerous applications like wireless sensors. For advanced applications the actual position and the tracking of RFID tags is from importance. Therefore for battery operated devices a method for RFID position estimation with low power consumption is needed.

The principles of position estimation of RFID devices can be separated into two groups. First, the RFID device is detected by its ID response if it is powering up in the vicinity of a base station. If a RFID device is supplied with energy from an external device, the standard ISO/IEC 14443 [1] defines that the RFID's ID will be periodically transmitted. Based on this principle, the position of a RFID device can be roughly estimated from the maximum transmission distance of the base station [2]-[4]. A second principle for position estimation is given by base station connected to a directional antenna. RFID tags are located on known position and if the base station irradiates one of the RFID tags, it powers up and transmits its ID. From the angle of the directional antenna and the known position on the RFID tags, the position of the base station can be estimated [5][6]. This principle is commonly used for moving objects like robots. In general, the performance of position estimation can be improved by using the received signal strength (RSS) as an additional indicator [7]-[9].

II. SYSTEM DESIGN

In this study, a principle for wireless position estimation of RFID devices based on time of arrival (ToA) and phase of arrival calculation of a transmitted broadband spread spectrum signal is described (Figure 1).

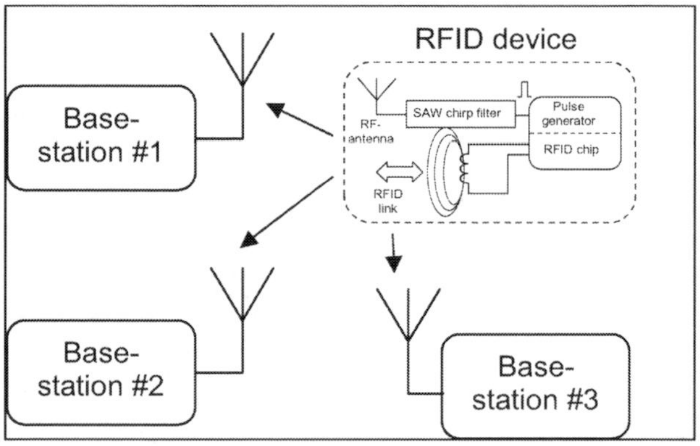

Figure 1. Transmission of linear chirp signals for ToA measurement.

The used spread spectrum waveforms are broadband chirp signals which are generated by passive surface acoustic wave devices (SAW). The impulse response of the used SAW filters is a linear chirp signal with center frequency f_0=250MHz and a bandwidth of B=80MHz (Figure 2). The chirp signal is generated by exciting the SAW chirp-filter with a short pulse which is delivered by the RFID unit on the tag. To transmit a powerful chirp signal from the RFID tag to the base stations a pulse generator based on an avalanche transistor was developed. With this method, high energy pulses with rise times below 3ns are generated for exciting the SAW chirp filter. The chirp signal is transmitted via a RF antenna to RFID base-stations which are located within the transmission range.

a)

b)

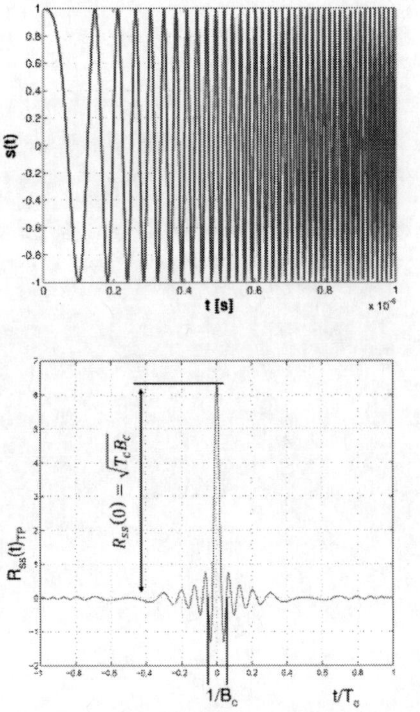

Figure 2. **a)** Linear frequency modulated signal (chirp signal), **b)** compressed chirp signal after matched filter detection (autocorrelation function ACF).

The RFID is not continuously in the active mode but will normally be set in the low-power sleep state and powered up only at scheduled time points or on request by a received wake-up signal. After wake-up, the RFID unit starts a periodic transmission of chirp signals to receivers within the transmission range. To gain a high signal to noise ratio (SNR) at the receiver a signal matched filter having the time inverse impulse response of the transmitted signal is used which generates in the matched filter case the chirp-autocorrelation function at the output with a compression gain proportional to the time-bandwidth product of the chirp (Figure 2b).

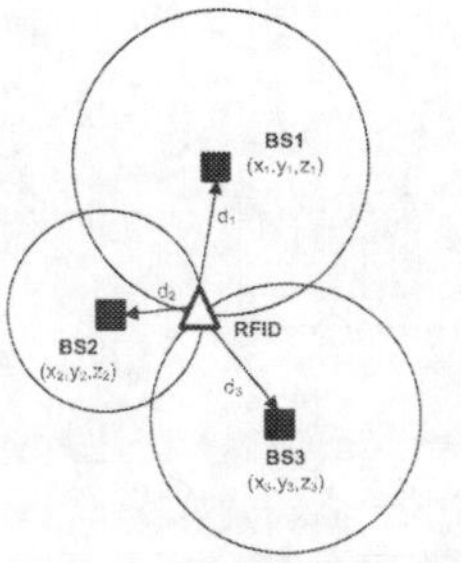

$$d1 = c\Delta t_{12} = \sqrt{(x_1 - x)^2 + (y_1 - y)^2 + (z_1 - z)^2}$$
$$d2 = c\Delta t_{23} = \sqrt{(x_2 - x)^2 + (y_2 - y)^2 + (z_2 - z)^2}$$
$$d3 = c\Delta t_{31} = \sqrt{(x_3 - x)^2 + (y_3 - y)^2 + (z_3 - z)^2}$$

Figure 3. Trilateration principle for 3D RIFD position estimation.

The position estimation is done by trilateration [1-3] where the time of arrival differences of the chirp signals at the receivers is calculated (Figure 3). If the position of more than none RFID tag should be estimated, each RFID transmits its unique code for separation. The coding of the transmitted chirp signals is done by pulse position modulation where the chirps are located in different time slots.

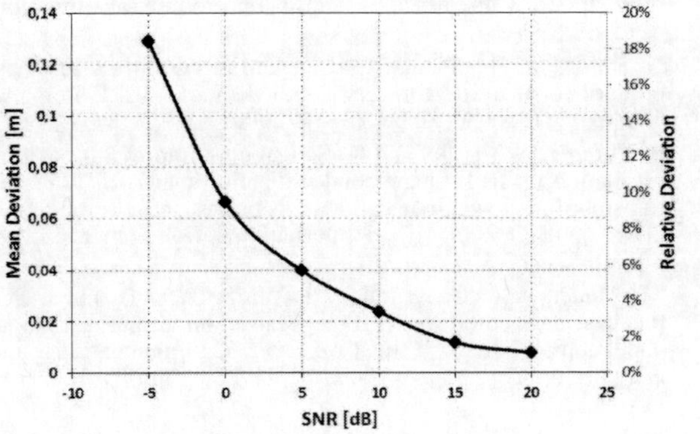

Figure 4. Mean accuracy of the RFID position estimation under AWGN conditions. N = 100.

The localization accuracy of the proposed method was determined under the assumption of an AWGN (additive white Gaussian noise) transmission channel where the received signal is corrupted with noise. The accuracy of position estimation based on chirp signals under LOS conditions is mainly given by the peak amplitude of the chirp ACF and the noise on the transmission channel. The simulation results for the accuracy of position estimation for different SNR values are depicted in Figure 4. It is shown that for SNR values above 10dB the position can be estimated with an error below 2%.

III. Conclusion

An accurate and power-saving principle for wireless position estimation of RFID devices was proposed. For correlative signal processing with a high immunity against interference in the transmission channel, linear chirp signals for locating RFID devices are used. The signal generation is carried out on the RFID tag by triggering a SAW-based chirp filter with short and broadband pulses. Several simulations of the chirp-based position estimation method under AWGN conditions underlie the accuracy and robustness of the proposed principle. Further simulations will be done under AWGN and indoor situations. The proposed position estimation principle should also be compared to different existing methods.

Acknowledgment

The authors thank the government of Lower Austria for funding this work and the European Commission (EFRE) for supporting our activities under project ID no. WST3-T-91/026-2012.

REFERENCES

[1] ISO14443. Available: http://www.openpcd.org/ISO14443, accessed: 08 March 2016.

[2] M. Bouet, and L. A. dos Santos, "RFID tags: Positioning principles and localization techniques," In Wireless Days, 2008. WD '08. 1st IFIP, pp. 1–5.

[3] C. Wang, H. Wu, and N.F. Tzeng, "RFID-based 3-D positioning schemes," In IEEE INFOCOM 2007. 26th IEEE International Conference on Computer Communications, pp. 1235–1243.

[4] N. Bulusu, J. Heidemann, and D. Estrin, "GPS-less low-cost outdoor localization for very small devices," IEEE Personal Communications, 7(5), pp. 28–34, 2000.

[5] P. Youngsu, W. L. Je, and K. SangWoo, "Improving position estimation on RFID tag floor localization using RFID reader transmission power control," In Robotics and Biomimetics, 2008. ROBIO 2008. IEEE International Conference on, pp. 1716–1721.

[6] M. Bouet, and G. Pujolle, "L-VIRT: A 3-D range-free localization method for RFID tags based on virtual landmarks and mobile readers," In Consumer Communications and Networking Conference, 2009. CCNC 2009. 6th IEEE, pp. 1–5.

[7] F. Manzoor, H. Yi, and K. Menzel, "Passive RFID-based indoor positioning system: an algorithmic approach," In RFID-Technology and Applications (RFID-TA) 2010. IEEE International Conference on, pp. 112–117.

[8] H. Koyuncu, and S. H. Yang, "A survey of indoor positioning and object locating systems," IJCSNS International Journal of Computer Science and Network Security, 10(5), pp. 121–128, 2010.

[9] H. Liu, H. Darabi, P. Banerjee, J. Liu, "Survey of wireless indoor positioning techniques and systems," IEEE Transactions on Systems, Man and Cybernetics, Part C (Applications and Reviews), 37(6), pp. 1067–1080, 2007.

A Novel Unambiguous CBOC Correlation Function With an Improved Main-Peak

Keunhong Chae and Seokho Yoon†
College of Information and Communication Engineering, Sungkyunkwan University, Suwon, Korea
†Corresponding author (Email: syoon@skku.edu)

***Abstract*—Conventionally, the design of a correlation function for unambiguous tracking of composite binary offset carrier (CBOC) signals has focused on only the elimination of the side-peaks causing the ambiguity in tracking without considering the loss in height and sharpness of the main-peak during the elimination process, thus resulting in a worse tracking performance compared with that corresponding to the CBOC-autocorrelation function. In this paper, we propose a novel correlation function with no side-peaks *and* a main-peak that is higher and sharper than those of the conventional correlation functions including the CBOC-autocorrelation function, thus enabling us to have not only unambiguity in tracking but also a better tracking performance over that of the CBOC-autocorrelation function. We first split the CBOC sub-carrier into multiple partial sub-carriers and correlate each of them with the received signal, yielding partial correlations. Then, we combine the partial correlations in a specialized way, where the side-peaks are canceled out and the main-peak becomes higher and sharper than that of the CBOC-autocorrelation function. Finally, the proposed correlation function is shown to have no side-peaks and to provide a better tracking performance than those of the conventional correlation functions including the CBOC-autocorrelation function.**

Keywords–Composite binary offset carrier; Tracking ambiguity; Galileo; global navigation satellite system;

I. INTRODUCTION

Recently, various global navigation satellite systems (GNSSs) have been developed due to increasing demands for location-based service [1]. Galileo is the GNSS developed by European Space Agency and is now operating with twelve satellites including six satellites launched in 2015 [2]. In Galileo, CBOC signals have been employed in E1 band to provide more precise location service than that of the conventional GNSSs: The CBOC signal provides an improved signal tracking performance compared with the phase shift keying (PSK) signals of the conventional global positioning system (GPS) due to its sharper correlation main-peak [3]. In addition, the CBOC signal enables Galileo to share the frequency band with GPS. The CBOC signal is generated by multiplying a pseudorandom noise (PRN) code and a CBOC sub-carrier obtained from a weighted sum of two sine-phased BOC sub-carriers, and is denoted by CBOC(x,y,α), where x and y are the ratios of the chip period $T_c = 1/(1.023 \times 10^6)$ of the PRN code to the sub-carrier periods of BOC(x,1) and BOC(y,1), respectively, and α represents that the power of the sub-carriers of BOC(x,1) and BOC(y,1) accounts for α and $1-\alpha$ of the power of the CBOC sub-carrier, respectively [3].

The main drawback of the CBOC signal is a problem of ambiguity in tracking caused by multiple side-peaks around the main-peak. The side-peaks could cause the tracking loop to be locked on one of the side-peaks, eventually incurring a biased tracking measurement. To tackle this problem, various unambiguous correlation functions have been proposed [4]-[12]. Several of them are for sine-phased or cosine-phased BOC signals only and are inapplicable to the CBOC signal [4]-[7]. Sousa proposed an unambiguous correlation function for the CBOC signal, removing the side-peaks completely [8]; however, the correlation function has a lower and blunter main-peak than that of the CBOC-autocorrelation function, and thus, leads to an inferior tracking performance compared with the CBOC-autocorrelation function. Although there are several correlation functions with a main-peak that is higher and sharper than that of Sousa, the improvement in height and sharpness of the main-peaks is not pronounced, and consequently, the tracking performances of the correlation functions do not exhibit a significant improvement over that of the CBOC-autocorrelation function [9]-[11]. In [12], a novel approach based on splitting the sub-carrier was presented for improvement of the main-peak and it was shown that the main-peak can be much higher and sharper compared with those of the correlation functions mentioned above through the approach. However, the splitting method is empirical and the number of the split sub-carriers is limited to four in the method.

Observing that a higher and sharper main-peak could be yielded by splitting the sub-carrier more, in this paper, we propose a *systematic* method for splitting the sub-carrier, by which the sub-carrier can be split into *any number* of partial sub-carriers, and consequently, a significantly improved main-peak can be obtained. We first split the CBOC sub-carrier into multiple partial sub-carriers, and subsequently, generate partial correlations by correlating each of the partial sub-carriers and the received signal. Then, we cancel out the side-peaks while making the correlation main-peak higher and sharper than that of the CBOC-autocorrelation function by combining the partial correlations in a specialized way.

The rest of this paper is organized as follows: In Section II, we describe the CBOC signal model. In Section III, we propose an unambiguous correlation function with an improved main-peak and no side-peaks. In Section IV, it is confirmed that the proposed correlation function provides a better tracking performance than those of the conventional correlation functions including the CBOC-autocorrelation function in terms of the tracking error standard deviation (TESD), and in Section V, conclusion is presented.

II. CBOC(6,1,1/11) SIGNAL MODEL

In this paper, the CBOC(6,1,1/11) signal, denoted by $B(t)$, is considered and it can be expressed as

$$B(t) = \sqrt{P} \sum_{i=-\infty}^{\infty} p_i r_{T_c}(t - iT_c) d(t) s_{sc}^i(t), \tag{1}$$

where P is the signal power, $p_i \in \{-1, 1\}$ is the ith chip of a PRN code with a period T, $r_\alpha(t)$ denotes the unit rectangular

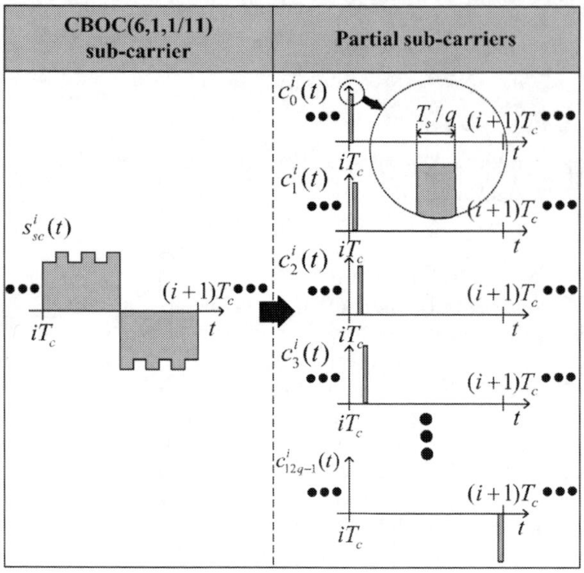

Figure 1. The sub-carrier and partial sub-carriers of the CBOC(6,1,1/11) signal.

pulse over $[0, \alpha)$, T_c is the chip period of the PRN code, $d(t)$ denotes the navigation data, and $s^i_{sc}(t)$ is the CBOC sub-carrier for the ith PRN code chip. In this paper, we assume that every chip of the PRN code is an independent random variable taking on +1 and -1 with equal probability and the code period T is sufficiently large compared with the chip period T_c. It is also assumed that a pilot channel for signal tracking is provided so that no data modulation is present during the tracking process (i.e., $d(t) = 1$). The sub-carrier $s^i_{sc}(t)$ of the CBOC(6,1,1/11) signal can be expressed as a weighted sum of the BOC(1,1) sub-carrier and the BOC(6,1) sub-carrier with a power split ratio of 1/11. Thus, the CBOC(6,1,1/11) sub-carrier can be expressed as

$$s^i_{sc}(t) = \sqrt{\frac{10}{11}} s^i_{\mathrm{BOC}(1,1)}(t) - \sqrt{\frac{1}{11}} s^i_{\mathrm{BOC}(6,1)}(t), \quad (2)$$

where $s^i_{\mathrm{BOC}(1,1)}(t)$ and $s^i_{\mathrm{BOC}(6,1)}(t)$ are the BOC(1,1) and BOC(6,1) sub-carriers for the ith PRN code chip, respectively, and can be expressed as

$$s^i_{\mathrm{BOC}(1,1)}(t) = \sum_{l=0}^{1} (-1)^l r_{6T_s}(t - iT_c - 6lT_s) \quad (3)$$

and

$$s^i_{\mathrm{BOC}(6,1)}(t) = \sum_{l=0}^{11} (-1)^l r_{T_s}(t - iT_c - lT_s), \quad (4)$$

respectively, where $T_s = T_c/12$, i.e., the pulse period of the $s^i_{\mathrm{BOC}(6,1)}(t)$. The CBOC(6,1,1/11) sub-carrier is depicted on the left-hand side of Figure 1.

III. Proposed Unambiguous Correlation Function with an Improved Main-Peak and No Side-Peaks

To obtain an unambiguous correlation function with an improved main-peak and no side-peaks, (i) we split the CBOC sub-carrier into multiple partial sub-carriers and (ii) combine the partial correlations in a specialized way.

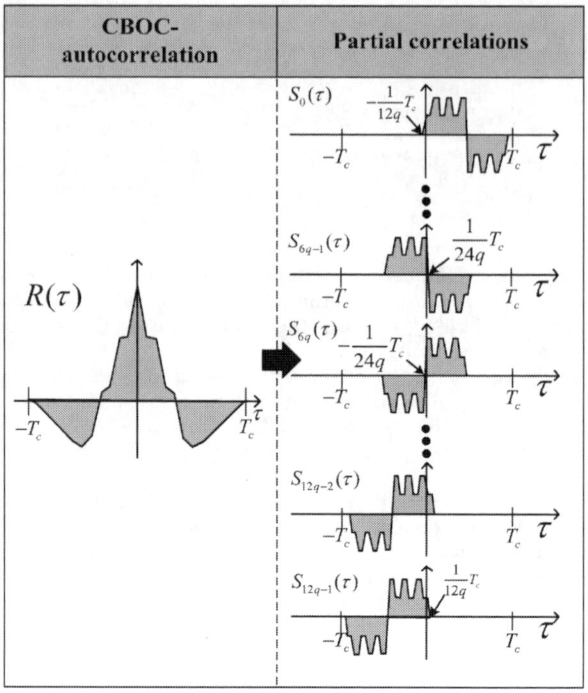

Figure 2. The autocorrelation and partial correlations for the CBOC(6,1,1/11) signal.

A. Splitting the CBOC sub-carrier

First, we evenly split the CBOC(6,1,1/11) sub-carrier $s^i_{sc}(t)$ into $12q$ partial sub-carriers, where q is a natural number (i.e., $q = 1, 2, 3, \cdots$). Thus, the pulse duration of each partial sub-carrier is given by T_s/q, and the CBOC(6,1,1/11) sub-carrier can be expressed as the sum of the partial sub-carriers:

$$s^i_{sc}(t) = \sum_{m=0}^{12q-1} c^i_m(t), \quad (5)$$

where $c^i_m(t)$ is the mth partial sub-carrier for the ith PRN code chip as depicted on the right-hand side of Figure 1, and $\{c^i_m(t)\}_{m=0}^{12q-1}$ are used as locally-generated signals instead of the CBOC sub-carrier.

The normalized CBOC-autocorrelation function shown on the left-hand side of Figure 2 can be expressed as

$$\begin{aligned} R(\tau) &= \frac{1}{PT} \int_0^T B(t)B(t+\tau)dt \\ &= \frac{1}{\sqrt{PT}} \sum_{m=0}^{12q-1} \sum_{i=-\infty}^{\infty} \int_0^T B(t)c^i_m(t+\tau)p_i r_{T_c}(t+\tau-iT_c)dt \\ &= \sum_{m=0}^{12q-1} S_m(\tau), \end{aligned} \quad (6)$$

where $S_m(\tau)$ is the mth partial correlation shown on the right-hand side of Figure 2.

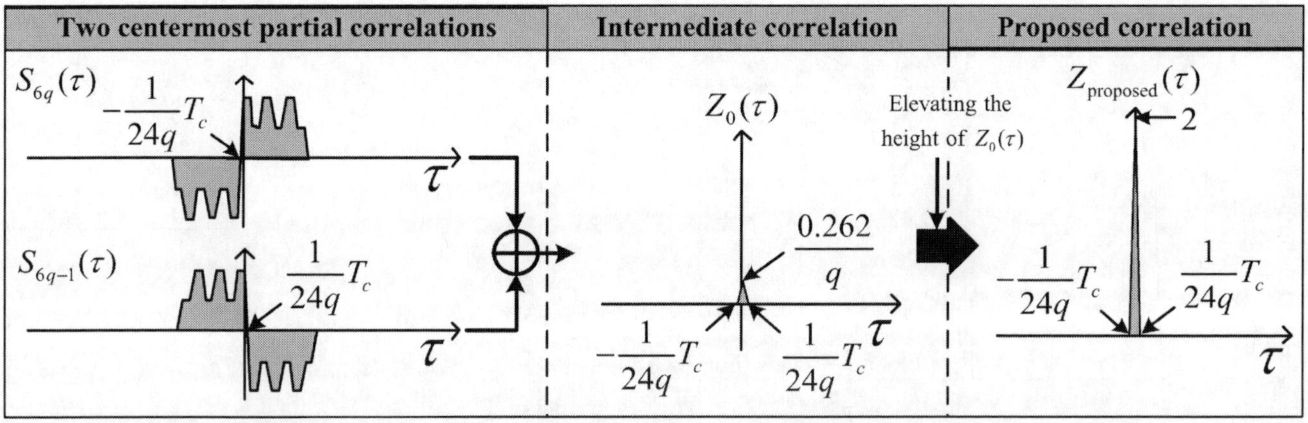

Figure 3. The cancelation of the side-peaks and improvement of the main-peak through combining of the partial correlations.

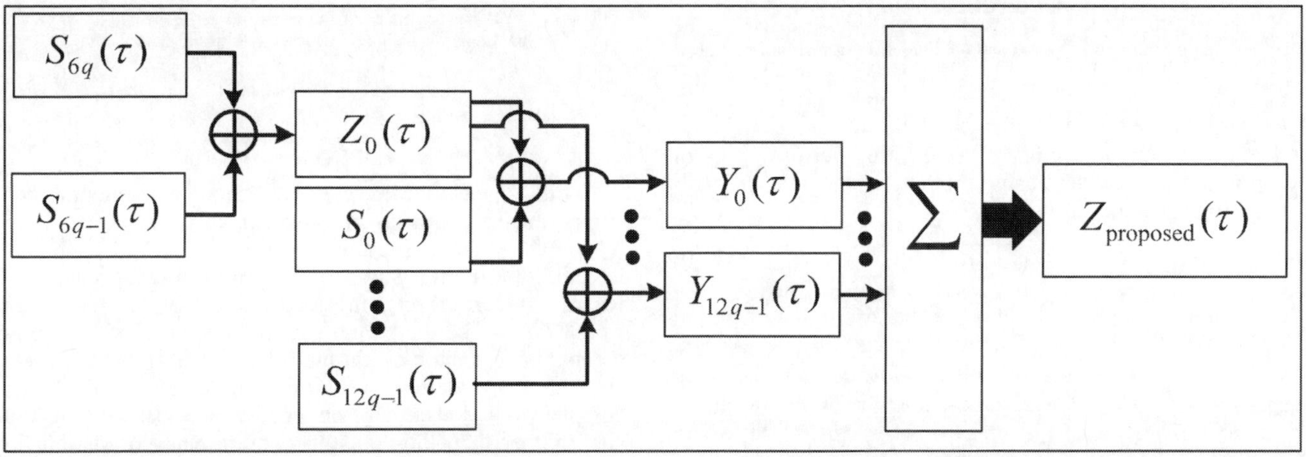

Figure 4. The generating process of the proposed unambiguous correlation function.

B. Combining the partial correlations

Now, we cancel out the side-peaks by combining two centermost partial correlations $S_{6q-1}(\tau)$ and $S_{6q}(\tau)$. Specifically, we use the following arithmetic relation: $|x|+|y|-|x-y|=0$ for $xy \leq 0$ and $|x|+|y|-|x-y|>0$ otherwise. Since the product value of the partial correlations $S_{6q-1}(\tau)$ and $S_{6q}(\tau)$ is positive and negative when $|\tau| < \frac{1}{24q}T_c$ and $|\tau| > \frac{1}{24q}T_c$, respectively, we can eliminate the side-peaks as follows:

$$Z_0(\tau) = S_{6q-1}(\tau) \oplus S_{6q}(\tau), \tag{7}$$

where $A(\tau) \oplus B(\tau) = |A(\tau)| + |B(\tau)| - |A(\tau) - B(\tau)|$, and $Z_0(\tau)$ is an intermediate correlation function obtained right after eliminating the side-peaks and is shown in Figure 3. In fact, we could employ other partial correlations besides $S_{6q-1}(\tau)$ and $S_{6q}(\tau)$ in (7); yet, we found that the combination of $S_{6q-1}(\tau)$ and $S_{6q}(\tau)$ yields the sharpest intermediate correlation function. For example, the half-width of the intermediate correlation function would be $\frac{1}{12q}$ if $S_0(\tau)$ and $S_{12q-1}(\tau)$ are used, which is twice the half-width ($\frac{1}{24q}$) of the intermediate correlation function obtained when $S_{6q-1}(\tau)$ and $S_{6q}(\tau)$ are used, and so, the corresponding intermediate correlation function would be half as sharp as that obtained with $S_{6q-1}(\tau)$ and $S_{6q}(\tau)$.

Next, we increase the height of $Z_0(\tau)$, which is much lower than that of the CBOC-autocorrelation function; moreover, decreases as the value of q increases, and so, is not useful in obtaining a good tracking performance. We observe that similar correlation functions to $Z_0(\tau)$ are obtained by combining each of the partial correlations and $Z_0(\tau)$ as in (7), and propose the following correlation function

$$Z_{\text{proposed}}(\tau) = \sum_{m=0}^{12q-1} S_m(\tau) \oplus Z_0(\tau). \tag{8}$$

Figure 4 shows the whole process for generating $Z_{\text{proposed}}(\tau)$, where $Y_m(\tau) = S_m(\tau) \oplus Z_0(\tau)$. Figure 5 shows the normalized proposed and conventional correlation functions, where we can observe that the proposed correlation function is much sharper than the conventional correlation functions including the CBOC-autocorrelation function, and also, that the difference in sharpness becomes larger as the value of q increases, implying that we can further improve the tracking performance by using a larger value of q. However, it should be noted that the computational complexity is expected to increase as the value of q becomes larger, and thus, an appropriate value of q should be selected according to given system design requirements.

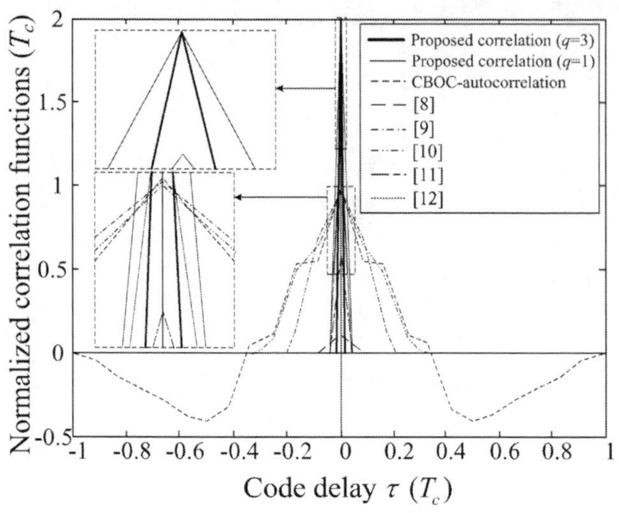

Figure 5. The normalized proposed and conventional correlation functions.

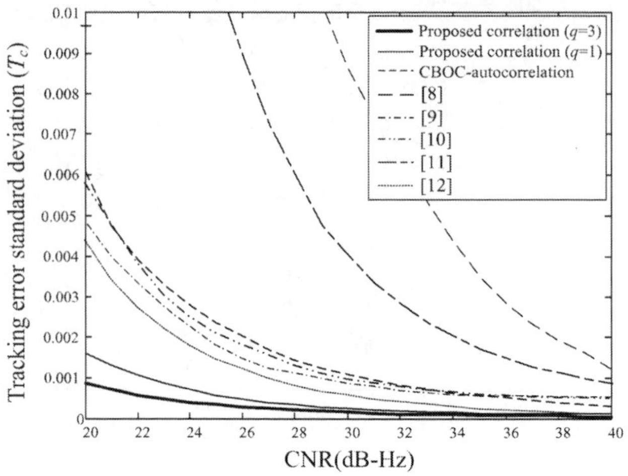

Figure 6. TESD performances of the proposed and conventional correlation functions as a function of the CNR when $\Delta = T_c/96$.

IV. NUMERICAL RESULTS

In this section, we compare the tracking performances of the proposed and conventional correlation functions in terms of the TESD defined as

$$\frac{\sigma}{G}\sqrt{2B_L T_I}, \quad (9)$$

where σ is the standard deviation of the discriminator output $D(\tau)$ at $\tau = 0$, G is the discriminator gain at $\tau = 0$, i.e., $G = \frac{dD(\tau)}{d\tau}\Big|_{\tau=0}$, B_L is the loop filter bandwidth, and T_I is the integration time [13]. The discriminator output $D(\tau)$ can be expressed as $D(\tau) = Z^2_{\text{proposed}}(\tau+\frac{\Delta}{2}) - Z^2_{\text{proposed}}(\tau-\frac{\Delta}{2})$, where Δ is the early-late spacing for a delay lock loop (DLL). For simulations, we consider the following parameters: q=1 and 3, B_L = 1 Hz, $\Delta = \frac{T_c}{96}$, $T = T_I$, and 20,000 Monte Carlo runs are used for each carrier to noise ratio (CNR) defined as P/N_0 dB-Hz, where N_0 is the noise power spectral density. In addition, we consider T_c^{-1} = 1.023 MHz and T = 4 ms, which have been employed in the CBOC signal of Galileo E1 band [3]. For several conventional schemes which have additional system parameters [9][11], the optimized parameters of them are used for simulations, and thus, the best tracking performances of them are compared with those of other correlation functions including the proposed correlation function.

Figure 6 shows the TESD performances of the proposed and conventional correlation functions as a function of the CNR. From the figure, it is clearly confirmed that the proposed correlation function provides a significant improvement in TESD performance over the conventional correlation functions in the CNR range of 20 $\sim$ 40 dB-Hz of practical interest. Specifically, the proposed correlation function gives a performance improvement of more than 5 dB-Hz and 8 dB-Hz when q = 1 and 3, respectively, over all of the conventional correlation functions in the CNR range of practical interest. This stems from the fact that the proposed correlation function is not only unambiguous (i.e., the proposed correlation function has no side-peaks), but also is the highest and sharpest. In addition, as expected, the tracking performance becomes better, as the value of q increases. Specifically, the tracking performance of the proposed correlation function is improved by more than 3 dB-Hz when the value of q is changed from 1 to 3 as shown in Figure 6.

V. CONCLUSION

In this paper, we have proposed an unambiguous correlation function with an improved main-peak for tracking of the CBOC signal. Splitting the CBOC(6,1,1/11) sub-carrier into multiple partial sub-carriers and correlating each of the partial sub-carriers and the received CBOC(6,1,1/11) signal, we have obtained the partial correlations, and then, combining the partial correlations through a specialized way based on an arithmetic relation, we have canceled out the side-peaks completely, and also, have obtained a main-peak that is higher and sharper than those of the conventional correlation functions including the CBOC-autocorrelation function. Numerical results have confirmed that the CBOC tracking loop using the proposed correlation function offers a significant improvement over that using the conventional correlation functions in terms of the TESD in the CNR range of practical interest.

ACKNOWLEDGMENT

This work has been supported by the National GNSS Research Center program of Defense Acquisition Program Administration and Agency for Defense Development and by Basic Science Research Program through the National Research Foundation (NRF) of Korea under Grant 2015R1D1A1A01057327 with funding from the Ministry of Education.

REFERENCES

[1] J. W. Betz, "Binary offset carrier modulations for radionavigation," *J. Inst. Navig.*, vol. 48, no. 4, Dec. 2011, pp. 227-246.

[2] "GNSS modernization," Mar. 2016, URL: http://www.unavco.org/projects/project-support/gnss-support/gnss-modernization/gnss-modernization.html/ [retrieved: Mar., 2016].

[3] J. Nurmi, E. S. Lohan, S. Sand, and H. Hurskainen, GALILEO Positioning Technology, Springer, 2015.

[4] O. Julien, C. Macabiau, M. E. Cannon, and G. Lachapelle, "ASPeCT: unambiguous sine-BOC(n, n) acquisition/tracking technique for navigation applications," IEEE Trans. Aer., Electron. Syst., vol. 43, no. 1, Jan. 2007, pp. 150-162.

[5] Z. Yao, M. Lu, and Z. Feng, "Unambiguous sine-phased binary offset carrier modulated signal acquisition technique," IEEE Transactions on Wireless Commun., vol. 9, no. 2, Feb. 2010, pp. 577-580.

[6] Z. Yao, X. Cui, M. Lu, Z. Feng, and J. Yang, "Pseudo-correlationfunction-based unambiguous tracking technique for sine-BOC signals," IEEE Trans. Aer., Electron. Syst., vol. 46, no. 4, Oct. 2010, pp. 1782-1796.

[7] H. Chen, J. Ren, W. Jia and M. Yao, "Simultaneous perturbation stochastic approximation for unambiguous acquisition in cosine-BOC signals," Radioengineering, vol. 22, no. 2, June 2013, pp. 578-585.

[8] F. Sousa, F. Nunes, and J. Leitao, "Code correlation reference waveforms for multipath mitigation in MBOC GNSS receivers," in Proc. ENG-GNSS, Toulouse, France, Apr. 2008, pp. 1-10.

[9] Z. Yao, M. Lu, and Z. Feng, "Unambiguous technique for multiplexed binary offset carrier modulated signals tracking," IEEE Signal Process. Lett., vol. 16, no. 7, July 2009, pp. 608-611.

[10] D. Xu, M. Liu, and F. Shen, "Ambiguity mitigating technique for multiplexed binary carrier signal tracking," IEEE Communications Letters, vol. 17 ,no. 11, Nov. 2013, pp. 2021-2024.

[11] J. W. Ren, G. Yang, W. Jia, and M. Yao, "Unambiguous tracking method based on combined correlation functions for sine/cosine-BOC CBOC and AltBOC modulated signals," Radioengineering, vol. 23, no. 1, Apr. 2014, pp. 244-251.

[12] K. Chae, S. R. Lee, H. Liu, S. Yoo, S. Y. Kim, G.-I. Jee, D.-J. Yeom, and S. Yoon, "A novel unambiguous composite binary offset carrier(6,1,1/11) tracking based on partial correlations," Computers and Electrical Engineering, vol. 50, Feb. 2016, pp. 54-66.

[13] A. J. Van Dierendonck, P. Fenton, and T. Ford, "Theory and performance of narrow correlator spacing in a GPS receiver," J. Inst. Navig., vol. 39, no. 3, Fall 1992, pp. 265-283.

Ontology Driven Reputation Model for VANET

Renata M. P. Vanni[1]
Departamento de Informática
Federal Institute of Sao Paulo (IFSP)
Araraquara, Brazil
rportovanni@ifsp.edu.br
rporto@icmc.usp.br

Luz Marina S. Jaimes[1]
Engineering of Systems
University of Pamplona
Pamplona, Colombia
lsantos@unipamplona.edu.co
lsantosj@icmc.usp.br

Glenford Mapp
Department of Computer Science
Middlesex University
London, UK
g.mapp@mdx.ac.uk

Edson Moreira
[1]Instituto de Ciências Matemáticas e de Computação (ICMC)
University of Sao Paulo (USP)
São Carlos, Brazil
edson@icmc.usp.br

***Abstract*— As Vehicle *Ad Hoc* Networks (VANETs) become a key component of Intelligent Transportation System (ITS), trust is important in applications that besides traditional security requirements need to evaluate the behavior of different entities in VANETs. Highly dynamic environments of vehicles need an adapted form of trust establishment. There are efforts for evaluating trust in VANETs, based on reputation mechanisms. In this paper, we propose a definition of the reputation relying on the use of an ontology of VANETs, ensuring both an optimal coverage of the domain and a deep semantic rooting. This definition is based on the identification of the key aspects requiring the support of the ontology for their evaluation.**

Keywords- trust; ontology; VANETs; reputation model

I. Introduction

Vehicular Ad Hoc Networks (VANETs) are a special type of Ad Hoc networks, formed by vehicles with processing and wireless communication ability, traveling on streets or highways. Commonly, the vehicles can communicate directly or by the use of a roadside unit (RSU) [1] – Fig. 1. Through this infrastructure, vehicles can access network services and obtain data from other networks, such as the Internet. Due to this nature, VANETs can be established in different environments such as in urban centers and highways [2]. The communication takes place both between vehicle-to-vehicle (V2V) and vehicle-to-infrastructure (V2I), aiming to enable automated cooperation between different vehicles on the road.

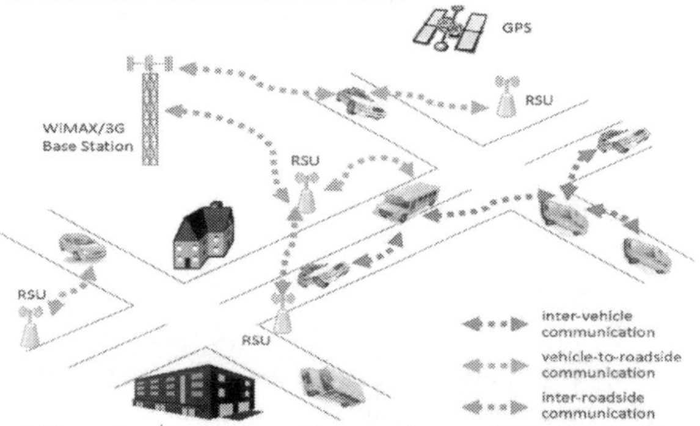

Figure 1. Example of an Intelligent Transport System (ITS) scenario [1]

The emergence of VANET has generated new challenges and requires an even deeper consideration of reputation, as it is one of the ways to trust in vehicles or drivers sending messages. Reputation mechanisms are meant to offer insightful information about the capacity of nodes in a system to accomplish specific actions. Inter-vehicle communications can only occur when two vehicles are within the transmission range of each other, which we refer to as opportunistic forwarding. One key design question is: how do the vehicle/driver decide to (or not to) forward the data to adjacent vehicle/driver when the type of message requires trustworthiness based on node's reputation?

By nature, VANETs' users may expect for opportunistic message forwarding than usual mobile users, as they intend to share information about traffic and road condition, for example. As such, the reputation of vehicles and drivers impact not only forwarding hops choice but also VANETs' users relying on each other, driving users toward trying to build and maintain higher reputation. We suggest that not only the vehicles are evaluated. For instance, drivers are also part of the ecosystem, and have to correctly use services. Given this consideration, it becomes natural that reputation has to be envisaged as a characteristic of message forwarding service, but also a characteristic of vehicles, drivers and passengers if associated with this service. This research considers that reputation management based on ontology could drive many aspects of VANETs, and more particularly can serve as a reference for the production of feedback that will then feed the Reputation of the nodes. A formal specification of conceptualization permits data interoperability and attributes of reputation among the different entities involved in transportation systems. Trust relations can be built by the nodes through the definition of trust rules. Based on these rules, the users will be able to decide to forward the data to the neighbor node.

In this paper, we propose the complexity of reputation by defining a model relying on the use of an ontology of VANET. This ontology ensures semantic consideration of the different elements and provides the necessary expressiveness, openness and mechanisms to fully represent their intrinsic complexity. The remainder of this paper is organized as follow. Section II describes the decision process of opportunistic message forwarding. Section III addresses the reputation model researched. Section IV goes into details with respect to the proposed reputation model for VANET. Discussion and future work conclude the article.

II. OPPORTUNISTIC FORWARDING DECISION

Everyday, vehicles transit in a city and along their trajectories they encounter other vehicles. The frequency of these encounters is influenced by many factors, such as: vehicle speed, destination, traffic condition, and the period of the day.

A possible scenario is a road with two roadways, where vehicles can receive, generate and forward messages between them (V2V) or with the infrastructure (V2I). To simplify, the vehicles can forward one message at a time (it is not possible to send in bulk) and the types of messages that are taken into account for each transaction should require a node reputation level. This model consists of three phases (discovery, forwarding and feedback) in six steps as follow.

The phase of discovery uses a HELLO-RESPONSE technique for detecting approaching vehicles. Vehicles carrying data (Message – M) send out periodic HELLO beacon [3]. If a neighboring node hears a HELLO message, it will send a RESPONSE message to announce its presence. The HELLO (H) and RESPONSE (R) messages will also contain reputation information about the nodes – Fig. 2.

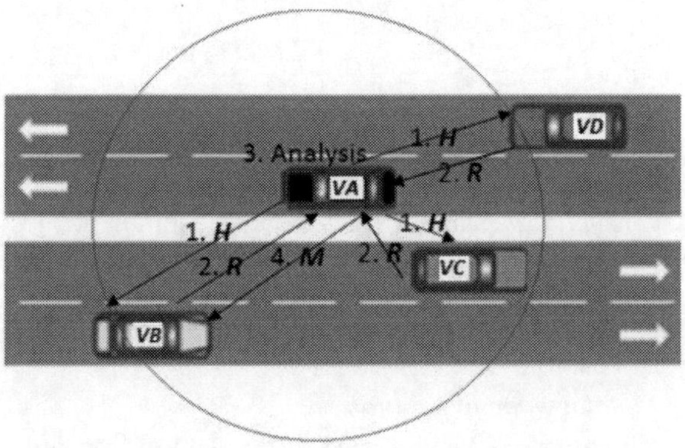

Figure 2. Scenario to opportunistic forwarding decision

The vehicle A (VA) sends "hello" beacon to its neighborhood. If vehicle B (VB) in the vicinity wants to interact with that VA, then it sends its reputation by a "response" beacon to VA.

Step 1 – Hello message.

VA is carrying data and waiting for a peer to forward its messages (M). VA sends out HELLO beacon every x seconds. Vehicles inside of range hear the HELLO message from VA and can send a RESPONSE message to announce their presence.

Step 2 – Response message.

VB hears a HELLO message from VA and sends a RESPONSE message to announce its presence.

In second stage, phase of forwarding, VA executes the process which defines the next hop of the message M forwarding. First, VA listens the responses then determines, through the application of the opportunistic forwarding algorithm, which neighbor vehicles could forward the message. Aspects as vehicles' direction, position, and relative velocity could be taken as inputs to the algorithm [3]. After that, VA analyzes the reputation of vehicles based on opportunistic forwarding algorithm to select the vehicle with the highest reputation to the next hop.

Step 3 – Analysis of reputation.

VA verifies the reputation of VB, VC and VD, and then decides which vehicle has the highest reputation to receive M, in the example, VB. The selected vehicle must be in the list of vehicles that sent responses to VA.

Step 4 – Forwarding Message.

VA adds to M its identification with its reputation and sends M to VB. If VB is not the final destination, VB will store M in cache and will restart from step 1, and so on, till M reaches its destination.

In third phase, phase of feedback, when M reaches the final destination, the destination node performs the process of feedback of each vehicle involved in forwarding phase.

Step 5 – Feedback.

The destination node elaborates feedback of VA that generated M and feedbacks of the intermediary vehicles that forwarded M. Vehicles VA, VB and VK will receive feedbacks with weights according to the ontological structure (section IV). It is important to notice that no feedback will be generated if message M do not reach the destination. Feedbacks of intermediary vehicles depends on their mutual collaboration. Feedback of VA that generated M will be based in a subjective feedback related to message content.

Step 6 – Feedback Reporting.

The destination node sends the feedbacks to a Reputation Server via RSU/4G/LTE, as shown in Fig. 3. In the server, the reputation of each vehicle is recalculated based on old and new feedbacks and updated. We represent feedback and reputation in section III.

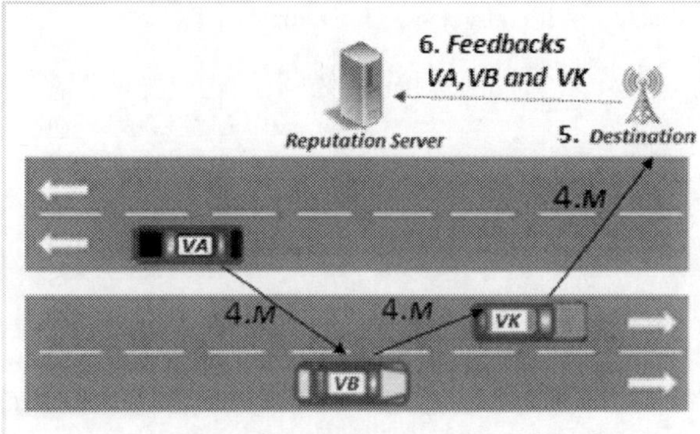

Figure 3. Feedbacks in opportunistic forwarding decision

Besides the feedback, other aspects should be considered to calculate the reputation, for example type of message, content, context, time to delivery, etc,.

III. Reputation Model

We initiated our research from the work of Hamadache [4][5], which provided the basis for the construction of an ontology driven reputation model for service-oriented computing in clouds. According to the general consensus, the reputation of service-oriented computing is characterized by an aggregation of the feedback provided by the different actors of the service ecosystem. Starting from this idea, the first concept to formalize is 'feedback'. Different representations of feedback have been provided in the literature [6], according to the needs of their associated reputation. In our research, we decided to adopt a variation of Sabater [7] and Hamadache's feedback tuple [4] using a 6th element "time – T".

$$\text{Feedback: F} = (\text{A, S, K, X, V, T}). \quad (1)$$

Equation (1) defines Feedback as a 6-tuple composed of the following elements: A is the actor (vehicle, driver, passenger, etc.) giving the feedback, S is the service on which the feedback is given, K stands for the service characteristic evaluated by the feedback (forwarding, alert, chat, etc.), X represents the context in which the feedback was given, V is the value of the feedback, and finally, T is the time at which the feedback was provided. The actual Feedback "F" represents the evaluation of the characteristic K of service S, by actor A in context X, at time T. Context can encompass a wide range of information, from the neighborhood on which the feedback was given, to the type of message being sent at the time of feedback.

The time dimension provides information for different aspects of the reputation. The aspect "decay", for example, will be associated to a lower weight to older feedback.

As suggested by Hamadache[4], the following notations will help to represent sets of feedback matching certain patterns. Equation (2) is the first notation, it follows a similar approach as the one used by Sabater [7] and depicts the set of feedback provided by a specific actor A.

$$\text{Actor Feedback Set: AFS} = \{\text{F} \mid (\text{a, -, -, -, -, -}). \quad (2)$$

From this first notation, a set of similar notations is derived for the different elements of the feedback:

$$\text{Service Feedback Set: SFS} = \{\text{F} \mid (\text{-, s, -, -, -, -}). \quad (3)$$

Service Feedback Set contains all the feedback given about a specific service.

$$\text{ASK Feedback Set: ASKFS} = \{\text{F} \mid (\text{a, s, k, -, -, -}). \quad (4)$$

ASKFS contains feedback provided by an actor on the characteristic of a specific service. A wide range of additional notations can be used, such as those used as illustrative samples.

A. Individual Perception

Starting from this consideration of feedback information (Feedback Set – FS), it is possible to build the individual perception (IP) of a service characteristic (SK) for a given actor (A) at a period of time ^{t}.

$$\text{SKIP}^{t}(ASKFS) = \textstyle\sum_{SKIP \in Fi} \rho(\text{t}, \text{t}i).\text{V}i. \quad (5)$$

Here it is considered all feedback (Fi) provided by the actor (A) on the service characteristic (SK). Then it is aggregated the value (Vi) of each feedback by weighting them according to the time it was given. In this perspective, $\rho(\text{t}, \text{t}i) \in [0,+1]$ is a function giving higher values to more recent feedback. This function is used as a basis to compute the individual perception of the service itself. The principle of computing this value relies on the aggregation of all feedback provided on all the characteristics of the service and weighting each characteristic, not only according to the service but also according to its context. This leads to formula (6):

$$\text{SIP}^{t}(ASFS) = \textstyle\sum_{Fi \in ASFS} \Upsilon(Fi).\rho(\text{t}, \text{t}i).\text{V}i. \quad (6)$$

On (6), $\Upsilon(Fi)$ is the weight of the characteristic K_i. This weight is not always the same from one execution to another, as the actor may have varying expectations over time and may have, for example, sent/forwarded different message type, implying variability in the importance of the service characteristic. In order to compute this weight, it was proposed by Hamadache [4] to base the function on the ontological representation of service execution's context.

B. Ontology and Reputation

The term ontology is used in the field of semantic web and refers to a structured set of concepts in a particular field of knowledge. There are generally two global entities in ontology. The first aims terminology, which defines the nature of the elements making up the field of ontology in question, as the definition of a class in oriented object programming in definition of the nature of the objects that we will manipulate later. The second part of ontology contains explicit relationships between multiple instances of the classes defined in the terminology. Thus, within ontology, concepts are defined in relation to each other (a graph model of the organization of knowledge), which enables reasoning and manipulation of knowledge.

We can identify at least two functions that should be computed with the help of ontology.

1) Weight of Message Type

All characteristics of a message do not convey the same importance of the user and it may be completely irrelevant to consider that a message is sent/forwarded well but did not reach the final destination. Several approaches can be envisaged to tackle this need: establish a mapping between message types and importance of characteristics, asking users explicitly when they provide the feedback to rank the importance of the different parameters, or deducing the importance level from the context in which the message is sent and from the interaction between the peers.

Finding an efficient way to evaluate the importance of characteristics implies to consider what would be user's loss if the characteristic fails. Comparing the needs of each type of message and establishing a rank between them should evaluate this importance – (see (7)).

$$\gamma(F_i) = \begin{cases} \text{importance evaluated by user} \\ \gamma_r\,(F_i, K^s) \end{cases} \quad . \quad (7)$$

The rank of characteristic K_i within the set of characteristics K^s of the service with feedbacks (F_i) of user (r) – $\gamma_r\,(F_i, K^s)$ – should take advantage of the previous evaluation of characteristic weight.

2) Similarity of Message Types

This is an important aspect of our work. Defining the similarity of message types, it is possible to prioritize the forwarding of some message types, define the necessary level of trust for each group, and associate the context during the execution of the message forward.

IV. REPUTATION MODEL FOR VANET

The proposed Reputation Model for VANET (REMOVAN) considers the ideas suggested by The Regret system [7]. The Regret system structure is based on three dimensions of reputation. If we consider only direct interactions between nodes to establish reputations it is said that the decision is based on the **individual dimension**. If information coming from other nodes and their social relations are used, we are talking about the **social dimension**. Finally, if we consider that the reputation of a node is not a single and abstract concept but rather a multi-facet concept, it is considered an **ontological dimension**. For example, the reputation of being a suitable forwarding node summarizes the reputations of respond HELLO messages and generates messages about road conditions. The different types of reputation and how they are combined to obtain new types are the bases of the third dimension of reputation, the ontological dimension.

A. Individual Dimension

The individual dimension models the direct interaction between two nodes. The reputation that takes into account this dimension is the most reliable. This is because it takes into account all the peculiarities of the target node. The called *outcome reputation* (noted as $R\ a \rightarrow b\ (\delta)$ where δ is the reputation type) is the reputation calculated from direct interactions between nodes.

The subset of issues of an outcome taken into account to calculate a given reputation type δ is domain dependent. It is defined by a grounding relation (*gr*) as the relation that links a reputation type δ with a list of issues (*i.e.*, other reputations). This set of issues allows the selection of the right subset of outcomes from the general outcomes' database. Each issue is a tuple with the form $(I_i, \{+, -\}, \alpha_i)$ [7]. The first parameter (I_i) is a label that identifies the issue. The second parameter $(\{+, -\})$ indicates how an increment of the value of the issue affects the reputation, that is, a + means that if the value of the issue increases, the reputation also increases while a − means that if the value of the issue increases, the reputation decreases. Finally, the last parameter is the weight that issue has in the general calculation of the reputation. As an example, the grounding relation for an intermediate node, which could forward a message, in our scenario should be defined as in TABLE I.

TABLE I. TABLE TYPE STYLES

$\boldsymbol{\delta}$	**gr($\boldsymbol{\delta}$)**
To_forward_message	{(Forward, +, 0.8)}
To_generate_message	{(Generate, + 0.2)}
To_refuse_message	{(Refuse, −, 0.8)}
To_have_ traffic_ticket	{(Traffic_ticket, −, 0)}

To calculate an outcome reputation it is desirable to use a weighted mean of the outcomes evaluation, giving more relevance to recent outcomes [4].

B. Social Dimension

For an interaction between two nodes, past experiences of direct interaction is the most reliable source of information to define a reputation [1]. Unfortunately, the social dimension of VANETs does not permit the generation of reputation based just on direct experiences. Not only because the node can be a newcomer but also because for large networks such as the Internet, there will be a considerable amount of direct interactions to evaluate. We suggest indirect reputation processed by a broker of System Reputation. That reputation should be based on all direct experiences sent to a centralized database and used to calculate the individual reputation.

C. Ontological Dimension

Along the individual and social dimensions, reputation is always linked to a single behavioral aspect (an issue). With the ontological dimension it is added the possibility of combining reputations on different aspects to calculate complex reputations [5]. To represent the ontological dimension, graph structures are used.

Fig. 3 shows an ontological dimension for a vehicle in our scenario. In this case, the reputation of being a **suitable vehicle** to forward a message is related with the reputation of forwarding messages and the reputation of generate messages about road conditions. For the owner of this ontological structure, having traffic ticket is something irrelevant to be considered as a suitable vehicle to forward. Hence, to calculate a given reputation taking into account the ontological dimension, the reputation has to be calculated for each of the related aspects that, in turn, can be a node of another subgraph with other associated aspects. The reputations of those nodes that are related with an atomic aspect of the behavior are calculated using the individual and social dimensions. For instance, using the ontological structure in Fig. 3, we can calculate the reputation of B as a suitable vehicle to forward a message from A's perspective using (8):

$$R_{A\to B}(suitable) = 0.8* R_{A\to B}(to\_forward) + 0.2*R_{A\to B}(to\_generate\_message). \quad (8)$$

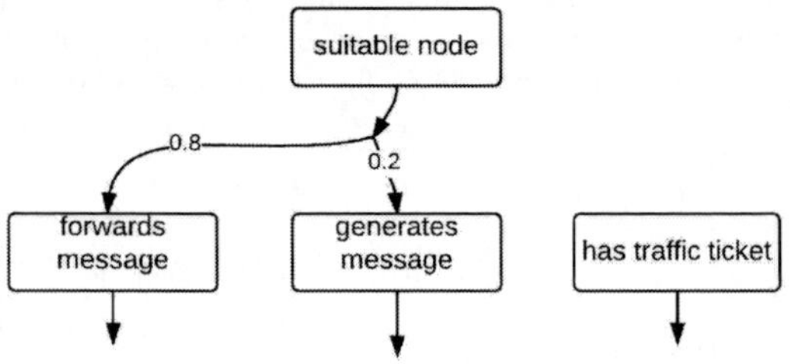

Figure 4. Ontological structure for a suitable vehicle

V. RELATED WORK

Reputation modeling has attracted the interest of researchers in the field of e-commerce and cloud computing [4]-[6]. Hamadache *et al.* [4][5] has focused on reputation of services in cloud computing in the basis of ontologies for Service Level Agreements. Vavilis *et al.* [6] has investigated reference models for reputation systems using subjective user's feedbacks in e-commerce. However, these works mainly focused on the description of the rules and the math involved in reputation calculation. They do not propose a hybrid model from different sources for evaluating feedbacks based on collaborative activity as message forwarding. Our work goes one step further, since it attempts to monitor and update the evaluation of the feedbacks during the whole message forwarding, including the context of user feedback to create and feed a meaningful reputation management system for VANETs.

VANET research Group at Middlesex University is developing a set of simulations to evaluate a VANET mobility model [8]. At University of Sao Paulo, we are using a simulation environment to evaluate our model and integrate it with their work. Our environment is composed by those tools: Simulation of Urban Mobility (SUMO) [9] to set up the mobility model, object-oriented modular discrete event network simulation framework (OMNET++) [10] to support the network model, and the framework Vehicles in Network Simulator (Veins) [11] to implement the propagation model and communications between vehicles. In our mobility model, a grid scenario of 1 Km^2 is considered. A group of 100 vehicles enter to the scenario and stay there, traveling the time it takes the simulation; a RSU is fixed in the center of the scenario and it is connected to the reputation server. The maximum speed of the vehicles is 13.9 m/s. We configured 20% of vehicles generating messages. The final destination is located in a fixed position. REMOVAN is being implemented on the WAVE Short Message Protocol (WSMP) stack [12]; it has adopted the standard IEEE 802.11p [13] and the Simplified Path-Loss model. In TABLE II is showed the parameters of mobility and network.

The goal of our simulations is to evaluate the performance of the reputation system in VANETs. So, the response variable that will be evaluated at the beginning is the average of the reputation of the vehicles in the reputation server. We supposed an initial reputation with neutral value (0), each time the destination receives a message; it generates and sends the feedbacks to the reputation server. The server will increase the reputation of the vehicles that generated and forwarded messages.

TABLE II. SIMULATION PARAMETERS

Parameter	Value
Urban area	(1km x 1km) $1km^2$
Number of vehicles	100
Packet format	WAVE Short Message
Beacon Interval in the RSU	1s
MAC Protocol	802.11p
Transmission rate	6Mbps
Communication range	320m
Simulation time	600s

The main concepts of the ontology to be used in our model and their relationships are described in Figure 5. The main concepts are: Actor, Message, Feedback, Reputation and Broker. Context was omitted from this representation; it will be included into the ontology in next simulation. A Message *is generated by* an Actor. Car *is an* Actor, as are Passenger and Driver. So a Message can be *generated by* one of them. We are also categorizing cars in their types (Truck, Bus, Taxi, etc) to be further used on Context. A Message *has a* Content; Subjective Feedback *is based on* it, in other words, a Destination *gives* Feedback (Subjective Feedback) *based on* a Content of a Message. A Destination also gives Objective Feedback, but in this case, a route table is consulted in order to list all intermediary cars, which collaborated in message forwarding. A Message *is addressed to* a Destination. In future simulations, it should be addressed to more than one Destination or to all in the way, for example, an alarm message. A Broker (Reputation Server) *receives* Feedbacks and *generates* Reputation. Then Reputation *is generated by* a Broker. Reputation, as was said before, is an important concept in this work because message forwarding will take it into account. Note that Car *has* Reputation and not all Actors. It happens because Driver and Passenger will be linked to a car.

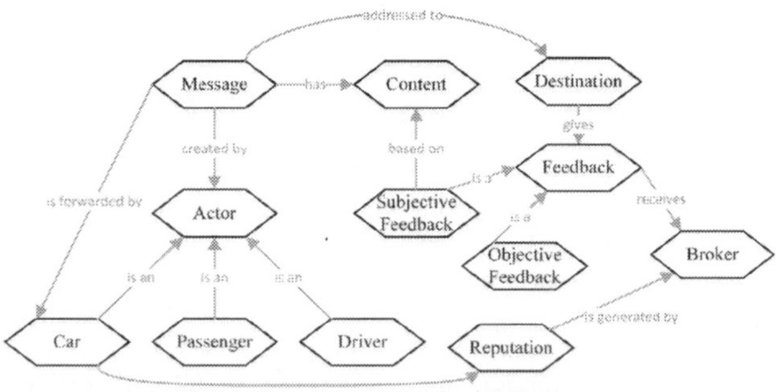

Figure 5. Ontology High Level Concepts

VI. CONCLUSION

In this paper, we have presented our reputation model for VANET. The very next steps for this research will consist in the refinement of ontological structure and testing implementation of the proposed algorithms and their evaluation against simulated scenarios and from real testbeds [8]. This will ensure the coherence and the common ground on which ontologies are built. By ensuring the coherence, the goal is the long-term evolution of feedback and reputation.

ACKNOWLEDGMENT

Federal Institute of Education, Science and Technology of São Paulo (IFSP) supports this work of post doctorate. University of Pamplona, Vehicle Ad-Hoc Networks Research group at Middlesex University and at University of Sao Paulo (USP) support the collaboration of coauthors.

REFERENCES

[1] VANET research Group at Middlesex University. [Online]. Available: http://www.vanet.mdx.ac.uk/. [retrieved: March, 2016].

[2] A. Boukerche, H. A. B. F. Oliveira, E. F. Nakamura, and A. A. F. Loureiro, "Vehicular ad hoc networks: A new challenge for localization- based systems," Computer Communications, vol. 31, no. 12, July 2008, pp. 2838– 2849

[3] J. LeBrun, Chen-Nee Chuah, D. Ghosal, and M. Zhang, "Knowledge-based opportunistic forwarding in vehicular wireless ad hoc networks," in Vehicular Technology Conference, 2005. VTC 2005-Spring , vol.4, May 2005, pp. 2289-2293 , doi:10.1109/VETECS.2005.1543743

[4] K. Hamadache, "Ontology Driven Reputation Model for the Cloud," in IEEE 6th International Conference on Cloud Computing Technology and Science (CloudCom), Singapore, December 2014, pp. 735-738. doi: 10.1109/CloudCom.2014.156

[5] K. Hamadache and S. Rizou, "Holistic SLA Ontology for Cloud Service Evaluation," Advanced Cloud and Big Data (CBD), 2013 International Conference on, Nanjing, 2013, pp. 32-39. doi: 10.1109/CBD.2013.18

[6] S. Vavilis, M. Petković, and N. Zannone, "A reference model for reputation systems", in Decision Support Systems, vol. 61, May 2014, pp. 147–154, doi:10.1016/j.dss.2014.02.002

[7] J. Sabater and C. Sierra, "REGRET: A reputation model for gregarious societies," in Proceedings of the Fourth Workshop on Deception, Fraud and Trust in Agent Societies, 2001, pp. 61-69, Montreal, Canada,. doi:10.1145/375735.376110

[8] A. Ghosh,, V. V. Paranthaman, G. Mapp, O. Gemikonakli and J. Loo, "Enabling seamless V2I communications: toward developing cooperative automotive applications in VANET systems," in Communications Magazine, IEEE , vol.53, no.12 December 2015, pp.80-86, doi:10.1109/MCOM.2015.735557

[9] Intitute of Transportation Systems - DLR, "Sumo – simulation of urban mobility," 2014. [Online]. Available: http://www.dlr.de/ts/en/desktopdefault.aspx/tabid-9883/16931_read-41000/. [retrieved: May, 2016]

[10] OMNeT++, "Omnet++ community," 2014. [Online]. Available: http://www.omnetpp.org/. [retrieved: May, 2016]

[11] C. Sommer, "Veins - vehicles in network simulation," 2014. [Online]. Available: http://veins.car2x.org/. [retrieved: May, 2016]

[12] IEEE Standard for Wireless Access in Vehicular Environments (WAVE) - Networking Services," in IEEE Std 1609.3-2010 (Revision of IEEE Std 1609.3-2007), Dec. 30 2010, pp.1-144, doi: 10.1109/IEEESTD.2010.5680697

[13] D. Jiang and L. Delgrossi, "IEEE 802.11p: Towards an International Standard for Wireless Access in Vehicular Environments," Vehicular Technology Conference, 2008. VTC Spring 2008. IEEE, Singapore, 2008, pp. 2036-2040. doi: 10.1109/VETECS.2008.458

User Experience Evaluation Based on Arbitration QoS Parameters in Video Stream Using NetFPGA in a Controlled Environment

Rafael S. Jacaúna
Federal University of Sergipe (UFS)
Sergipe - Brazil
e-mail: rjacauna@gmail.com

Edward David Moreno
Universidade Federal de Sergipe (UFS)
Sergipe - Brasil
e-mail: edwdavid@gmail.com

Ricardo José P. de B. Salgueiro
Universidade Federal de Sergipe (UFS)
Sergipe - Brasil
e-mail: ricardo.salgueiro@gmail.com

***Abstract*—A streaming video has some features that are different from others, such as the occupation of a large amount of bandwidth, and the possible scenes variation with a consequent increase or decrease in the amount of transmitted bytes. Applications for the video streaming transmission (YouTube, Vimeo, Netflix, Telecine Play, etc) have aroused the interest of the scientific community regarding to the networks behavior. The purpose of this paper is to measure, through a video stream, the user experience, also known as Quality of Experience (QoE) based on the arbitration of QoS parameters in a controlled environment using NetFPGA.**

Keywords–QoS; QoE; DiffServ; Correlation Models; NetFPGA.

I. INTRODUCTION

This paper presents some initial results that validate the environment tests in a simple scenario, with only one customer receiving the streaming video server. Its purpose is to measure the user experience in a controlled environment through Differentiated Services techniques (DiffServ) to adjust the routing of packets between client and server, following the appropriate adjustments according to the QoS parameters (Jitter, packet loss, latency and bandwidth) and their application (codec, latency, resolution). In our work, we have inserted one NetFPGA hardware among routers to compose a cloud of higher performance without QoS treatment.

From researches based on Alreshodi et al. [1] and Arousi et al. [2] works on QoS/QoE correlation models, it was possible to realize that these authors did not address papers related to wireless networks; Gahbiche et al. [3] investigated external/environmental factors that could affect the user experience without considering the QoS requirements of the network layer; Bingjin et al. [4] and Kyeong et al. [5] have developed/implemented methods for evaluating QoS, using simulators like the Object-Oriented Modular Network Simulator (OMNET) [6]. They used those simulators to shape the effect of traffic from Internet Services Providers (ISP). On the other side, Valente [7] proposed a prototype for QoS/QoE provisioning of wireless networks, using NS2 for its evidences.

The objective of this paper is to demonstrate the user experience in a real world scenario with router vendors that have contributed to the adoption of open Standards, as the Cisco example on the RFC 2475 and 2597 recommendations, which determine the behavior of the packet to each passage among routers on the Internet.

It is important to mention that the paper has been divided into six Sections: the first one is related to the introduction; the second one is dedicated to QoS and QoE concepts. The NetFPGA board characteristics are described in Section 3. Section 4 presents the scenario used in the experiment, and some preliminary results have been presented in Section 5. The last one, Section 6, suggests some ways to cover and to assess the proposed problem.

II. QUALITY OF SERVICE AND QUALITY OF EXPERIENCE

Works on the user experience analyze the seven layers of the Open Systems Interconnection (OSI) reference model. In this paper only two layers will be considered: the network and the application ones. According to Siller and Woods [8], we can see a pseudo-layer over both, and inside it the authors designed the user experience. These academics have defined QoS as "the experience perceived by the user being presented by the Application Layer, which acts as a front-end user presenting overall results of the individual Quality of Service".

Hohlfeld et al. [9] deal with the specifics of the differences between QoS and QoE, i.e., the first one is centered on the network, while the second one, centered on the user. The QoE depends on a multidimensional perceptual space that includes: factors of influencing system (such as QoS measures, transport protocols, or specific parameters of devices); the influence of human characteristics (such as humor, personality traits or expectations) and the context characteristics (location, activities or costs) [9].

Quality of Experience is based on the Mean Opinion Scores(MOS) Methodology. However, in Seshadrinathan et al. [10] work, the research focuses on the difference of the Difference MOS (DMOS). This technique was based on the Video Quality Assessment (VQA) that considers the objective aspects and the subjective human perceptions [10].

A. *Quality of Service*

The network layer allows the transfer of packets between origin and destination, which might go through several hops routers in order to get to the destination. In terms of services of this layer, TCP/IP model seeks to deliver the same packets with the "least effort". There are two ways of implementing services on this layer: the oriented and the connectionless ones. Despite of the Internet adopting connectionless services, Tanenbaum [11] makes a highlight in four aspects that must be resolved regarding the QoS:

1) What network applications are required;
2) How to regulate traffic entering the network;
3) How to reserve resources in routers to ensure performance, and;

4) If the network can accept more traffic safely. No isolated technique deals, effectively, with all these aspects. In practice, there are two versions of QoS that are widely used in many Internet routers: Integrated Services and Differentiated Services.

1) Integrated Services: It is a service designed for unicast and multicast applications that are able to deliver multimedia flows through the Resource Reservation Protocol (RSVP) [11]. This, in turn, it operates as following: each group of stations is assigned and addressed. For each transmitter that sends data, these places address to the group in their own packets; then a routing algorithm, through a multicast, builds a spanning tree covering all members (this algorithm is not part of RSVP). The Integrated Services have the key requirements admission control and the resource reservation. In essence, real-time services require some sort of service guarantee, but it is important to be careful on the use of this term. It would be more appropriate to use "enough" or even "acceptable" [12].

2) Differentiated Services: This service is based on the "class" concept, where there is no need for resource reservation to "ensure" the packet delivery, hence there will be no channel exclusivity after the connectionless establishment. It can be offered in a cloud of routers belonging to the same domain. Classes are defined as "Per-Hop Behaviors" (PHB) [11], each hop is a router, and each packet that is to arrive at a hop, after being sent back to the network, will not have any guarantee of delivery to the destination. This is a function of the Transport layer.

B. Quality of Experience

Siller and Woods [8] have defined QoE as "the experience perceived by the user that is being presented by the Application layer, which acts as a front-end of the user who has the overall result of quality individual services".

The QoE can be measured in all layers of the OSI model, as it was presented in the Introduction part. The most common action is to control the parameters of the network layer (bandwidth, delay, loss and change) to prevent the user to receive a stream with any low quantity during the playback. As it will be presented in the next Section, subjectivity in the user perception is a factor in his/her experience, like how to evaluate his/her level of satisfaction during the involvement in a particular site, or his/her enjoyment in a game, in real time [13].

C. Correlation between QoS and QoE models

There are two methodological approaches to evaluate the correlation between QoS and QoE models. They are the objective and the subjective assessments [1]. These techniques, whenever are observed separately, do not evaluate properly the user experience. The models evaluated by Alreshoodi and Woods were:

- IQX hypothesis (*exponential interdependence of quality*): based on a generic formula in which the parameters of QoS and QoE are connected through an exponential relationship [14].
- VQM (*Video Quality Metric)-based Mapping Model*: function *n* dimensional QoS (in which "*n*" is the number of different QoS parameters) [15].
- QoE *Model using Statistical Analysis method*: it is a technique employed that correlates QoS parameters and estimates QoE perceptions, and identifies the degree of influence of each of the QoS parameters on user perception [2].
- QoE *Models based on Machine Learning methods*: It is a new approach for the construction and adaptive QoE prediction models using classification algorithms in machine learning, with trained data for subjective tests [16].
- QoE *model using Crowdsourcing for subjective tests*: it is based on Microworkers platform, it allows driving *surveys* on-line tests as YouTube [17].
- QoE *model using a Resource Arbitration System*: it is based on the integration between the Network and Application layers (NQoS and AQoS) [8].
- QoE *model considering equipment and environment factors*: it is a technique that can be used when the source signal interference in the environment wireless (such as frame error rate, and delay variation) can occur. Different QoS parameters can be applied to the user equipment. Then, parameters such as noise, jitters and ambient light forming the interference environment in which QoE different parameters are used [4].
- QoE *model based on Quantitative and Qualitative Assessment*: this model is a combination of both of these approaches. The Set Gross Theory (RST) has been used here for the Quantitative Evaluation, while CCA framework (catalogue, categorize and analyze) has been used for the Qualitative one [1].

For finishing this section, we would like to highlight that it is necessary that the methodology for evaluating the user experience includes the QoS requirements. This work has studied the relationship between QoS and QoE influencing this experience, since all the authors that studied this subject have been treating these issues, most of them, by focusing between network layer and the application one. Issues on physical layer also have directly influenced the outcome after a broadcast, like the Cyclic Redundancy Check (CRC) errors during a Voice Communication over IP (VoIP).

Those who worked in the telephony industry during the migration to VoIP, were able to observe what the biggest problems were during this transition. There were constant complaints from the users related to interference during phone calls. The main reason was the CRC errors, and the main cause was related to the cabling, which was totally obsolete.

III. Features of the NetFPGA

The NetFPGA board, designed to assist researchers in research projects for computer networks, is flexible and operates at the rated speed of the Ethernet interfaces.

NetFPGA is the concept of Field Programmable Gate Array (FPGA) dedicated to computer networks. The NetFPGA has been increasing since its inception in 2001, being available in 03 plate versions: NetFPGA, 1G-CML, NetFPGA 10G and NetFPGA SUME. The NetFPGA 1G version was discontinued. The NetFPGA 1G-CML model will be soon presented.

A. *NetFPGA CML model*

This model was designed to operate under a PCIe 4X second generation interface. This model has four (04) Gigabit Ethernet ports, incorporating the Kintex-7 325TFPGA, Xilinx. This platform had been designed to support NetFPGA architecture, developed by Stanford University, with reference models available through GitHub NetFPGA community. It is totally compatible with the Xilinx Vivado software and ISE Suite Design, as well as embedded software projects of Xilinx SDK. The board has the following characteristics:

- A FPGA (physical chip);
- Four network ports Gigabit Ethernet;
- *Quad Data Rate Static Random Access Memory* (QDRII+ SRAM) - 36MBit (4.5MBytes);
- Double-Date Rate Random Access Memory (DDR3 DRAM), capable of 512MBytes;
- PCI Express Gen. 2;
- SD card storage and memory *flash* BPI (*Byte Peripheral Interface*)
- Expansion Interface (FMC and PMOD connectors);
- Additional features such as PIC micro-controller and USB, RTC, chip with Crypto authentication;
- PCIe standard *Form Factor*;
- Flexible, open source.

The purpose of using this hardware is to make it available to implement routing algorithms both at software (through Microbloze processor), and hardware levels, using the FPGA resources.

B. *FPGA Configuration*

All system programming logic is stored in SRAM Memory, and for the fact that it is a type of volatile memory, the device is setup each time it is powered up. The data configuration is known as bit-stream, whose formats are used as "bit" or "mcs". It can be configured via BPI flash, USB drive off-board or via PC. Another very important feature is the Hardware Description Language (HDL), that allows to create an Intellectual Property (IP), in which the most populars are VHDL and Verilog, or use the creation of others. Among the possible uses for the NetFPGA card, we can mention an IP for Image and Video Processing Manipulation (Image Characterization).

IV. PROPOSED SCENARIO

In order to simulate the closest testing environment of an Internet user, the following scenario has been created as depicted in Figure 1.

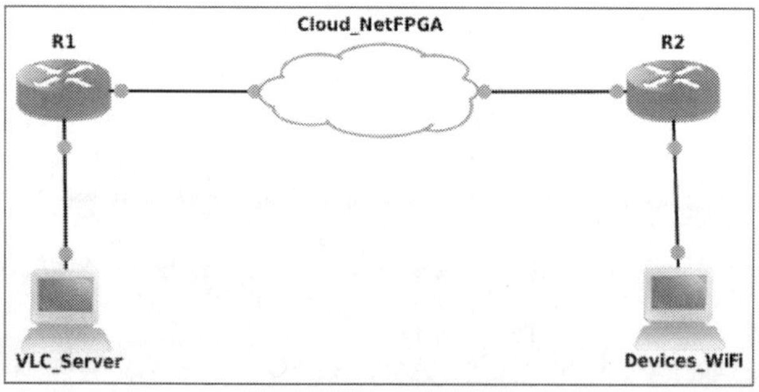

Figure 1. Proposed scenario.

In Fig. 1, the "VLC_Server" represents a streaming server executing the VLC software; the "Devices_WiFi" represents the devices on the LAN; R1 and R2 are the border routers that will make the QoS requirements. The Cloud_NetFPGA represents the various Internet routers, allowing the passage of simulated traffic generated by one of the following tools: iPerf, Harpoon or RUDE/CRUDE.

A. *Real Scenario*

The routers used in our test environment are the Cisco 1841 model. The streaming server is an HP Pavillion desktop, with Intel i3 CPU and 4GB RAM. The physical connection between VLC_server and R1 is Fast-Ethernet (100Mpbs), as well as the connection between routers and the NetFPGA cloud. The wifi devices are smartphones, notebooks and desktops with interface, and infrastructure as a router DLINK DIR-610 802.11n model, and that device it is connected to the router R2 via Fast-Ethernet. In order to capture frames, we will use Wireshark version 1.10.6 for the analysis of packets, forensic tool CapAnalysis 1.2.1 for the captured packets from the NetFPGA board interfaces, and for the Cisco routers counters analysis, we use the ManageEngine NetFlow Analyzer Tool. The PRTG tool has been evaluated here, although it has shown some inconsistencies regarding the counter reading on routers.

B. *Expected Experiments*

Through this research, it has been aimed to measure the quality of the user experience, such as, for most part of them, the mobile device, as well as smartphones and laptops. The use of a residential router reflects, in general, the infrastructure in the user's homes. Tanenbaum has mentioned that with 1Mbps, it is possible to watch a video from the Internet, using data compression, with reasonable quality [11]. If somebody wants to watch movies in High Definition (HD) quality with at the same rate, it probably will not be a pleasant experience since high-definition movies occupy an average of 2.5Mbps bandwidth. This situation is critical in some countries, like Brazil, where the average bandwidth contracted is 1Mbps [18].

V. PRELIMINARY ANALYSIS

This preliminary analysis consisted on watching two different movies, in order to realize their characteristics and aspects. The first film, " Insurgent", was played with a resolution of 1,920 x 800 dip per inch (dpi), frame rate equal to 23.97 frame per second (fps) and codec H.264. During playback, the image was freezing for several seconds, but the audio quality was good at all times. The second one, "The Silver Dollar", was presented at a resolution of 632 X 352 dpi, MPEG4 codec, frame rate equal to 25 fps and the movie was reproduced satisfactorily. In the first case, the codec has the characteristic of consuming a lot of processing, both for the image compression and decompression, but it uses low bandwidth (something around 2,5 Mbps). However, the MPEG-4 codec, from "The Silver Dollar" movie, did not present frame loss. Fig. 2 depicts the bandwidth consumed in this same movie (lower curve), and the amount of bandwidth consumed in transmitting the "Insurgent" movie. It is important to highlight that in both cases, we had a 100Mbps bandwidth, and we had used 2.5Mbps, but the user experience in the first movie was not satisfactory.

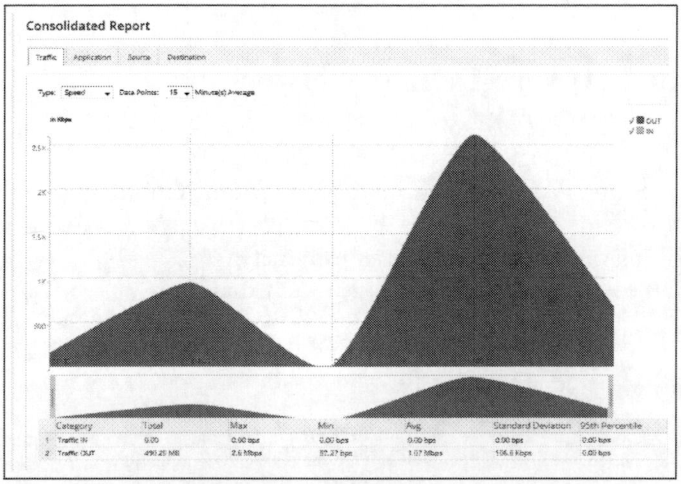

Figure 2. Use the channel during the transmission of movies.

In both cases, by unchecking the "activate transcoding" option at the VLC server, all processing happens to be executed on the client. When the resolution of the movie is performed in FULL HD mode, the CPU consumption increases considerably enough to stop its reproduction for several seconds. If this option has been checked, the processing reduces and the movie playback becomes acceptable, but it will depend on the processor speed and the amount of memory on the user device.

VI. Conclusion

In this paper we have shown that the problem associated to QoE is strongly dependent on multidimensional spaces, such as QoS measures, transport protocols and specific parameters of used devices, besides the influence of human and contextual factors. In spite of these dependences, many of the studies and researches have forgotten this correlation. For this reason, in our proposal we have suggested a real scenario for measuring the user experience in an environment controlled by Differentiated Services techniques to adjust the routing of packets between clients and servers, with appropriate adjustments to the QoS parameters (jitter, packet loss, latency and bandwidth) and application (codec, latency, resolution). We have used a NetFPGA hardware which is inserted among routers to represent a high performance cloud.

This experiment showed that it was necessary to make adjustments in the Internet layer and Application. Despite the low consumption of the channel, the film presented in FULL HD had frames loss during playback. A probable cause was the high consumption in the CPU processing on the client to decompress the bit-stream generated by the H.264 protocol. Another possible factor was the adjustment of the latency for video playback on the user device. If the player has been configured with low latency, frame loss increased considerably; if set to maximum latency, losses frames were reduced by the same proportion.

For future works we would like to suggest a deeper study and research about the real contribution and usage of NetFPGA in this experiment, to measure the quality of communication and different real scenarios using different QoE and QoS models.

Acknowledgment

It is important to thank CNPq, CAPES, FAPITEC, UFS and IFS for their financial support and help.

References

[1] M. Alreshoodi and J. Woods, "Survey on QoE\QoS Correlation Models for Multimedia Services," International Journal of Distributed and Parallel systems, 2013.

[2] S. Aroussi and A. Mellouk, "Survey on machine learning-based QoE-QoS correlation models," 2014 International Conference on Computing, Management and Telecommunications, ComManTel 2014, 2014, pp. 200–204.

[3] H. Gahbiche Msakni and H. Youssef, "Is QoE estimation based on QoS parameters sufficient for video quality assessment?" 2013 9th International Wireless Communications and Mobile Computing Conference, IWCMC 2013, 2013, pp. 538–544.

[4] B. Han, X. Zhang, Y. Qi, Y. Gao, and D. Yang, "QoE model based optimization for streaming media service considering equipment and environment factors," Wireless Personal Communications, vol. 66, 2012, pp. 595–612.

[5] H. long Kim, B. K. Kim, H. H. Choi, and S. G. Choi, "Implementation of QoS control system with QoE parameters on multimedia services," Advanced Communication Technology (ICACT), 2010 The 12th International Conference on, vol. 2, 2010, pp. 1035–1040.

[6] K. S. Kim, "The effect of ISP traffic shaping on user-perceived performance in broadband shared access networks," Computer Networks, vol. 70, 2014, pp. 192–209. [Online]. Available: http://dx.doi.org/10.1016/j.comnet.2014.06.001

[7] W. M. Valente, "Arcabouço para Aprovisionamento de QoS e QoE em Redes Sem Fio Heterogêneas WiMAX / Wi-Fi com Garantia de Equidade entre Vazões Arcabouço para Aprovisionamento de QoS e QoE em Redes Sem Fio Heterogêneas WiMAX / Wi-Fi com Garantia de Equidade entre Vazões," Dissertação, UFPA, 2011.

[8] M. Siller and J. Woods, "Improving quality of experience for multimedia services by QoS arbitration on a QoE framework," pp. 1–7, 2003. [Online]. Available: http://citeseerx.ist.psu.edu/viewdoc/download?doi=10.1.1.194.7031{\&}rep=rep1{\&}type=pdf

[9] O. Hohlfeld, E. Pujol, F. Ciucu, A. Feldmann, and P. Barford, "A QoE Perspective on Sizing Network Buffers," Proceedings of the 2014 Conference on Internet Measurement Conference - IMC '14, 2014, pp. 333–346. [Online]. Available: http://dl.acm.org/citation.cfm?doid=2663716.2663730

[10] K. Seshadrinathan, R. Soundararajan, A. C. Bovik, and L. K. Cormack, "Study of subjective and objective quality assessment of video." IEEE transactions on image processing : a publication of the IEEE Signal Processing Society, vol. 19, no. 6, Jun. 2010, pp. 1427–41.

[11] J. W. Tanenbaum, Andrew S; David, Redes de Computadores, 5th ed., P. P. Hall, Ed. São Paulo: Pearson Education do Brasil, 2011.

[12] X. P. R. Brad, ISI, D. Clark, MIT, S. Shenker, "Integrated Services in the Internet Architecture: an Overview Status of this Memo," p. 28, 1994. [Online]. Available: https://www.rfc-editor.org/rfc/rfc1633.pdf

[13] P. Brooks and B. r. Hestnes, "User measures of quality of experience: Why being objective and quantitative is important," IEEE Network, vol. 24, no. April, 2010, pp. 8–13.

[14] P. Fiedler, M., Hossfeld, T., Tran-Gia, "A generic quantitative relationship between quality of experience and quality of service," Network, IEEE, vol. 24, no. April, 2010, pp. 36–41.

[15] M. Pinson and S. Wolf, "A new standardized method for objectively measuring video quality," Broadcasting, IEEE Transactions on, vol. 50, no. 3, Sept 2004, pp. 312–322.

[16] M. Katsarakis, V. Theodosiadis, and M. Papadopouli, "On the Evaluation of a User-centric QoE-based Recommendation Tool for Wireless Access," Department of Computer Science, University of Crete, and Institute of Computer Science, Foundation for Research and Technology - Hellas, Tech. Rep., 2014.

[17] T. Hoßfeld, M. Seufert, M. Hirth, T. Zinner, P. Tran-Gia, and R. Schatz, "Quantification of YouTube QoE via crowdsourcing," Proceedings - 2011 IEEE InternationalSymposium on Multimedia, ISM 2011, 2011, pp. 494–499.

[18] CETIC.BR, "Velocidade Máxima para Download Contratualmente Fornecida Pelo Provedor de Internet nos Últimos 12 Meses," 2014.

High Availability WLANs Based on Software-Defined Networking

Hwi Young Lee, Young Min Kwon, Jung Wan Shin, Won Jin Lee, and Min Young Chung

College of Information and Communication Engineering, Sungkyunkwan University,
Email: {lhy152, ko116, withmyjw, reign0208, mychung}@skku.edu

***Abstract*—The software defined networking (SDN) has become one of the popular subject in the domain of information and communication technology and a huge amount of research has been conducted in this area. However, most of these existing research works only provide theoretical SDN concepts and they hardly show any implementation or testbed results. In order to market the SDN technology, useful real-time practical applications of SDN controller are required. Therefore, in this paper we propose a novel SDN based high availability (HA) solution for wireless local area networks (WLAN). The proposed solution uses open network operating system (ONOS) controller as a SDN controller. Our experimental results under real-time network environment show that the ONOS controller can be used to manage the overall WLANs.**

***Index Terms*—Software defined networking; High availability WLAN; Open network operating system.**

I. Introduction

Recently, the software defined networking (SDN) has attracted a lot of interest. The main characteristics of SDN is to decouple the control and data planes of a network and provide the freedom of programmability to development more efficient network applications [1]. Furthermore, the SDN also results in less complex and more flexible wired networks [2]. Due to these characteristics, many research works consider to employ SDN architecture to wireless networks such as mobile networks and wireless local area networks (WLANs) [3]-[7].

The existing studies in this area of wireless networks mainly focus on the theoretical SDN concepts of wireless networks and they rarely provide any real-time SDN based results. It is due to the fact that the implementation of real-time SDN controller is very difficult. Furthermore, the existing research works hardly discuss any useful application of SDN controllers. However, in order to market SDN technology the industry requires valuable practical SDN applications. Therefore, in this paper we study the feasibility of SDN controller by implementing a real-time WLAN. As shown in Figure 1, our proposed high availability (HA) scheme aims to provide HA solution for WLAN by using open network operating system (ONOS) controller . In our proposed scheme. When the ONOS controller detects that a WLAN AP is unavailable due to some unexpected system failure, it instructs its neighboring WLAN APs to accommodate the abandoned stations (STAs) which were previously associated with malfunctioned AP. In addition, the ONOS controller also instructs the OpenFlow switches to update their flow tables for efficient and reliable data transfer. As a result, the STAs is not severely affected by the failure of the WLAN AP. The rest of the paper is organized as follows. Section II presents the preliminaries regarding our proposed scheme. In Section III, we introduce the system architecture and procedures for the proposed HA WLANs. Section IV contains the detailed performance evaluation of the proposed HA WLAN and Section V provides the conclusion of this paper.

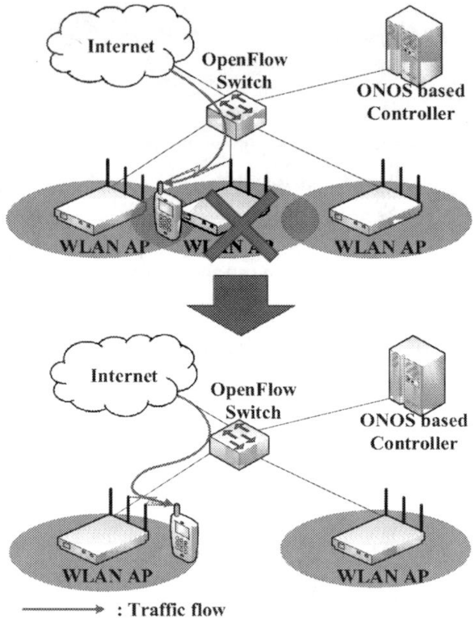

Fig. 1. Solution for High Availability WLANs

II. Preliminaries

For better understanding of our proposed scheme, this section provides a brief introduction of both OpenFlow and ONOS controller.

A. OpenFlow

OpenFlow is a standard protocol to provide interface between the control and forwarding layers of SDN architecture [8]. OpenFlow protocol identifies the common features in the flow tables of the Ethernet switches [9] and it manages the flow table of the switch. It enable the user to control switches without any technical support from vendors [10]. The main objective of OpenFlow is to provide a platform to test the newly developed networking ideas [9]. Due to these advantages several vendors around the globe are taking keen interest in the standardization procedure of OpenFlow protocol. The OpenFlow standardization procedure is carried out by Open Networking Foundation (ONF) founded in 2011 [10].

OpenFlow network has centralized characteristic where a single controller can manage multiple switches. In OpenFlow network, single controller can analyze traffic statistics and control the traffic flows. OpenFlow network consists of three components: an OpenFlow switch, a OpenFlow channel, and a controller [11]. An OpenFlow switch is comprised of one or more flow tables and a group table. Each flow table of the OpenFlow switch has a set of flow entities including match fields, counters, and instructions for traffic packets. A group table contains group entities with action buckets dependent on group types. The action indicates the additional processing and forwarding features such as multi-path, fast rerouting, and link aggregation. Based on these flow tables and a group table, the OpenFlow switch examines and forwards data packets. An OpenFlow channel is an interface for the OpenFlow switch to communicate with an external controller. Through the OpenFlow channel, the OpenFlow switch can receive the control message to add, update, and delete its flow tables from the controller.

B. Open Network Operating System (ONOS)

During the past several years, open source SDN controllers such as NOX [12], Beacon [13], and POX [14] had been developed. The objective of these controllers is to explore and demonstrate SDN potential. Since these controllers have primitive programming and devices-oriented abstractions, SDN applications for these controllers are tightly coupled to OpenFlow protocol such as network device drivers. Therefore, these controllers are hard to provide the key features such as scalability and HA.

In order to provide these key features, ONOS is developed [15]. Since ONOS is a network operating system, it is responsible for the following functions: management for finite resources on behalf of resource consumers, isolation and protection of ONOS users from each other, efficient resource management, and security from the outside world. The architecture of ONOS consists of distributed core, Northbound abstraction/APIs, Southbound abstraction/APIs, and software modularity.

- **Distributed core**: It is required to provide the scalability, and HA of the SDN control plane. ONOS can be deployed as a service on a cluster of servers running the same ONOS software. If system failure occurs in an ONOS server, the distributed core enables rapid failover. In addition, a cluster of multiple ONOS servers can perform applications and control network devices from a single platform. This feature makes ONOS more scalable.
- **Northbound abstraction/APIs**: ONOS enables users to easily develop application with the help of Northbound abstraction/APIs. ONOS includes network graph and application intents to ease development of control, management, and configuration services. There are two powerful Northbound abstractions; intent framework and global network view. The intent framework allows an application to request a service from the network without information of how the service will be performed. And, the global network view provides the application a view of the whole network.
- **Southbound abstraction/APIs**: The Southbound abstractions provides the interfaces between OpenFlow control plan and network devices. The Southbound abstraction enables ONOS to control or manage multiple diverse devices, even if they use different protocols such as OpenFlow, NetConf, etc.
- **Software modularity**: ONOS provides the freedom to develop, debug, maintain, and upgrade ONOS as a software system. Because of the modularity, new applications or new protocol adapters can be added according to user requirement. In addition, software modularity provides a architectural integrity and coherence, easy maintenance with fewer side effects of changes, and extensibility and customization of components.

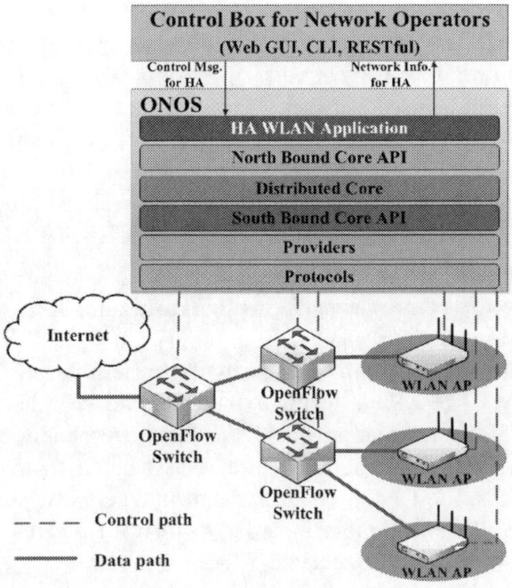

Fig. 2. System Architecture

III. Proposed Scheme

In this Section, we introduce a SDN-based HA WLAN solution. For implementation of HA WLAN, we propose the system architecture, the monitoring procedure for WLAN APs, and the flow control and failover procedure.

A. System Architecture

Figure 2 shows the proposed system architecture for supporting the HA WLAN application based on the ONOS controller. The system architecture consists of three components; control box for network operators, ONOS controller, and OpenFlow-based network. The control box provides the abstractive view of OpenFlow-based network. Network operators can check the status of OpenFlow-based network and control the OpenFlow-based network via Web graphic user interfaces (GUI), command line interface (CLI), or RESTful of the control box.

The ONOS controller performs the procedures for supporting HA WLANs. It periodically monitors the state of WLAN APs. If the ONOS controller detects the system failure in one or more WLAN APs, it instructs the available WLAN APs to support the re-association of STAs which are abandoned by the dead AP. When the STAs are re-associated to available WLAN APs, the ONOS controller directs OpenFlow switches to update their flow table in order to forward the respective data traffic to newly associated STAs.

The OpenFlow-based network is comprised of several OpenFlow switches and WLAN APs. Since the OpenFlow switches support the OpenFlow protocol, they can be managed by ONOS controller. WLAN APs are entities which provide wireless accesses to their associated STAs. For implementation of HA WLANs, WLAN APs also have interface to receive the control messages from ONOS controller and report their state to the controller.

B. Monitoring Procedure for WLAN APs

In order to provide HA WLAN, the ONOS controller should detect the system failure of one or more WLAN APs. It is impossible for the ONOS controller to perceive the exact time when the system failure occurs in a WLAN AP. Hence, the ONOS controller should periodically confirm the state of WLAN APs as shown in Figure 3.

The proposed monitoring procedure for state of WLAN APs is as follows: In Step 1, ONOS controller sends *hello* messages to WLAN APs, and then it waits for the response for a predefined time in Step 2. Based on the type of response, the ONOS controller confirms the state of the WLAN APs. As shown in Step 3-a) of Figure 3, if the ONOS controller receives the *ok* messages from a WLAN AP before the timer expires it perceives the state of the WLAN AP as the *available* state. If the ONOS controller receives the *WiFi Failure* message from a WLAN AP such as Step 3-b), it recognize the state of the WLAN AP as the *WiFi-disabled* state which indicates that the WLAN AP is running but its WiFi radio does not work. On the other hand, If the ONOS controller does not receive any message from a WLAN AP after the predefined time such as Step 3-c), it perceives that a system failure has occurred and the WLAN AP is dead. Thus, the ONOS controller sets the state of WLAN APs to the *unavailable* state.

Even if some WLAN APs are malfunctioning, the proposed HA WLAN system should provide seamless services to users and in order to do this, ONOS controller determines alternative WLAN APs which can accommodate the abandoned STAs. If

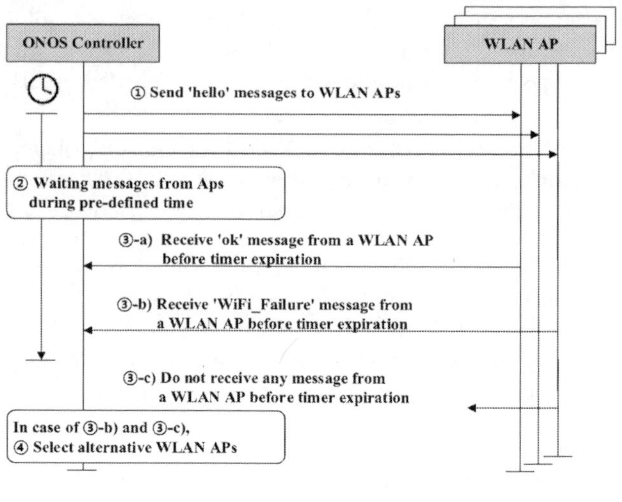

Fig. 3. Procedure to monitor the state of WLAN APs

ONOS controller detects a WLAN AP under the *WiFi-disabled* or *unavailable* (Step 4), it requests the re-association and re-authorization for the abandoned STAs to the newly assigned APs.

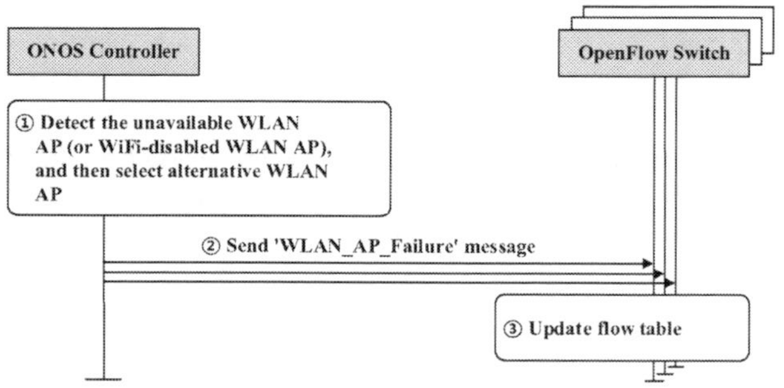

Fig. 4. Procedure to control traffic flow

C. Flow Control and Failover Procedure

ONOS controller should adjust the traffic path in order to prevent the data from being forwarded to the disabled WLAN AP. If ONOS controller detects a disabled WLAN AP under the *WiFi-disabled* or *unavailable* state, it sends *WiFi AP Failure* messages to OpenFlow switches as shown in Figure 4. A *WiFi AP Failure* message includes IP addresses and port numbers of the disabled WLAN AP and its alternative WLAN AP. Based on the information of the *WiFi AP Failure* message, OpenFlow switches delete their flow tables and stop forwarding data packets to the faulty WLAN AP. Then, they add new flow tables and forward the data packets to the alternative WLAN AP.

If state of a malfunctioned WLAN AP is the *WiFi-disabled*, it means that the WLAN AP is still running with null WiFi signal. In this case, ONOS controller can command the

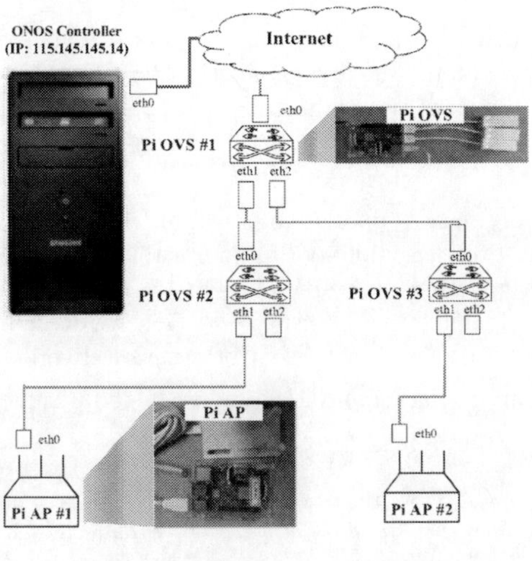

Fig. 5. Network components for test environment

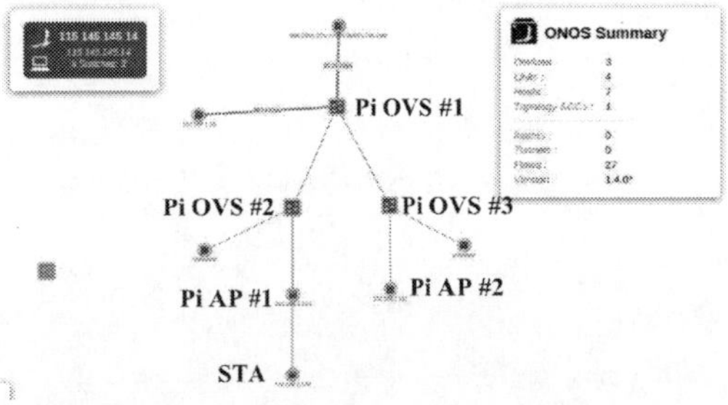

(a) Before turning off the power of Pi AP 1

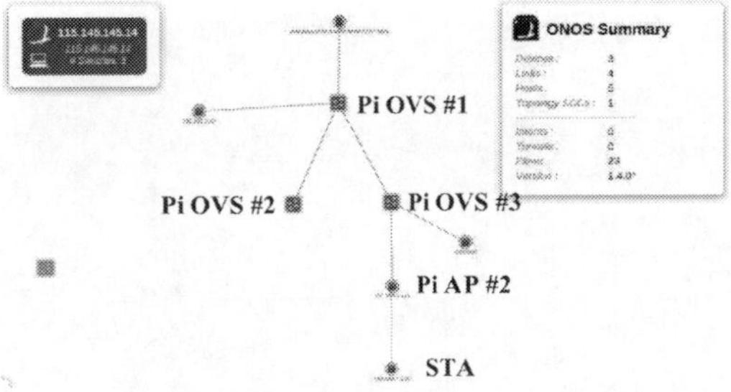

(b) After turning off the power of Pi AP 1

Fig. 6. Network topology in the Web GUI of ONOS

WLAN AP to reboot. After rebooting, if the WLAN AP successfully recovers, the ONOS controller confirms the state of the WLAN AP by performing the monitoring procedure, and then it changes the state of the WLAN AP from the *WiFi-disabled* state to the *available* state. The ONOS controller requests that the WLAN AP performs the re-association and re-authorization for its STAs. Simultaneously, it sends the *WiFi AP Failover* message with IP addresses and port numbers of the WLAN AP and its alternative WLAN AP. By using *WiFi AP Failover* message, OpenFlow switches update the flow tables of OpenFlow switches in order to forward data packets to the WLAN AP.

IV. Performance Evaluation

In this Section, a detailed description of our test environment for the performance evaluation of HA WLAN is provided. Under the real-time test environment, we measure and analyze the data rate by using WireShark application [16].

A. Test Environment

For performance evaluation of HA WLAN, we construct test environment with one ONOS controller, three OpenFlow switches, and two WLAN APs as shown in Figure 5. The ONOS controller is made by installing the ONOS Drake package (version 1.3.0) on a desktop PC. Since the ONOS controller has fixed global IP address, OpenFlow switches can be connected with the ONOS controller via Internet.

For implementation of OpenFlow switch and WLAN AP, Raspberry Pi [17] which is one of open source hardware (OSHW) platforms is utilized. The Raspberry Pi supports the Raspbian OS based on the debian linux [17]. It can perform the functionalities of OpenFlow protocol by installing the Open vSwitch packages [18]. In our test environment, we define the Raspberry Pi using Open vSwitch as Pi OVS. As shown in Figure 5, three Pi OVSs are deployed as a binary tree, where all Pi OVSs manages the packet forwarding based on their flow tables. Two WLAN APs used in our test environment comprise WLAN USB adaptors having MediaTek RT5572 chipsets and Raspberry Pi. The Raspberry Pi can perform the functionalities according to IEEE 802.11 standards by installing the hostapd package [19]. We define the WLAN APs as Pi AP. The Pi APs 1 and 2 are connected with Pi OVSs 2 and 3, respectively. One laptop PC with IEEE 802.11 WLAN radio interface is used as a STA. In our test environment, Pi APs and the STA utilize the 5GHz ISM band to communicate with each other, which is not used by any other WLAN hot spot in the neighborhood.

B. Experimental Result

Under our test environment, we consider a test scenario to confirm feasibility of our proposed HA WLAN solution. In the HA WLAN scenario, we consider that the STA is associated with the Pi AP 1. We configure that the Pi AP 2 is the alternate WLAN AP of the Pi AP 1. In case that the power of a WLAN AP (i.e., PI AP 1) is turned off, we check whether the STA associated to the PI AP 1 is reconnected to the alternative WLAN AP (i.e., Pi AP 2) or not. Since ONOS controller provides the Web GUI showing the network topology, we confirm the execution of the our proposed HA WLAN solution through the Web GUI of ONOS controller as shown in Figure 6. Figure 6(a) shows the initial condition where the Pi AP 1 with an STA is running normally. When the power of Pi AP 1 is cut off (that is, the Pi AP 1 is disabled), an STA will be re-associated to the Pi AP 2 due to HA WLAN solution of ONOS controller. By Figure 6(b), we confirm that the STA is successfully re-associated to the Pi AP 2.

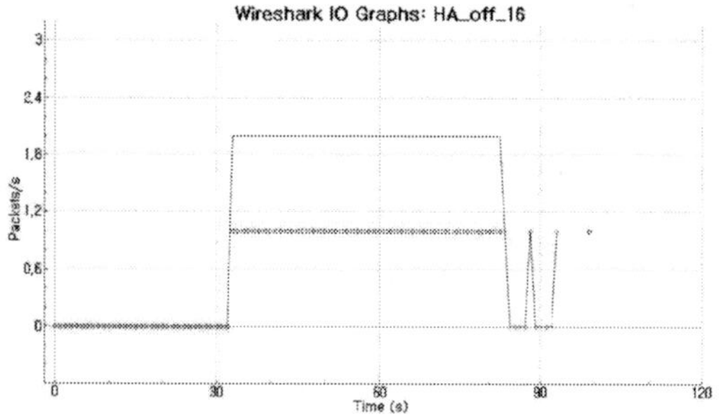

(a) Not employing HA WLAN solution

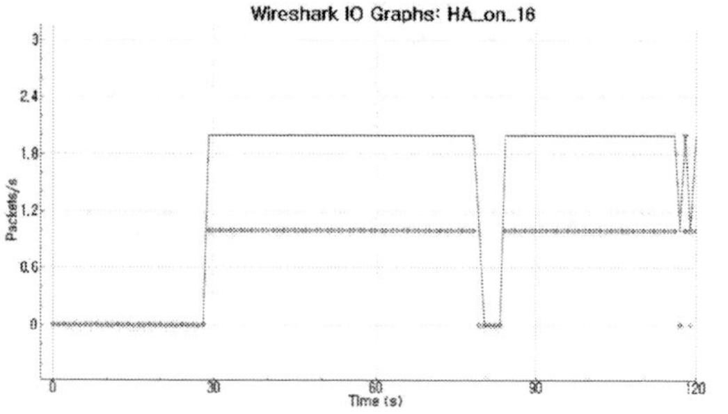

(b) Employing HA WLAN solution

Fig. 7. Packet data rate

For estimating the effect of HA WLAN, we measure the packet data rate by using WireShark application [16]. Figure 7(a) and 7(b) show that the effect of our proposed scheme for high availability when WLAN AP is disabled. We send packets from domain name system (DNS) server of google IP to STA, then power off Pi AP 1 at 80 seconds. As shown in Figure 7(a), STA can not receive the packets after Pi AP 1 is disabled. It means that other WLAN AP (i.e., PI AP 2) do not recognize the disconnection between Pi AP 1 and STA in the ordinary environment. However, Figure 7(b) presents the successful re-association from Pi AP 1 to the Pi AP 2 with HA WLAN solution of ONOS controller. After being disabled Pi AP 1, Pi AP 2 can associate with STA by using HA WLAN solution of ONOS controller. Thus, after 4 seconds, STA can receive the packet from Pi AP 2 instead of Pi AP 1. Through these experimental results, we confirm the feasibility of our proposed scheme.

V. Conclusion

In this paper, we introduced an ONOS SDN controller based HA WLAN solution for WLANs. Unlike previous research works where only theoretical concepts of SDN are discussed, we developed a real-time ONOS controller based WLAN test environment. Furthermore, we also implemented and evaluated the performance of our proposed HA WLAN solution. According to our proposed scheme, the SDN controller periodically monitors the state of its attached WLAN APs and in case of an AP failure it re-associates it abandoned STAs to a neighboring functional AP. Through experimental results, we confirm the successful implementation of our proposed HA WLAN scheme. As part of our future work, we plan to reduce the re-association time by enhancing the algorithm and to make the scenario more realistic.

Acknowledgment

This work was supported by Institute for Information & communications Technology Promotion(IITP) grant funded by the Korea government(MSIP) (B0190-15-2013, Development of Access Technology Agnostic Next-Generation Networking Technology for Wired-Wireless Converged Networks)

Prof. Min Young Chung is the corresponding author.

References

[1] W. Xia, Y. Wen, C. H. Foh, D. Niyato, and H. Xie, "A survey on software-defined networking," *IEEE Commun. Surveys & Tutorials*, Vol. 17, no. 1, pp. 27-51, Jun. 2014.

[2] D. Raumer, L. Schwaighofer, and G. Carle, "Monsamp: A distributed SDN application for QoS monitoring," in *Federated Conference on Computer Science and Information Systems (FedCSIS)*, pp. 961-968, Sep. 2014.

[3] T. Chen, M. Matinmikko, X. Chen, X. Zhou, and P. Ahokangas, "Software defined mobile networks: concept, survey, and research directions," *IEEE Communications Magazine*, Vol. 53, no. 11, pp. 126-133, Nov. 2015.

[4] F. Granelli, et al. "Software defined and virtualized wireless access in future wireless networks: scenarios and standards," *IEEE Communications Magazine*, Vol. 53, no. 6, pp. 26-34, Jun. 2015.

[5] D. Zhao, M. Zhu, and M. Xu, "Supporting One Big AP illusion in enterprise WLAN: An SDN-based solution," *Sixth International Conference on Wireless Communications and Signal Processing (WCSP)*, pp. 1-6, Oct. 2014.

[6] R. Riggio, M. Marina, J. Schulz Zander, S. Kuklinski, and T. Rasheed, "Programming Abstractions for Software-Defined Wireless Networks," *IEEE Transactions on Network and Service Management*, Vol. 12, no. 2, pp. 146-162, Jun. 2015.

[7] D. Zhao, M. Zhu, and M. Xu, "SDWLAN: A flexible architecture of enterprise WLAN for client-unaware fast AP handoff Computing," *International Conference on Communication and Networking Technologies (ICCCNT)*, pp.1-6, Jul. 2014.

[8] OpenFlow, Accessed on 11 April 2016. [Online]. Available: https://www.opennetworking.org/sdn-resources/openflow

[9] N. McKeown, et al. "Openflow: enabling innovation in campus networks," *ACM SIGCOMM Computer Communication Review*, Vol. 38, no. 2, pp. 69-74, Apr. 2008.

[10] A. Lara, A. Kolasani, and B. Ramamurthy, "Network Innovation using OpenFlow: A Survey," *IEEE Communications Surveys & Tutorials*, Vol. 16, no. 1, pp. 493-512, 2014.

[11] OpenFlow Switch Specification, v1.3.2, 2013.

[12] N. Gude, et al. "Towards opportunistic flow management in OpenFlow," *ACM SIGCOMM Computer Communication Review*, Vol. 38, no. 3, pp. 105-110, July 2008.

[13] What is Beacon? Accessed on 11 April 2016. [Online]. Available: https://openflow.stanford.edu/display/Beacon/Home

[14] POX wiki, Accessed on 11 April 2016. [Online]. Available: https://openflow.stanford.edu/display/ONL/POX+Wiki

[15] ON.LAB White paper, Introducing ONOS - a SDN network operating system for Service Providers, 2014.

[16] WireShark, Accessed on 11 April 2016. [Online]. Available: https://www.wireshark.org/

[17] Raspberry Pi, Accessed on 11 April 2016. [Online]. Available: https://www.raspberrypi.org/

[18] Open vSwitch, Accessed on 11 April 2016. [Online]. Available: http://openvswitch.org/

[19] hostapd: IEEE 802.11 AP, IEEE 802.1X/WPA/WPA2/EAP/RADIUS Authenticator, Accessed on 11 April 2016. [Online]. Available: https://w1.fi/hostapd/

Implementation of an Energy Detection Based Cooperative Spectrum Sensing on USRP Platforms for a Cognitive Radio Networks

Zdravka Tchobanova, Galia Marinova
Faculty of Telecommunications,
Technical University - Sofia
Sofia, Bulgaria
e-mail:{z.chobanova, gim}@tu-sofia.bg

Amor Nafkha
SCEE,
CENTRALE-SUPELEC,
Rennes, France
e-mail:amor.nafkha@centralesupelec.fr

***Abstract*— The paper describes a centralized cooperative spectrum sensing system, implemented on Universal Software Radio Peripheral (USRP) hardware platforms driven by the Genuinely Not Unix (GNU) Radio software. Spectrum sensing is realized by energy detection and a new block of energy detector with uncertainty is developed using GNU Radio out-of-tree implementation. A centralized scheme for cooperative spectrum sensing is applied and a hard global decision is taken in a fusion center which collects the local decisions from secondary users, selects those of them which will be taken for global decision estimation and performs classical decision fusion logic, such as AND, OR, MAJORITY rules. Based on measured data, the probabilities of detection for different Signal-to-noise ratios (SNRs) are built for each secondary user and for different scenarios of cooperative sensing.**

Keywords — Cooperative Spectrum Sensing;, Energy Detector; Fusion center; USRP; GNU Radio.

I. INTRODUCTION

In cooperative spectrum sensing, multiple secondary users (SUs) cooperate to overcome the unpredictable wireless environment which includes multipath fading, shadowing, and noise power uncertainty. By exploiting the spatial diversity, it has been proven that cooperative spectrum sensing outperforms single-user sensing [1].

In centralized cooperative sensing each local decision from SUs is collected in a central unit called fusion center (FC), which merges sensing data or local decisions and makes selection of the secondary users which will contribute to the global decision [13]. Then it takes a global decision through an algorithm often based on counting (voting), obtained by the classic logic rules such as AND, OR, MAJORITY applied on local decisions of SUs. The global decision is transmitted back by the FC to the SUs through a control channel. Different schemes of cooperative sensing, as well as issues, are considered in [7]. Two stage cooperative sensing with coarse and accurate stages in perspective to reduce power consumption and sensing time is proposed in [8]. Hard and soft information combined algorithms for cooperative sensing are described in [9], whereas [10] focuses on hard decision solutions. A widely used technique for spectrum sensing is energy detection [2] [3] [12]. The impact of noise uncertainty on the energy detector performances is considered in [6]. Recent papers are proposing some hardware implementations of energy detector and cooperative spectrum sensing schemes. An implementation of energy detector on USRP is presented in [4]. An implementation of centralized cooperative spectrum sensing with two SUs, realized on USRPs is described in [5] and its functionality is illustrated through a video transmission. In [15], probabilities of detection in cooperative sensing system implemented with 3 USRPs with 3 scenarios are compared – individual sensing, hard (OR) and soft decision. In [16], a validation of the advantages of cooperative sensing over individual sensing is proposed, through a hardware set-up with 2 SUs on USRPs and applying Roy's Largest Root Test algorithm for sensing decision. Joint energy-and-bandwidth spectrum sensing with GNU radio and USRP is proposed in [11]. Kullback-Leibler distance-based optimization to determine the decision thresholds for cooperative sensing and its scalability with the number of SUs is implemented in [14]. These implementations have quite limited applications and a more profound study is needed.

The paper describes a centralized cooperative spectrum sensing system, implemented on USRPs hardware platforms using GNU Radio software. Spectrum sensing is realized by energy detection and a new block of energy detector with uncertainty is developed in GNU radio. A centralized scheme for cooperative spectrum sensing is applied and a hard global decision is taken in FC which collects the local decisions from SUs, selects those of them which will be taken for global decision estimation and performs AND, OR, MAJORITY estimates of the global decision. Based on measured data, the probabilities of detection for different SNRs are built for each SU and for cooperative sensing with different scenarios.

The rest of the paper is organized as follows. Section 2 describes the Energy detector used for spectrum sensing and the GNU radio block built. Section 3 describes the Cooperative spectrum sensing scheme applied, the experimental setup, based on USRPs, as well as GNU radio flowgraphs constructed for the FC global decision making. Section 4 presents simulation results based on measurements and processing in GNU radio. Section 5 contains conclusion remarks.

II. ENERGY DETECTOR BLOCK WITH GHU RADIO

A. Theoretical aspects of energy detector

The energy detector (ED) is based on the idea that if a signal is present in the channel, there will be significantly more energy than if signal is absent. The block diagram of ED is shown on Fig. 1. Detection technique is available for every primary user (PU), without knowledge about any PU's signal, and it includes a threshold on the collected energy from the channel. The threshold is used by the ED to make the decision.

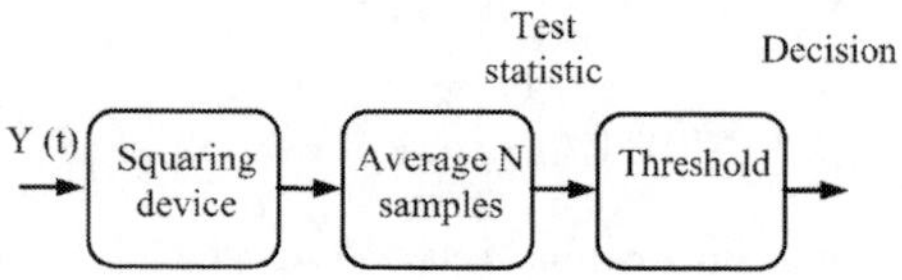

Figure1. Energy detector's block diagram

The PU signal is modeled by a random signal $\boldsymbol{s}$ with additive white Gaussian noise (AWGN) $\boldsymbol{w}$. The received signal $\boldsymbol{y}$ is sampled and it can be presented as a zero mean stationary Gaussian process with variance $\sigma_w^2 + \sigma_s^2$. The noise samples are assumed as a random variable with mean zero and variance σ_w^2. The received signal detection at the SU can be specified as binary hypothesis:

$$H_0 : y[n] = w[n] \Rightarrow signal\ is \quad absent \tag{1}$$

$$H_1 : y[n] = s[n] + w[n] \Rightarrow signal\ is \quad present$$

$$n = 1,\ldots,N.$$

where $y[n]$ is the received signal, $w[n]$ is the additive noise, $s[n]$ is the PU signal, and N is the number of received samples corresponding to the length of the interval of interest. The signal received is only noise when H_0 is true or signal plus noise when H_1 is true. The test statistic Λ, is a sum of squared input samples and it is compared with the detection threshold λ:

$$\Lambda = \sum |y(n)|^2 = \begin{cases} > \lambda & \text{under } H_1 \\ < \lambda & \text{under } H_0 \end{cases} \tag{2}$$

The ED threshold λ depends on the probability of detection P_d or the probability of misdetection P_{md} or the probability of false alarm P_{fa}, which are defined and interconnected, as follows.

$$P_d = P_r[\Lambda > \lambda \mid H_1] \tag{3}$$

$$P_{fa} = P_r[\Lambda > \lambda \mid H_0] \tag{4}$$

$$P_{md} = P_r[\Lambda < \lambda \mid H_1] = 1 - P_d \tag{5}$$

The choice of a suitable threshold is particularly important for good performance of the ED. If the threshold is too high, the SU can decide that there is free space in the spectrum when the PU signal is present, and its transmission will interfere with the PU transmission. If the value is too low, the detector will not react to the absence of a signal in the channel and the SU will then miss the opportunity to use the spectrum.

When the number of samples and the noise variance are known, the threshold is calculated with a constant false alarm probability P_{fa}. The IEEE 802.22 wireless regional area network (WRAN) limits P_{fa} down to 10% [2]. In practice, the exact value of the noise variance is not always available and first the noise in the channel must be evaluated.

Using the Central Limit Theorem (CLT) when $N \to \infty$, the test statistic Λ could be approximated by Gaussian distribution and evaluated, as follows:

$$P_{fa} \approx Q\left(\frac{\lambda - \sigma_w^2}{\sqrt{\frac{2}{N}\sigma_w^2}}\right) \tag{6}$$

$$P_d \approx Q\left(\frac{\lambda - (\sigma_w^2 + \sigma_s^2)}{\sqrt{\frac{2}{N}(\sigma_w^2 + \sigma_s^2)}}\right) \tag{7}$$

When it has included uncertainty in the noise model [5], the P_d and P_{fa} are calculate by:

$$P_{fa} \approx Q\left(\frac{(\lambda - (1+\rho)\sigma_w^2)}{\sqrt{\frac{2}{N}}(1+\rho)\sigma_w^2}\right) \tag{8}$$

$$P_d \approx Q\left(\frac{\lambda - ((1+\rho)^{-1}\sigma_w^2 + \sigma_s^2)}{\sqrt{\frac{2}{N}}((1+\rho)^{-1}\sigma_w^2 + \sigma_s^2)}\right) \tag{9}$$

where

$$Q(x) = \frac{1}{2} erfc\left(\frac{x}{\sqrt{2}}\right) \tag{10}$$

is the tail probability of the normal Probability density function. The parameter ρ defines the level of the noise uncertainty. The threshold can be calculated as follows:

$$\lambda_\alpha = (1 - \sqrt{2}.erf^{-1}(2(1-\alpha))\frac{\sqrt{2}}{\sqrt{N}}))\sigma_w^2 \tag{11}$$

$$\lambda_\beta = (1 - \sqrt{2}.erf^{-1}(2(1-\beta))\frac{\sqrt{2}}{\sqrt{N}}))\sigma_w^2 \tag{12}$$

$$Q^{-1}(P_{fa}) = \sqrt{2}.erf^{-1}(1 - 2P_{fa}) \tag{13}$$

where: erf^{-1} is the inverse error function and α (resp. β) is the upper (resp. lower) false alarm probability. Then, if the test statistic Λ is greater than λ_α (resp. lower than λ_β), the detector decide H_1 (resp. H_0).

B. Energy detector block in GNU radio

A new block of ED is developed and implemented in the GNU Radio Companion's libraries [17]. The input parameters of the ED block are the number of samples, the noise variance and the parameters α and β that specify the level of uncertainty.

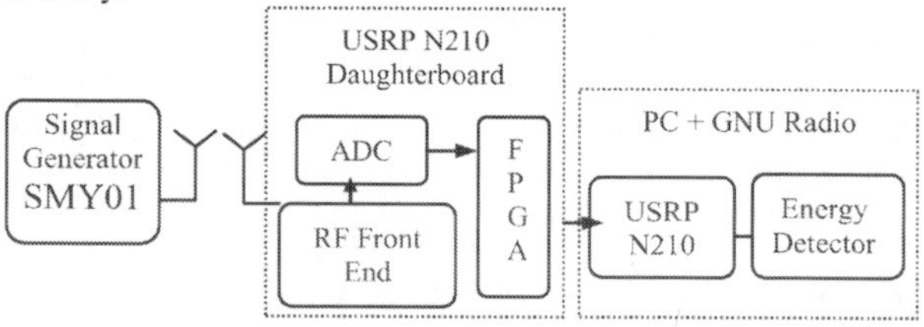

Figure 2. Block diagram of the experimental set-up for testing the energy detector

The ED developed is tested, as shown on the block diagram of the experimental set-up from Fig. 2. A signal generator SMY01 9 kHz – 1.040 GHz Rohde & Schwarz is used for transmitter. It is connected with broadcast antenna by Bayonet Neill–Concelman (BNC) coaxial cable. The generator is set to a frequency of 433MHz, with FM modulation with a deviation of 200 kHz. The generator provides different values of the transmitted signal in the range -30 dBm to 10 dBm with step of 2 dBm. The receiver is implemented with USRP N210 of Ettus Research, connected to a PC via Gigabit Ethernet, installed with a GNU Radio.

III. Cooperative Spectrum Sensing scheme and experimental set-up using USRPs and GNU Radio

The system considered consists in a single PU and four SUs, all located in a laboratory. One of the SUs - SU1 is put behind a screen. During the experience no change in noise conditions is considered. The SUs detect the spectrum for the presence of the PU signal and a FC takes the global decision after a preliminary selection of the PUs to be involved in the decision process. Hard decision combining rules are applied in the FC, for making decision about the presence of PU signal. The SUs make local decision and send 1 bit decision to the data FC. The FC combines sensing results and makes the global decision by AND, OR and MAJORITY rule. The function OR decides that the PU signal is present when any SU has reported "1". The function AND decides that the PU signal is present when all SUs have reported decision "1". In MAJORITY rule, if half or more SUs have reported a local decision "1", FC decides that PU signal is present. The block diagram of the experimental set-up is shown on Fig. 3. Here, also a signal generator SMY01 9 kHz – 1.040 GHz Rohde & Schwarz is used as a transmitter. It is connected with broadcast antenna by BNC coaxial cable. The generator is set to a frequency of 433MHz, with FM modulation with a deviation of 200 kHz. The generator provides values with different of the transmitted signal in the range – from 30 dBm to 10 dBm with a step of 2 dBm/5 dBm.

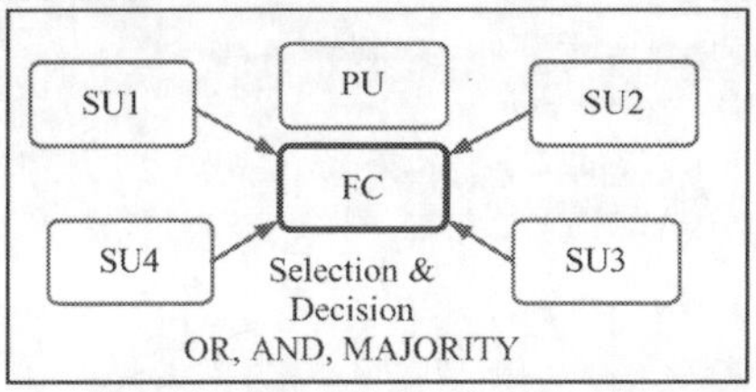

Figure 3. Block diagram of the model of cooperative sensing system

The receivers are implemented with 4 USRP N210 of Ettus Research, connected to a host personal computer (PC) via Gigabit Ethernet installed with a GNU Radio.

Photos of the experimental set-up are shown and the flowgraph in GNU Radio for saving measurement data files at Fig. 4. Data are saved for 2 minutes at each emitted power. Fourteen files are created for each one of the 4 SUs. The first group of 4 measured files is obtained when signal is missing and only noise is received. The EDs in the SUs calculate in that case the noise variance σ_w^2 estimations. These estimations are used later as input data for each one of the EDs in the SUs. The values obtained are presented in Table I.

TABLE I. Noise variance estimations σ_w^2 in SUs

SU	SU1	SU2	SU3	SU4
σ_w^2	14.7nW	46.5nW	43.6nW	46.1nW

Combining rule block diagrams for functions OR/AND applied for decision making in the FC are built in GNU Radio companion. On Fig. 5 is shown the flowgraph for global decision taking in FC, using the function OR. The sequences emerging at the output of the detector are collected by the block File Sink and they are saved in files. The files are binary type, and they can be opened in MATLAB. The FC decisions for MAJORITY function are calculated in MATLAB.

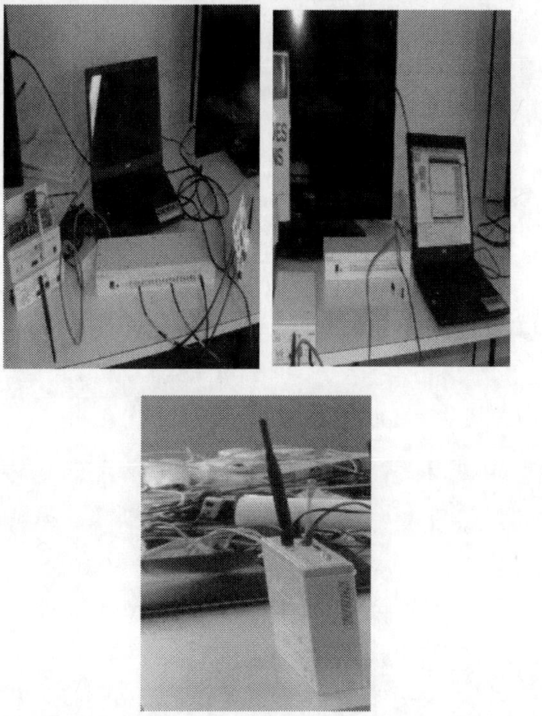

Figure 4. Experimental set-up for cooperative sensing and flowgraph in GNU Radio for saving measured data files

IV. Results from Cooperative Spectrum Sensing based on measurement data

The ED's performance characteristic of the probability of detection P_d as a function of SNR is built, based on subsets of the first 700000 data of each file from the experimental file set for the 4 SUs. Fig. 6 presents the P_d(SNR) curves for all 4 SUs.

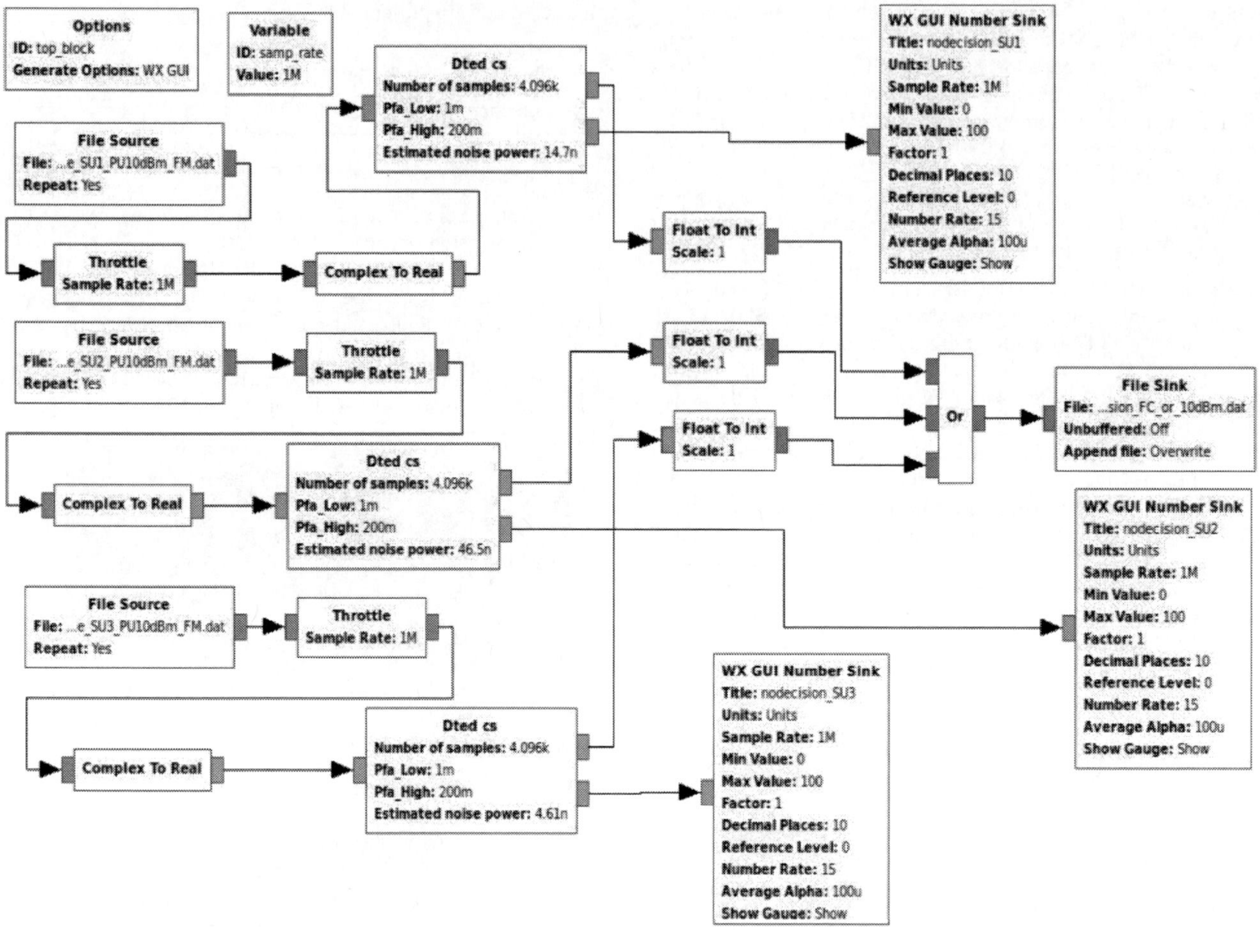

Figure 5. Flowgraph in GNU radio for global decision taking in a fusion center, using the function OR on the local decisions of SUs

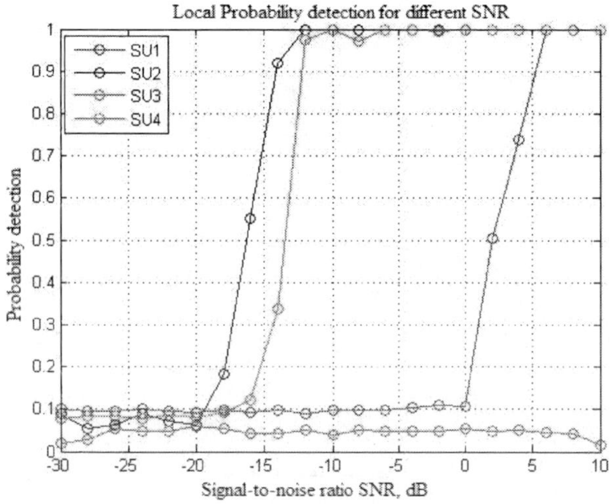

Figure 6. Pd(SNR) curves for all 4 SUs

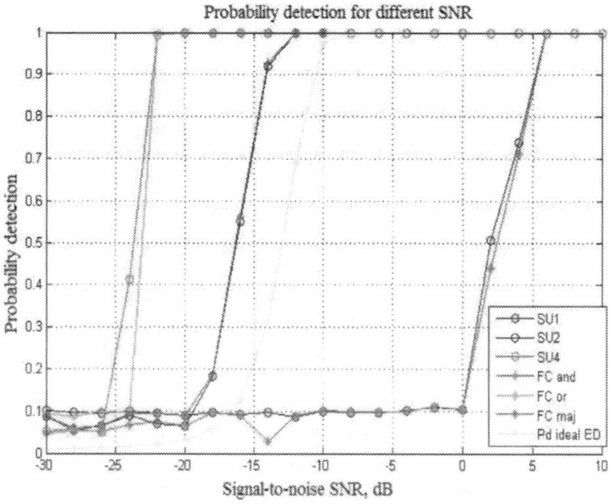

Figure 7. P_d(SNR) curves of 3 SUs selected by FC, P_d(SNR) curves of FC using functions OR, AND, MAJORITY and MATLAB curve as reference

The observation of the 4 curves show that 3 of the Pd curves for SU1, 2, 4 are typical ED curves and the P_d curve for SU3 is almost invariant. It's a good illustration of the need of selection procedure in the FC for security and reliability reasons. Outliers and sharply differing curves have to be discarded to avoid skewed result for the global decision.

Here, the criterion proposed in [12], for discarding SUs with invariant curves by the FC, before decision making, is applied. So, the global decision, taken by the FC is based on results from SU1, 2, 4. Three SUs, often used in cooperative sensing experiments [7][15], are enough to give meaningful results for MAJORITY function, which is not possible with 2 SUs [5][16].

Three rules - OR, AND, MAJORITY combinations of the local decisions of the three SUs are experimented. Fig. 7 presents the P_d(SNR) curves of the 3 SUs, selected by FC and the P_d(SNR) curves of the FC when using functions OR, AND, MAJORITY on the local decisions of these 3 SUs. As it can be noticed, the OR function gives the best result in this particular experience. The yellow curve comes from simulation in MATLAB and it's given as reference. The results on Fig. 7 are obtained after 100 minutes long simulation on a notebook. The results on Fig.7 fully correspond to theory. Functions OR and MAJORITY in FC decision allow to overcome the late detection from SU1 which is behind the screen. The MAJORITY curve is the closest to the MATLAB simulation curve and it's the recommended function for the FC since the risk in the OR function is that in case of false alarm in only one SU, it will be transmitted to the FC decision.

V. Conclusion

The paper presents the results of a research on the implementation on USRP and GNU Radio of cooperative sensing system with EDs. The experimental setup realized permits to perform experiments using different scenarios as OR, AND, MAJORITY rules for decision making in FC on the basis of local decisions of SUs. More research on the performance of each function in cases of lower and higher thresholds in the EDs is foreseen. Special attention is given to selection function which is important to be included in the FC in order to discard outlying and misleading results, thus improving reliability and security of the system. Further work is foreseen focused on uncertainty influence and overcoming in cooperative sensing systems.

Acknowledgement

This research is partly supported by the project Bg:DRILA01/10/17.04.2015 from Fund "Nauchni izsledvania", Fr: Project №34281ZM. Additional information on the project can be found on www.phcrila15.free.bg.

References

[1] S. Mishra, A. Sahai, and R. Brodersen, "Cooperative sensing among cognitive radios," Proc. IEEE ICC 2006, vol.4, pp.1658-1663, june 2006

[2] S. Atapattu, Ch. Tellambura, and H. Jiang, "Energy Detection for Spectrum Sensing in Cognitive Radio", Springer Briefs in Computer Science, pp. 11-26, 2014,

[3] Sh. Hossain, I. Abdullah, and M. A. Hossain, "Energy Detection Performance of Spectrum Sensing in Cognitive Radio", I.J. Information Technology and Computer Science, pp.11-17, November 2012.

[4] A. Nafkha, M. Naoues, K. Cichon, and A. Kliks, "Experimental Spectrum Sensing Measurements using USRP Software Radio Platform and GNU-Radio", CROWNCOM June 2014, Oulu, Finland, pp. 429- 434.

[5] Y. Fu, D. Liu, Zh. Li, and Q. Liu, "Implementation of Centralized Cooperative Spectrum Sensing Based on USRP", International Conference on Logistics Engineering, Management and Computer Science, pp.962-966, May 2014.

[6] S. Bahamou, et al., "Noise uncertainty analysis of energy detector: Bounded and unbounded approximation relationship," in Proceedings of the 21st European Signal Processing Conference, , pp. 1-4, September 2013.

[7] Ian F. Akyildiz, and B. F. Lo, R. Balakrishnan, "Cooperative spectrum sensing in cognitive radio networks A survey", Physical Communication 4, March 2011, pp.40–62

[8] N. Zhao, F. R. Yu, H. Sun, and A. Nallanathan, "Energy-efficient cooperative spectrum sensing schemes for cognitive radio networks", EURASIP Journal on Wireless Communications and Networking, pp.1-14,May 2013.

[9] D.Teguig, B.Scheers, and V.Le Nir, "Data Fusion Schemes for Cooperative Spectrum Sensing in Cognitive Radio Networks", Communications and Information Systems Conference (MCC), pp.1-7,October 2012 Military.

[10] Sh. Hossain, M. Rahman, I. Abdullah, and M. A. Hossain, "Hard Combination Data Fusion for Cooperative Spectrum Sensing in Cognitive Radio", International Journal of Electrical and Computer Engineering , pp. 811-818, December 2012.

[11] Y. Zhao, J. Pradhan, J.Huang, Y.Luo, and L.Pu, "Joint energy-and-bandwidth spectrum sensing with GNU radio and USRP", Newsletter ACM SIGAPP Applied Computing Review, pp.40-49, December 2014.

[12] J. D. Gadze, Oyibo, A. Michael, Ajobiewe, and N. Damilola, "A Performance Study of Energy Detection Based Spectrum Sensing for Cognitive Radio Networks", International Journal of Emerging Technology and Advanced Engineering, pp.21-29, April 2014

[13] H. Rifà-Pous, M. J. Blasco, and C. Garrigues, "Review of Robust Cooperative Spectrum Sensing Techniques for Cognitive Radio Networks", Springer Science+Business Media, LLC, pp. 175-198, November 2011.

[14] D. Bielefeld, G. Fabeck, M. Zivkovic, and R. Mathar, "Optimization of Cooperative Spectrum Sensing and Implementation on Software Defined Radios", Applied Sciences in Biomedical and Communication Technologies (ISABEL), 3rd International Symposium, pp.1-5, November 2010.

[15] A. Haniz, M. Rahman, M. Kim, and J. Takada, "Implementation of a Cooperative Spectrum Sensing System using GNU Radio and USRP", IEICE General Conference, p.667, 2010

[16] R.Yoshimura et al. "A USRP based scheme for cooperative sensing networks" IV Workshop de Redes de Acesso em Banda Larga (WRA), pp. 67-76, May 2014.

[17] GNU radio, the free and open software radio ecosystem, http://gnuradio.org/[retrieved:April, 2016]

Software-Defined Networking for Industry 4.0

Theo Lins,
Mauricio Jose da Silva and
Ricardo Augusto Rabelo Oliveira

iMobilis Laboratory - DECOM
Federal University of Ouro Preto
Ouro Preto - MG - Brazil
Email: theosl,badricio,rrabelo@gmail.com

***Abstract*—The growing interest in Industry 4.0 increased the search for technologies that can help in its implementation. This technology has also evolved over the years enabling an increasing deployment of these industries. The Internet of Things (IoT), communication machine-to-machine (M2M) and Cypher Physical Systems (CPS) are essential for the implementation of Industry 4.0, while the Software Defined Networks (SDN), arrives as a new concept that can help in communicating devices that are part of the network that works with these industries. In our paper, we present an SDN architecture that implements the control plane together with the production control of an industry, where production decisions are passed directly to the SDN controller. In addition to the implementation of SDN communication, we also show the communication using a traditional network of computers. To validate the SDN architecture, we perform some simulation in scenarios of Industry 4.0, where success was obtained in the communications of industrial components.**

Keywords–Industry 4.0; SDN; IoT; M2M; CPS.

I. INTRODUCTION

With the emergence of new technologies over the past few years, several industry sectors have benefited from advances. The trend is that more and more technologies are created in to assist us in everyday tasks. But for this to happen, we must use them efficiently and effectively.

Among these technologies, we can highlight the Internet of Things, which are physical objects with some kind of technology such as Radio Frequency Identification (RFID) tags or sensors connected to the computer network, known as smart devices. These smart devices enable the integration of various processes such as communication devices themselves, production information, environmental information, equipment status and many other services.

New global requirements, such as environmental awareness also benefit from the use of these technologies, which have changed the way of production in industries with the use of green products and energy efficiency Based on these changes and developments, the main purpose of our paper is to propose a architecture of communication that can help in the technological evolution of industries, better known as Industry 4.0, making the communication more agile and efficient.

In Section II, we will present the technologies used in Industry 4.0. In Section III, we will present the SDN architecture for communication in Industry 4.0. In Section IV, we will perform the simulation with the proposed architecture, and finally in Section V, we present the conclusion and future work.

A. Problems and Goals

In the Industry 4.0, there may be hundreds of smart devices, devices that require network connections to cooperate with each other, and to perform increasingly complex tasks without manual assistance.

In addition to the proposal for an architecture that can connect the various components of Industry 4.0, from sensors to customers, there are also specific goals that would approach the requirements necessary for the operation of Industry 4.0.

Some requirements for the implantation of Industry 4.0 highlight some cited by Shrouf et al. [1]:

- Mass customization: Production processes have to meet varying requirements of production orders. It allows individuals to be included in the design, and enables last minute changes.
- Flexibility: Intelligent production processes and self configuration have to consider different aspects; such as time, quality, price and the ecological aspects.
- Factory visibility and optimized decision-making: Making the right decisions at anytime is a key to succeed in the market. IoT provides end-to-end transparency almost in real time (e.g., production status), allowing for optimization across factory sites in the area of production, and then improvement in factory efficiency.
- Connected Supply Chain: IoT will help manufacturers gain a better understanding of the supply chain information that can be delivered in real time. By connecting the machines and equipment to suppliers, all parties can understand interdependencies, the flow of materials, and manufacturing cycle times.
- Energy management: Energy efficiency improvement requires awareness of energy consumption behavior at production line and machine level. Smart meters can provide real time data, and take decisions based on their capabilities and in collaboration with external services.
- Creating values from big data collected: New improvements and value can be provided by the analysis of large quantities of data connected by IoT devices (i.e. big data).
- Remote monitoring: IoT technology will enable involvement by a third party (e.g., suppliers) in monitoring, operating and the maintenance of factories with

new services.

- Proactive maintenance: Monitoring production system and collecting performance data in real time will have a positive impact to improve proactive maintenance.

B. Contributions of Work

To achieve our main goal, we implemented an architecture of computer networks for Industry 4.0 using the paradigm of SDN to connect the components of Industry 4.0. With the new architecture we can mention some of the contributions:

- External communication for devices through Gateway SDN.
- Connection and management of data a cloud.
- Dynamic management of smart devices.
- Feed of data and automatically decision-making.
- Optimization and fault tolerance in production lines.
- Connection of customers and suppliers directly with Industry 4.0.
- We create scenarios for Industry 4.0 and run tests with simulators.

II. Industry 4.0 and its Technologies

The next step in the industrial development will be related to smart devices and the interaction of the products that are a part of the manufacturing process. Also called the New Industrial Revolution, Industry 4.0 or Intelligent Industry aims to transform the product which is usually a passive object into an active object, it is essential for decision-making and optimization of its manufacturing.

Among the main features of smart devices is the ability to self-monitor, detect faults, alter flows, perform calculations, and the main function is to communicate with other components.

Some recent research already addresses the Industry 4.0, Varghese et al. [2], discuss some of the challenges of wireless communication that must be met before it can be utilized in Industry 4.0. They describe how the 5G can help with the implementation, considering the communication m2m focused on latency, longevity, and reliability of communication. In our work in addition to addressing wireless communication and M2M communication, treat interoperability between communications technologies and validated through simulation, the implementation of an Industry 4.0. M2M communication, the study [3] Paelke show that the Intelligent Industry can also help users in manual tasks performed in the industry. An initial experience with an augmented reality system helps workers in an environment with constant changes in production decisions. The system helps workers in unfamiliar tasks through spatially registered task information in the users field of vision.

Gorecky et al. [4] also highlight the participation of users in Industry 4.0, with the flexibility proposed in this new concept, users will be faced with a wide variety of works ranging from the specification and monitoring, to also check production strategies. The aid technology will allow users to perform the management more accurately as well as control the production.

But there are still many essential concepts behind the Industry 4.0, such as Cyber Physical Systems, the Internet of Things and Machine-to-machine communication.

A. Cyber-Physical Systems

CPS are automated systems that enable connection of the operations of the physical reality with computing and communication infrastructures. Unlike traditional embedded systems, which are designed as standalone devices, the focus in CPS is on networking several devices. CPS goes with the trend of having information and services everywhere at hand, and its inevitable in the highly networked world of today [5].

The infrastructure of Industry 4.0 is composed of CPS, which makes the study of these systems necessary for correct implementation. Jazdi [5]present a prototype that demonstrates the essential aspects of Industry 4.0. In our work as well as evidenced in an architecture for network communication, we conducted several tests to validate the operation of the network.

B. Internet of Things

With the growth and popularization of the Internet emerged the IoT, this evolution is the future of communication and even computation. But for it to develop further, it depends on new technologies and service models that are being created and/or improved. For the IoT is a network of devices that make the integration between the physical and computational systems all through an infrastructure that collects and exchanges information.

To better understand the information circulating in IoT networks, Perera et al. [6] made a study of the context aware of this information. The work is an analysis of the context of the life cycle, and evaluates a subset of related projects. Based on these evaluations, they compare, highlight the lessons learned, and discuss the applicability to the Internet of Things.

In addition, the IoT is also one of the main factors involved in the implementation of Industry 4.0, if not the biggest supporter so that the next step is taken. This is due to its connectivity and interaction with many devices such as the Industry 4.0.

In [1], it is shown the relationship between IoT and Industry 4.0, which is created an architecture for Industry 4.0 based on IoT. They define the main characteristics of Industry 4.0 focused on sustainability. And propose an approach to power management in Intelligent Industries based on the paradigm IoT.

C. Machine-to-Machine

M2M technologies are used for communication between devices. Kim et al. [7] did a study on the M2M communication. They discuss the need for M2M platforms, comparing and analyzing the existing approaches and M2M solutions platforms, Thereby Identifying the requirements and functionality of the optimal service platform for M2M. Finally based on this information, the authors propose an architecture for M2M services platform (M2SP) and its features, then present the M2M ecosystem with this platform. Different application scenarios are presented to Illustrate the interaction between the components of the proposed platform.

So in the Industry 4.0 M2M, the communication between production components is allowed, enabling the exchange of information between them, facilitating decision making and speeding up the entire production process.

D. Software-Defined Networking

In recent years, the traditional networks have been limited compared to other technologies, as it relates to the management, performance, and scalability. Contrary to this limitation, a new paradigm in networks has shown to be the solution,

SDNs propose networks which have more flexible and dynamic computers.

The idea of SDN is to separate the control plane from the data plane while the data plan stays in the forwarding devices, the control plane stays in a central controller with a software responsible for the behavior of the network. The protocol OpenFlow is the most used for communication of SDN components and the main focus of recent related research because it allows the creation of SDN networks with common forwarding devices.

Despite many studies related to SDN and OpenFlow, so far there are few studies using SDN applied to IoT, some work as [8], presenthow the structure should be made, but does not simulate and generate statistic results. Already in [9] they designed an approach defined by software to an IoT environment in a scenario involving a heterogeneous wireless network. The prototype then uses a scenario with electric vehicles, locations for electric loading, and a smart grid infrastructure. But the IoT network vehicle has different requirements from a network of Industry 4.0, as a much greater mobility.

SDN can also address many challenges of Industry 4.0, since the adaptability which is one of the main characteristics of SDN to the energy efficiency that can be improved with communication between devices. Because the Industry 4.0 has a knack for effective communication as well as its flexibility and self-management, its exactly what the SDN has to offer. What makes SDN one with a potential tool for technology deployment Industry 4.0.

A well-known SDN limitation is centralized control. In Industry 4.0 network this limitation tends to be lower, due to the low data flow during production. But the network controller is a point of failure, meaning that if it stops working, the whole network stops. But this problem has been solved by using some techniques [10] of distributed network control.

In this paper, the SDN network is responsible for every connection made by smart devices and products. In order to have more efficient connections, favoring communication between devices, products, customers, suppliers, and administrators.

III. SDN ARCHITECTURE FOR INDUSTRY 4.0

The traditional computer networks are not prepared to adapt to constant changes that occur in the network flow and a lot of devices and information travels on it. These are the characteristics of most IoT networks. Based on these characteristics some authors have proposed SDN architectures for IoT [11][12][13], but to date none about Industry 4.0.

In Figure 1 it is shown an SDN architecture with applications and equipment used in Industry 4.0.

The application layer has applications that communicate with the SDN controller, and we implemented an Application Programming Interface (API) that communicates the SDN controller with the Production controller. The production controller is responsible for managing the production, as well as the one who makes all decisions related to production. When a decision is recieved, the production controller passes the information necessary to the SDN controller, in reverse the same thing is done when the SDN controller collects information related to the network, it transfers it to the production controller, all done through the API.

We also have the application layer of the cloud of data that

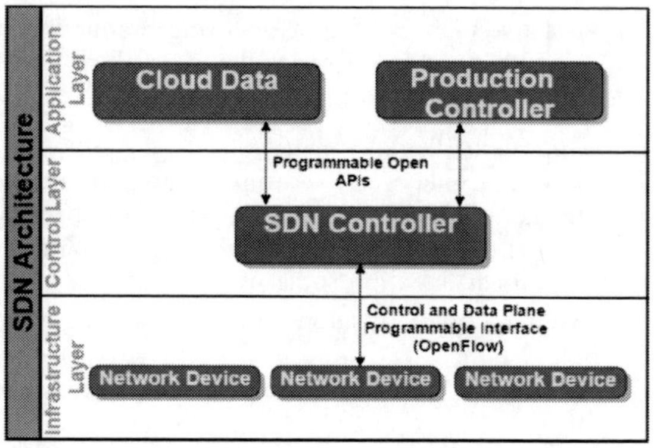

Figure 1. SDN architecture with the Production Controller.

is responsible for storing all the data collected. In the cloud, part of the production data can be accessed by customers and suppliers, who use this to follow the production process and to send data to the cloud, data that will be used by the production controller. While the production controller writes production data in the cloud, the Network Controller (SDN) enables automation of services, which is critical for cloud services. From the network details collected, all changes requested by cloud components are automatically reflected in the forwarding plane.

The control layer has the SDN Controller which is the central node of the industrys communications network, and responsible for all network management. The API that communicates with the application layer must be implemented in the same language of the controller. To communicate with the infrastructure layer a SDN protocol should be used, in our case, we use the OpenFlow.

In the infrastructure layer, all the SDN devices are managed by SDN controller, these devices have only the data plan that is sent by the controller, and any other decision is taken by the SDN controller, which has the control plane. While the switches receive and must perform packet forwarding, the gateway receives this and mounts their routes for communication. Status and information of sensors can be collected, as well as the necessary information to communicate with different networks and technologies, for example we can mention the cloud communications.

A. Packet Forwarding

The data path of an OpenFlow switch contains one or more flow tables. Each flow table in the switch contains a set of flow entries where each entry contains match fields, counters, and instructions. An entry is identified by its extensible match fields which comprise the switch ingress port and different packet header fields. For received packets on the data path, the switch tries to match the ingress port and packet headers with the match fields in the different flow entries.

If a flow entry field is wildcarded and has a value of ANY, it matches all possible values in the header. Only the highest priority flow entry that matches the packet must be selected. The counters associated with the selected flow entry must be updated and the included instruction set must be applied. If a matching entry is found, the instructions associated with the specific flow entry are executed. If no match is found in a flow table, the outcome depends on the switch configuration. The default in the OpenFlow switch specification version 1.2 is to send packets to the controller over the OpenFlow channel via a packet-in message. Another option is to drop the packet. The packet-in message may either contain the entire packet or just a fraction of the packet header [14].

IV. Simulation and Validation

Industry 4.0 implies the use of concepts that tangent state of the art, such as CPS, M2M and IoT, to create a smart production process, which is self-manageable and dynamic. SDN apply under this scenario allows a flexible management resource. In order to evaluate the performance of the communication mechanisms of an SDN network a different simulation was implemented in OMNeT ++ simulator [15] with an extension to OpenFlow call ofomnet [14]. In addition to the performance analysis of the SDN, we also provide an analysis of the capacity of a production process on Industry 4.0 to self-manage and self stabilize.

A. Scenarios

Based on some studies [16][17], about Industry 4.0, we developed a production scenario that addresses some characteristics in these industries. The chosen scenario is a generic factory that has N line productions, with several interconnected devices. In Figure 2 a production line used at work in Industry 4.0. Therefore, all applications used in the scenarios were implemented in the Industry 4.0 standards.

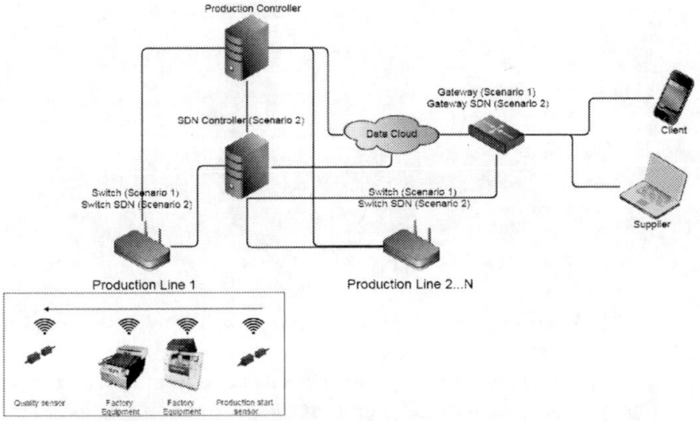

Figure 2. Scenario addressing Industry 4.0 on OMNeT ++.

To compare the possible deployments of Industry 4.0, we implemented two scenarios, the first scenario works with a traditional network of computers and is called Scenario 1. The second is Scenario 2 and works on an SDN network, in this case there is an additional network controller, and network switches are SDN, specifically OpenFlow.

Below is a description of each component of the scenario:

- Manufactured product: the product is an active object in production, where each product has an RFID tag, which will be used to identify the product, from the start of production until such time that it is ready to be sent to a client.
- Client: It is an agent, which can be a person or another industry, which should be able to place orders on demand and monitor the production process of your order. The manufacturing process is a response to a client request.
- Supplier: It is notified by Industry 4.0 when there is a need for more raw material for production.
- Production controller: Controls the entire process of production in Industry 4.0, in Scenario 2 some of its features are automated by the SDN. In addition to collecting information about each product throughout the production line, the production controller is able to make decisions such as:
    - When a production line is overloaded, the load is distributed with other production lines.
    - If the inventory level of raw material is low, more raw materials are required to go to the supplier
    - If the production line is idle, the line is used to produce another product.
- Data Cloud: The cloud stores all the information that is transmitted in Industry 4.0, and customers and suppliers also have access. The production control and data cloud could be implemented together, but for better organization and independence, we decided to implement them separately.
- SDN Controller: Is implemented using the OpenFlow protocol, and used in the scenario 2. The SDN controller is responsible for managing the Indust.ry 4.0 network. In the scenario 2, the SDN controller exchanges information with the production controller to make decisions about packet forwarding, and networking devices status check.
- Switch/Gateway: In the scenario 1 we use common switching devices. In scenario 2 everything is implemented using the OpenFlow protocol. In this case, the Switch/Gateway is managed by SDN controller, that mounts the data plan.
- Production start sensor (RFID Product): RFID sensor that collects product tags to begin the manufacturing process.
- Quality sensor (RFIDSize and RFIDWeigth): RFID sensors that are responsible for quality control. If the product does not have the quality requirements it is discarded and the request for a new product is sent to the server.
- Factory Equipment: The equipment is used in the manufacture of the product, and are also connected to the production controller by an switch. Eg laser cutting machine, laser welding system, bending machine, thermoforming machine, etc.

B. Testing and Results

In order to evaluate the use of traditional computer networks and SDN in Industry 4.0, we implemented two production lines that are able to attend the demand of a client automatically. Products used generically to illustrate that this process can be applied to other kinds of industry.

The simulation begins with a client requesting 100 products in producing. Throughout the simulation, the client makes 10 requests for 100 products in each. These requests are made periodically, and it is important to validate the properties of the industry cope with the demand scale, distributed production between the various production lines reducing the possibility that they are idle.

The production process begins when the production controller receives a client request. At this time, the production controller checks for raw materials in sufficient inventory to meet the new demand for products, if there is no stock of raw materials, or if the stock not enough, the production controller makes a request to the supplier for more feedstock. As we are dealing with a factory, it is common for some raw material is lost during the production process, therefore, the production controller considers it a waste rate of 10% when making a request to the supplier.

As noted above, a stock or raw material may exist, but this stock is not enough to attend the clients demands. In this case, the production controller requests the production of many products as the stock allows, and the other products of demand are produced when the production controller is able to guarantee enough stock to produce them.

Still with the objective of maintaining the tests applicable to other industries, monitoring the product within the production process is made by three sensors which represent: a sensor for registering the start of manufacturing of a product, from this moment the product is monitored until it is ready to be delivered to the customer.

The two other sensors represent quality tests to which products must attend. For each product, it is generated a random number between 0 and 1 with uniform distribution. If the generated number is greater than 0.9, the product is considered defective and the production process has to deal with such a problem requiring the production of a substitute product, guaranteeing that the client demand is met.

During the simulations, to meet customer demand of 1000 products, the error function used by the sensors detected in average 224 defective products in scenario 1 and 226 in scenario 2, that is, during the entire production process in average were produced 1224 products in scenario 1 and 1226 in scenario 2. Despite that error rate though it may seem large for a production process for our experiments it represents greater opportunities for communication, the greater amount of data transmitted and even still, an opportunity for more learning.

The simulations used parameters related to the Ethernet protocol, which can be seen in Table I. To generate the results we conducted 3 simulations for each scenario, then we averaged the results.

TABLE I. PARAMETERS USED IN THE SIMULATION.

Parameter	*Value*
Delay in channel	1μ
Transmission rate	$100Mbps$
Request package size	$200B$
Response package size	$1MB$

As a result the communication showed the most common metrics used in computer networks such as end-to-end delay, sent packets, and received packet. Figures 3 showed the end-to-end delay of main simulation devices, with the information of maximum delay, minimum delay, average delay, and standard deviation.

Made more comparisons between scenarios can be seen in the Figure 4, is made counting the number of incoming and outgoing packets in Mbytes, respectively. The communication usually begins with a request from a client that attends and is then answered by the server. As we can see in Table I, the size of the request and response packets are 200B and 1MB, respectively. That server usually answers the requests and the requests contain only 200B, which causes it to transmit fewer bytes than the other network nodes.

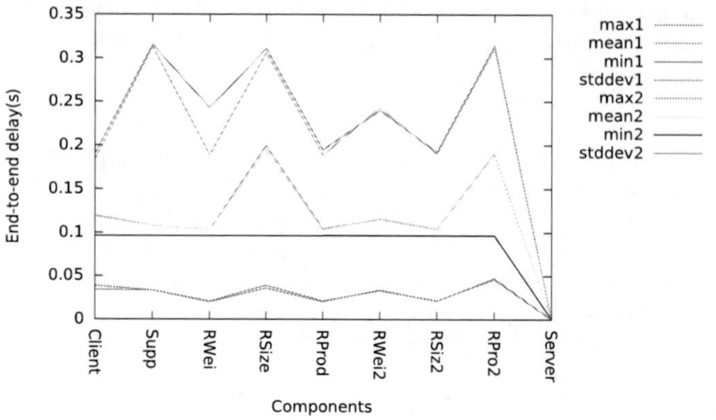

Figure 3. End-to-End delay - Scenario 1 and 2.

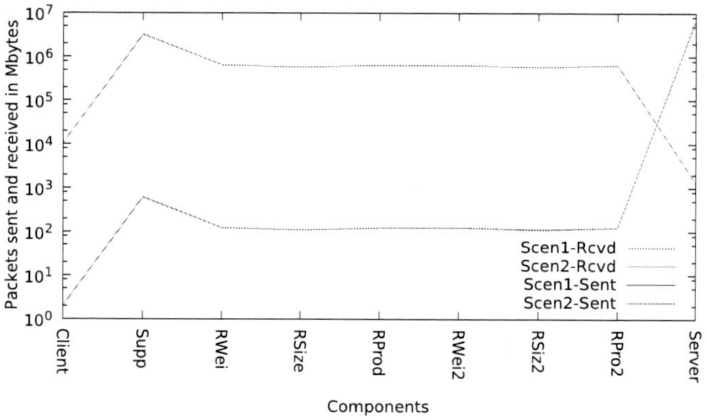

Figure 4. Number of packets sent and received in Mbytes.

To illustrate the benefits of using the SDN Industry 4.0, we made some simulations to show the efficiency of the use of SDN. In the simulation, a product takes on average 100s to finish, and a new product starts on the production line every 5s, thereby a production line has a maximum 20 products being produced.

In Figures 5 and 6, it is shown the simulation of 50 products in the same two scenarios with two Production Lines(PL1Cen1, PL2Cen1, PL1Cen2, PL2Cen2). In Figure 5, it is shown a number of products in process of production at an instant of time. The increasing number means new products being produced, and the declining number means products being finalized. During the simulation a failure occurs in a production equipment at 120s, between the interval of 60s and 180s.

In scenario 2, when a problem occurs in some equipment production, the moment in which the machine fails or stops the communicate, the Network Controller detects based on communication with the switch, and communicates the Production Controller. Then, the production controller changes the production line until the problem is resolved. In scenario 1, if the equipment fails, the production controller will not have a quick feedback, it will not know if the communication is slow or stopped. When the problem occurs in any network equipment, in scenario 2 it automatically can be solved by the network controller, which can change the route of communication, which can not be done in Scenario 1.

In Figure 6, it is shown the finished products where the scenario 1 finished all production in 355s, the scenario 2 finished the same amount of products in 305s. Other simulations were realized with some types of failures(Failure to equipment, switch overload, failure to sensors) and all had similar results.

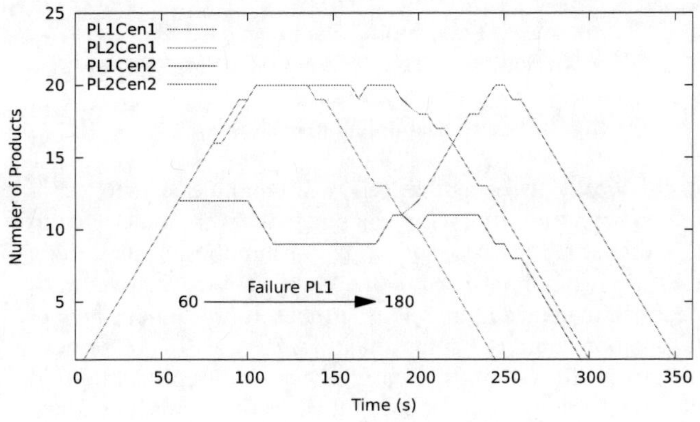

Figure 5. Production.

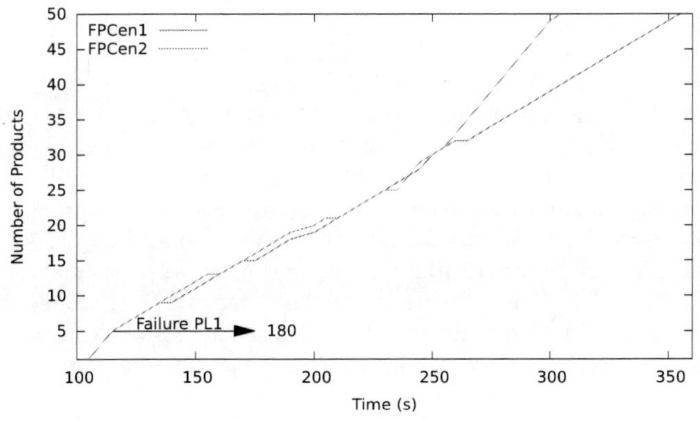

Figure 6. Finalized Products

From these results it is possible to observe that the bigger the number of production lines and equipment, the more evident will be the advantages of using the SDN.

V. Conclusion and Future Work

In the article, we propose an SDN architecture for network communication in Industry 4.0 based on SDN, which enables a flexible and effective management in the flow control of production and resources. The architecture uses the SDN Controller working together with the Production Controller, providing speed in decision making. Many APIs have been implemented and tested in a simulation in scenarios for Industry 4.0. The infrastructure has enabled customers and suppliers, consult and add information in real time on production.

The simulation results showed that it is possible to implement this new concept called Industry 4.0 and will soon be a reality for most industries. It was also shown that the features of technologies such as IoT, M2M, CPS and SDN are essential to the implementation of the Industry 4.0.

As future work we intend to simulate variations in the scenarios, implement new functions for SDN devices, and work on the security of network devices.

References

[1] F. Shrouf, J. Ordieres, and G. Miragliotta, "Smart factories in industry 4.0: A review of the concept and of energy management approached in production based on the internet of things paradigm," in Industrial Engineering and Engineering Management (IEEM), 2014 IEEE International Conference on. IEEE, 2014, pp. 697–701.

[2] A. Varghese and D. Tandur, "Wireless requirements and challenges in industry 4.0," in Contemporary Computing and Informatics (IC3I), 2014 International Conference on. IEEE, 2014, pp. 634–638.

[3] V. Paelke, "Augmented reality in the smart factory: Supporting workers in an industry 4.0. environment," in Emerging Technology and Factory Automation (ETFA), 2014 IEEE. IEEE, 2014, pp. 1–4.

[4] D. Gorecky, M. Schmitt, M. Loskyll, and D. Zuhlke, "Human-machine-interaction in the industry 4.0 era," in Industrial Informatics (INDIN), 2014 12th IEEE International Conference on. IEEE, 2014, pp. 289–294.

[5] N. Jazdi, "Cyber physical systems in the context of industry 4.0," in Automation, Quality and Testing, Robotics, 2014 IEEE International Conference on. IEEE, 2014, pp. 1–4.

[6] C. Perera, A. Zaslavsky, P. Christen, and D. Georgakopoulos, "Context aware computing for the internet of things: A survey," Communications Surveys & Tutorials, IEEE, vol. 16, no. 1, 2014, pp. 414–454.

[7] J. Kim, J. Lee, J. Kim, and J. Yun, "M2m service platforms: survey, issues, and enabling technologies," Communications Surveys & Tutorials, IEEE, vol. 16, no. 1, 2014, pp. 61–76.

[8] H. Huang, J. Zhu, and L. Zhang, "An sdn_based management framework for iot devices," in Irish Signals & Systems Conference 2014 and 2014 China-Ireland International Conference on Information and Communications Technologies (ISSC 2014/CIICT 2014). 25th IET. IET, 2013, pp. 175–179.

[9] Z. Qin, G. Denker, C. Giannelli, P. Bellavista, and N. Venkatasubramanian, "A software defined networking architecture for the internet-of-things," in Network Operations and Management Symposium (NOMS), 2014 IEEE. IEEE, 2014, pp. 1–9.

[10] A. Krishnamurthy, S. P. Chandrabose, and A. Gember-Jacobson, "Pratyaastha: An efficient elastic distributed sdn control plane," in Proceedings of the third workshop on Hot topics in software defined networking. ACM, 2014, pp. 133–138.

[11] N. Omnes, M. Bouillon, G. Fromentoux, and O. Grand, "A programmable and virtualized network & it infrastructure for the internet of things: How can nfv & sdn help for facing the upcoming challenges," in Intelligence in Next Generation Networks (ICIN), 2015 18th International Conference on. IEEE, 2015, pp. 64–69.

[12] L. Galluccio, S. Milardo, G. Morabito, and S. Palazzo, "Sdn-wise: Design, prototyping and experimentation of a stateful sdn solution for wireless sensor networks," in Computer Communications (INFOCOM), 2015 IEEE Conference on. IEEE, 2015, pp. 513–521.

[13] N. A. Jagadeesan and B. Krishnamachari, "Software-defined networking paradigms in wireless networks: a survey," ACM Computing Surveys (CSUR), vol. 47, no. 2, 2015, p. 27.

[14] D. Klein and M. Jarschel, "An openflow extension for the omnet++ inet framework," in Proceedings of the 6th International ICST Conference on Simulation Tools and Techniques. ICST (Institute for Computer Sciences, Social-Informatics and Telecommunications Engineering), 2013, pp. 322–329.

[15] A. Varga et al., "The omnet++ discrete event simulation system," in Proceedings of the European simulation multiconference (ESM 2001), vol. 9, no. S 185. sn, 2001, p. 65.

[16] H. Kagermann, J. Helbig, A. Hellinger, and W. Wahlster, Recommendations for Implementing the Strategic Initiative INDUSTRIE 4.0: Securing the Future of German Manufacturing Industry; Final Report of the Industrie 4.0 Working Group. Forschungsunion, 2013.

[17] M. Hermann, T. Pentek, and B. Otto, "Design principles for industrie 4.0 scenarios: A literature review," 2015.

Energy-Efficiency for Heterogenous Wireless Networks by using Hand-off Approach

Samet Öztoprak[1], M. Ali Aydın[2]
Department of Computer Engineering
Istanbul University
Istanbul, Turkey
sametoztoprak@hotmail.com[1], aydinali@istanbul.edu.tr[2]

Tülin Atmaca
Laboratoire Samovar
Télécom SudParis, CNRS, Université Paris-Saclay
Evry, France
tulin.atmaca@telecom-sudparis.eu

Abstract*—With the dense use of smart phones, the global mobile data traffic has increased from 0:2exabytes/month in 2010 to 2:5exabytes/month in 2014. With a growth of 1150% over 4 years it is expected that global mobile traffic will increase by a factor of 10 between 2014 and 2020 [1]. Mobile Base station (BS) cell sites consumed over 60% of the company total energy consumption for most mobile carriers, therefore current research has a significant focus on improving the energy efficiency of mobile access networks. In recent years, the increasing impact of networks on the environment has made energy efficiency in telecom networks an important theme for researches. In this context, heterogeneous wireless networks (HetNets) plays a key role in 4G and 5G due to offer easily access services anywhere and anytime. Our study is developed based on IPv4 protocol but our developed algorithm can apply too IPv6 easily. In this paper, we propose a new approaches which provides more energy efficient than Green Joint Radio Resource Management (JRRM) Architecture. Our proposed model has 2 stations, which are separated from each other. One of them, which is called macrocell, addresses the control of a vast territory. The other is located in more sophisticated and local areas. All calls come to the macrocell at first. According to the intensity of call rate microcells turn on or off. These actions are performed by a threshold located in the macrocell. Control of the macrocell achieves a good level of energy efficiency. As it is showed in the illustrations, Handoff Green JRRM Architecture is better than Green JRRM Architecture in the aspect of energy-saving, in any case. The energy-saving action changes the range from 45% to 70% in an average traffic load. Handoff Green's Dynamic Coverage Management (DCM) algorithm promises more opportunities in saving energy. Using a Markov model, the diagram of the states transitions is represented and some obtained performance results are showed by the figures.

Keywords-Energy efficiency; HetNets; joint radio resource management (JRRM); macrocell and microcell occupancy; green network design; threshold macrocell and microcell; Markov process; performance.

I. INTRODUCTION

In this paper, we have proposed a new algorithm for conserving energy in wireless networks which will be benefit economically for the power industry. The reason of these improvements to wireless networks is that the world of mobile communication growing at an amazing rate. Nowadays, Information Communication Technologies (ICT) consumes a significant portion of all energy that is produced in the world. It seems that ICT will continue to increase in the consumption of energy for many years to come. Due to this forecasted increase in energy consumption in the future, it is vital importance that some energy-saving actions must be taken in consideration. Furthermore, if precautions are not taken soon to improve this situation, there will be enormous negative effects on the environment. The production of electrical energy releases harmful gases that contribute to the Greenhouse Effect on the atmosphere. It is imperative that we make an effort to decrease this energy consumption as much as possible. One solution is finding "greener" ways to produce electricity, and another is to develop new technologies and methods of reducing the consumption of energy. In this paper, we have focused on the ways in which the consumption of electrical energy can be reduced.

The current forecasts predict that by 2018, high-speed coverage will reach over 85 percent of the world's population, and global traffic in mobile networks are going to rise with a compound annual growth rate (CAGR) of 50 percent, reaching a 12-fold increase since 2012 [2].

Nowadays, heterogeneous wireless networks (HetNets) 4G or 5G wireless networks allow to reach access services in everywhere and every time, the ICT carbon emission is comparable to that of the global aviation industry [3]. By 2020, this emission is foreseen to grow at a rate of 3.8 percent, expecting to contribute 2.3 percent of the global greenhouse gas emissions, which represents 1.27 $GtCo_2e^1$ [4]. The important part of this energy is consumed by Base Stations (BSs) [1]. This consumption is approximately 57% of the whole energies used by all ICT sector [5].

In our study, while lowering energy consumption we have to keep the performance of the system at acceptable level. Our developed algorithm defines a threshold value as a certain percentage of the whole capacity of the system. If the number of calls is lower than the defined threshold, the calls are accepted by macrocell and microcell is kept off. If the number of calls is equal or higher than the defined threshold, Calls are assigned to microcells from that are coming. The most engaged microcell is activated and its calls are transferred to their microcell. If microcell occupancy falls under predefined microcell threshold, the microcell transfers its calls to macrocell and closes itself. If microcell occupancy is greater than its threshold value, the microcell stays on working (on) state. Alternating microcells on working (on) and off states, we can save electrical energy.

In Section 2, we recall related works in this area and our contribution. In Section 3, we introduce general scheme and algorithm flow charts of the handoff green Joint Radio Resource Management (JRRM) algorithm that we developed. Besides, the explanation of our algorithm and it is shown the differences between green JRRM algorithm and handoff JRRM algorithm. Section 4 presents the modelling of our proposed scheme and the state transition diagram to compute blocking probability and idle state probability. Section 5 demonstrates the numerical results of energy-saving. One of them compares the two algorithms based on active microcell numbers. If we compare the number of active microcells, we will find the energy-saving ratio. In the last section, we talk about the future work to bring closer our experimented results to real ones by using real traffic and more microcells.

II. RELATED WORK

Falowo et al. [6] proposed the issue of unbalance in radio resources allocation among limited-capability heterogeneous mobile terminals in HetNets. They reproduced a terminal-modality based joint call admission control method that uses the RAT terminal capability and the network load as criteria for call admission control decisions.

Ngo et al. [7] addressed distributed RRM-based methods to optimally separate subcarriers and power in OFDM-based cognitive radio ad hoc networks. The issue of RRM is formulated as an optimization issue where the throughput is maximized subject to some network-related constraints such as the number of sub channels that each individual unlicensed user might engage, bearable interface at main network level, etc.

Guerrero-Ibanez [8] addressed a QoS-based dynamic pricing approach for services and besides resource supplying in HetNets. In their suggested scheme, an access network selection mechanism is proposed that assists choice the convenient network for every requested user's service and preferences.

Carvalho et al. [9] have proposed to build a green DCM algorithm which is based on a threshold. There are 2 layers which are called macrocell and microcell. Macrocell has the threshold making a decision whether or not microcell is needed to keep off.

In this study, the purpose of DCM algorithm is to ensure the energy efficient through the opening and closing of microcells on system by using a Markov model. Our contribution to this work is to reduce energy consumption by using handoff on macrocell and open the most engaged microcell.

Yao et al. [10] addressed the effectiveness of the derived centralized and decentralized QC-learning algorithms in balancing the tradeoff between energy saving and QoS satisfaction.

III. HANDOFF GREEN JRRM DESIGN

Our green JRRM algorithm is based on the following idea. We have to take into consideration the traffic load fluctuating during the day. The data is used as input values. Load of BSs is used to make a decision about the defining the threshold. The power-saving will be obtained by this threshold.

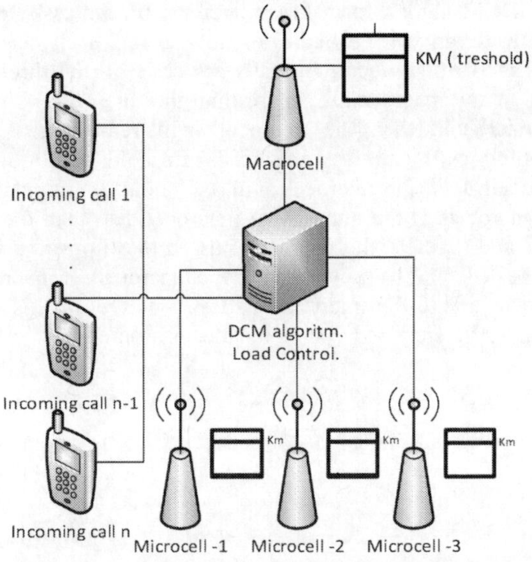

Figure 1 Handoff Green JRRM design

Figure 1 represents our green JRRM algorithm. It has two layers. One of them is called macrocell and the other is called as microcell. K is our Threshold value. According to K value, we are going to make a decision whether a BS is needed to be kept off or not. Load Control (LC) monitors the load of the system by certain periods. The decision of turning off a BS is made by DCM algorithm. In this architecture, macrocell always needs to be kept open. macrocell covers huge geographic territory generally considered as a country. Macrocell and microcells are completely independent of each other.

Figure 2 shows the flowchart of our algorithm. Let I_M be the call number of macrocell, let I_m be the call number of microcell and R_m is the number of calls continuing on microcell. After the calling reached to Green JRRM, it is necessary to determine their source, which requires recognizing whether or not the incoming calls are coming from the macrocell. After the call has been assigned as macrocell, and it is checked if this macrocell has the available capacity to handle the call, then if yes, the call will be accepted by the macrocell. However, if the capacity of the macrocell is full, the incoming call will be dropped. If the incoming call is defined as microcell call, then it is necessary to determine which microcell it belongs to. After the microcell is found, its density variable is increased by 1. All of the density variables of microcells are stored in the array. If they are less than the threshold value, the incoming calls will be handled by the macrocell. The microcells will continue to stay in off. Energy savings will be achieved as long as the microcells are kept off. If the value is greater than threshold (K) value or equal to K value, the most engaged microcell passes into an active position and accepts the call. At this point, the microcell is active, which means that it is consuming energy. The microcell has its own threshold as well. DCM algorithm makes a decision by the assist of its own threshold value whether or not the microcell needs to keep itself off. If incoming calls are equal to the threshold value of the macrocell, or more than the threshold value of the microcell, then the microcell will remain active. If incoming calls are less than the threshold value of the microcell, then the microcell will ask about the intensity of the macrocell. If the intensity of macrocell less than the sum of I_M and R_m calls, the microcell passed to off position itself and R_m calls will be transferred to the macrocell. If macrocell is not available the microcell will stay active. In this way, Energy-efficiency and system balance is assured.

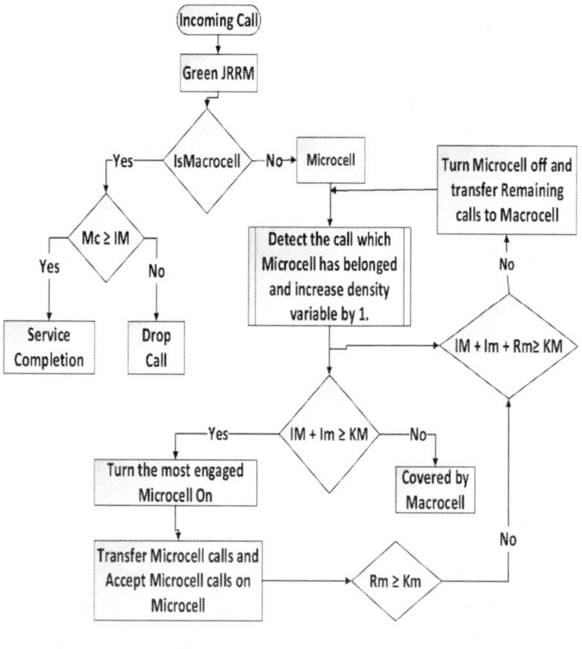

Figure 2 Handoff DCM-based green JRRM algorithm.

IV. Performance Model For Handoff

As we mentioned earlier, our model has 2 layers: macrocell and microcell. Arrival process are assumed to be Poisson in both layers with λ_M macrocell rate and λ_m microcell rate. In the green JRRM scheme, the state transition diagram for a small-scale system with M_{cell} =5, m_{cell} = 5, K=2. The number of macrocell and microcell channels are M_{cell} and m_{cell} respectively. K is considered as a threshold value defined by multiplying the capacity of macrocell by a certain coefficient, shown in Figure 3.

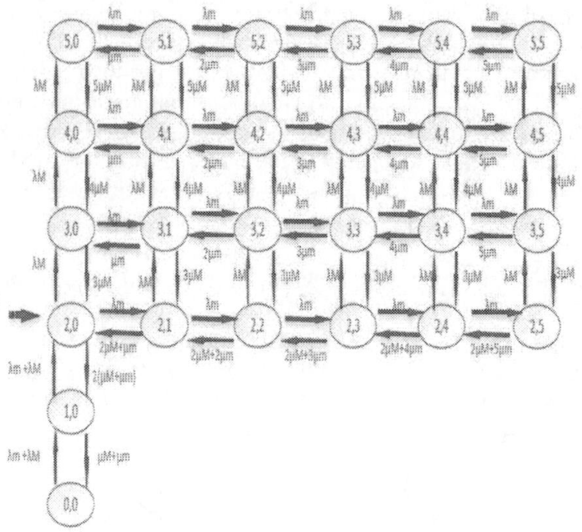

Figure 3 State transition diagram for the handoff green JRRM scheme with M_{cell} = 5, m_{cell} =5, K=2

Figure 3 represents the state diagram threshold value is calculated by multiplying the total capacity of the macrocell by 0.6 (NICIN 0.6) In this case, it is calculated as 3. Using bidimensional Continuous Time Markov Chain (CTMC) model, we define the state as:

$$\varphi = \{(I_M, I_m)\ 0 \le I_M \le M_{channel}, 0 \le I_m \le m_{channel}\}$$

From this point, formula 1, the blocking probability in the macrocell and formula 2, the blocking probability in the microcell are obtained as [9]:

$$P_{M_{blocking}} = \sum_{I_m=0}^{m_{channel}} \pi(I_M = M_{channel}, I_m) \quad (1)$$

$$P_{m_{blocking}} = \sum_{I_M=0}^{M_{channel}} \pi(I_M, I_m = m_{channel}) \quad (2)$$

Regarding DCM algorithm, formula 3, the probability of idle state of macrocell can be calculated as [9]:

$$P_{idle} = \sum_{I_M=0}^{M_{channel}} \pi(I_M, I_m = 0) \quad (3)$$

V. Performance Evaluation

In this section, we evaluate the performance of our DCM-based green JRRM scheme. The scenario of this experiment consists of 1 macrocell and 5 microcells and there is no any macrocell call to measure the performance of microcell call. We assume that the number of channels of the macrocell is 20, and the number of channels of the microcells is 10. The threshold value is 10. The threshold value is automatically determined so that the number of the macrocell's capacity is multiplied by 0.5 coefficients.

Scenario

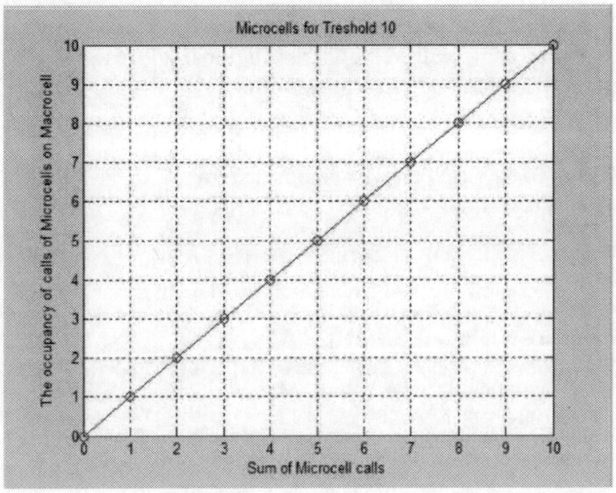

Figure 4 The occupancy of microcell calls on macrocell.

Figure 4 shows the sum of the number of incoming microcell calls. The number of incoming calls can't exceed the value of 10 due to fixing the threshold value to 10.

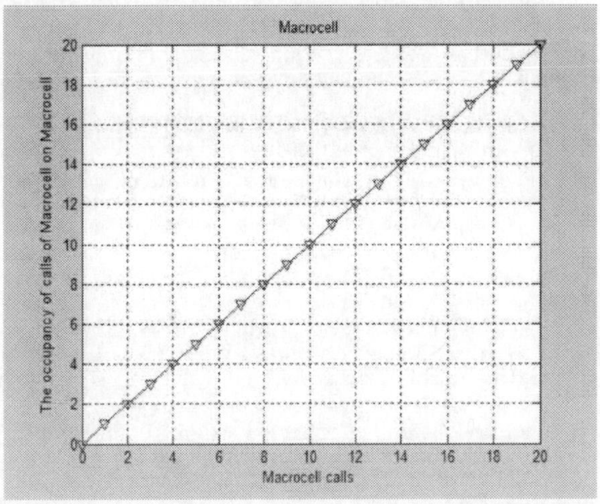

Figure 5 The occupancy of macrocell calls on macrocell.

Figure 5 shows the occupancy of macrocells which have occurred by the incoming calls on them. If there are not any microcell calls on the macrocell, then the macrocell has the right to consume all of the function of the macrocell's channels in order to recover its calls. The threshold value defined on the macrocell means that the sum of the number of microcell calls cannot exceed the threshold value. In our study, first of all, it is necessary to determine exactly the microcell to which the incoming call belongs. Secondly, the intensity variable of the microcell is increased by 1. When the sum of these calls reaches the threshold value, the most engaged microcell is activated, and the calls of this microcell are transferred to itself. Our aim is to underline the advantage of Handoff Green JRRM Architecture versus Green JRRM Architecture. If the number of incoming calls exceeds the threshold value, then the following incoming calls are diverted directly to microcells and will subsequently activate new microcells. The advantage of our approach is manifested at this point. The macrocell is alleviated after it has opened the most engaged microcell on the macrocell. Moreover, channels are opened for receiving new calls. For example, let us assume that the threshold value is 10 and we have 5 microcells. There are 10 calls. The distribution of these calls would be divided in such a way that there would be 4 calls coming from the first microcell, 3 calls coming from the second microcell, and 3 calls coming from the third microcell in a certain time period. In Green JRRM Architecture's approach, the fourth and fifth microcells will be opened even if there is only one call. In Handoff Green JRRM Architecture's approach, the most engaged microcell is activated and the calls are transferred. The other two microcells are covered by the macrocell until a total of 4 calls are keeping one microcell active. In this way, the green DCM algorithm is achieved. In the approach by Green JRRM Architecture, 2 microcells remain in an activated state. This example states that there is an energy savings of 50 %.

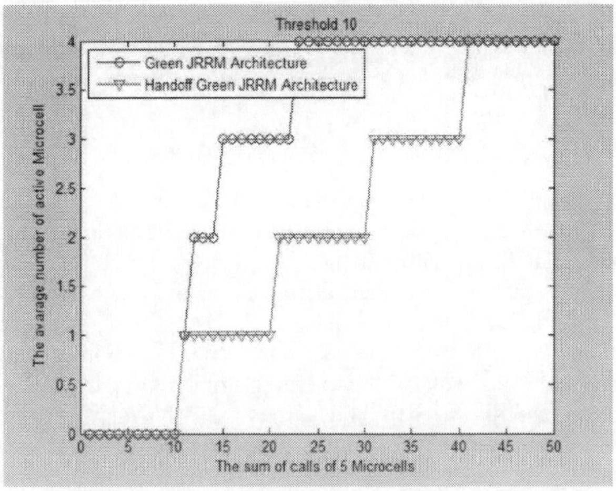

Figure 6 The average number of active microcell.

In Figure 6, the energy saving experiment is demonstrated by 5 microcells as shown above. The maximum number of microcell calls is 10 because of setting the threshold value to 10. As seen in Figure 6., there is a huge difference between the varying approaches made by Green JRRM Architecture and Handoff Green JRRM Architecture. The energy saving activity is made by closing the most engaged microcell. This action leads to alleviating the macrocell. In this way, the calls made by other microcells will continue being accepted on the macrocell.

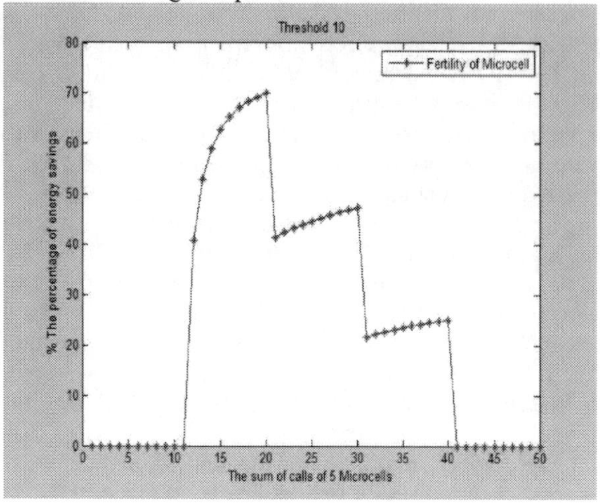

Figure 7 The percentage of energy savings versus Green JRRM Architecture.

In Figure 7, as seen, the energy saving action carried out by 5 microcells is shown as a percentage in Figure 7. It states that until threshold congestion occurs, both approaches act the same. Neither one of these approaches opened a microcell, nor were the calls handled by macrocells. With the average rate of call traffic, energy savings has been recorded in the range of 45% to 70 %. Further energy savings have been achieved by keeping the microcells closed. Energy saving opportunities were diminished by increasing the load of calls.

VI. Conclusion And Future Work

In this paper, we have introduced a new approach to the DCM-based energy efficient scheme for HetNets. Our Handoff DCM algorithm is based on 2 basic structures. One of them uses the Handoff mechanism and the other requires setting a threshold on the macrocell. Using both of these methods, we have obtained more energy savings and developed an anti-pollution algorithm. Green JRRM Architecture diverts new calls directly to the microcell by opening other microcells after the threshold is reached. Handoff Green JRRM Architecture is interesting in the way of opening the most engaged microcell by assigning incoming calls. The results have shown that Handoff Green JRRM Architecture has advantages in all ways, versus Green JRRM Architecture.

In future work, we are going to develop a smarter program by using statistics. We need not only instant data but also a database to assist making a decision which BS needs to open continuously to ensure more energy-efficiency. The next Generation Handoff Green JRRM algorithm will consist of a database and more complex decision mechanism. Further work will include adding more microcells and testing the real traffic load. This will enable us to understand the effect of various traffic loads on our new green DCM algorithm. It will be useful to take some precautions in order to avoid congestion as we strive towards our goal of reaching the pinnacle of energy-efficiency algorithm.

Acknowledgment

This work was partially supported by ANR/N-GREEN project (Project number ANR-15-CE25-0009/N-GREEN).

References

[1] G. Gonzalez, Energy Saving solution for integrated optical-Wireless Access Network Telecom SudParis and University of Paris VI, PhD thesis, July, 2015

[2] E. Chavarria-Reyes, Ian F. Akyildiz, Etimad Fadel, "Energy Consumption Analysis and Minimization in Multi-Layer Heterogeneous Wireless Systems" IEEE Transactions on mobile computing, vol. 14, no. 12, December, 2015, pp. 2474 – 2487.

[3] Gartner, "Gartner estimates ICT industry accounts for 2 percent of global CO2 emissions," April, 2007, http://www.gartner.com/newsroom/id/503867.

[4] The Boston Consulting Group, "GeSI SMARTer 2020: The role of ICT in driving a sustainable future," Global e-Sustainability Initiative, 2012, http://gesi.org/assets/js/lib/tinymce/jscripts/tiny_mce/plugins/ajaxfilemanager/uploaded/SMARTer%202020%20-%20The%20Role%20of%20ICT%20in%20Driving%20a%20Sustainable%20Future%20-%20December%202012.pdf

[5] Alactel-Lucent Strategic White Paper, "Information and Communication Technologies: Enablers of a low-carbon economy",http://www.alcatel-lucent.com/eco/docs/CMO7526101103\ICT\Enablers-eco\EN\StraWhitePaper.pdf, 2012

[6] O. E. Falowo and H. A. Chan, "Joint Call Admission Control Algorithm for Fair Radio Resource Allocation in Heterogeneous Wireless Networks Supporting Heterogeneous Mobile Terminals", Proceedings of 7th IEEE Consumer Communications and Networking Conference (CCNC), Las Vegas, NV, USA, January, 2010, pp. 1-5.

[7] D. T. Ngo and T. Le-Ngoc, "Distributed Resource Allocation for Cognitive Radio Networks With Spectrum-Sharing Constraints", IEEE Transactions on Vehicular Technology, vol. 60, no. 7, September, 2011, pp. 3436-3449.

[8] A. Guerrero-Ibanez, J. Contreras-Castillo, A. Barba and A. Reyes, "A QoS-based dynamic pricing approach for services provisioning in heterogeneous wireless access networks", Pervasive and Mobile Computing, vol.7, no. 5, October, 2011, pp. 569-583.

[9] G. H. S. Carvalho, A. Anpalagan, I.Woungang and S. K. Dhurandher, "Energy-Efficient Radio Resource Management Scheme for Heterogeneous Wireless Networks: a Queueing Theory Perspective" Future Technology Research Association International, vol. 3, no 4, December, 2012, pp. 15-22.

[10] Y. Yao, Q. Cao and A. Vasilakos, "Energy-Efficiency Oriented Traffic Offloading in Wireless Networks: A Brief Survey and a Learning Approach for Heterogeneous Cellular Networks" IEEE Journal on selected areas in communications, vol. 33, no. 4, June, 2015, pp. 627- 640.

Securing Vehicle ECUs Update Over The Air

Kevin Daimi
Computer Science and Software Engineering
University of Detroit Mercy
Detroit, USA
email:daimikj@udmercy.edu

Mustafa Saed, Scott Bone, Muhammad Rizwan
HATCI Electronic Systems Development
Hyundai-Kia America Technical Center
Superior Township, USA
email: {msaed, sbone, mrizwan }@hatci.com

***Abstract*—Present-day vehicles involve many Electronic Control Units (ECUs). Future vehicles will have even more ECUs. Currently, the firmware of these ECUs is updated at the dealership when there is a need. The updates are sent to the dealership using electronic media. This process is very time-consuming and lacks the possibility of performing these updates to all vehicles of a certain model in parallel. A future trend by auto manufacturers would be performing these updates over the air. Firmware Over-The-Air (FOTA) will be prone to a variety of attacks. This paper proposes a security architecture for the FOTA updates and discusses how this security architecture is implemented for vehicles at customer locations, dealership sites, and production lines.**

Keywords*—*ECUs; Firmware; FOTA; Security Architecture; Security Protocol

I. INTRODUCTION

There are a number of bus systems or protocols available in today's in-vehicle networks. Examples of these include Local Interconnect Network (LIN), Controller Area Network (CAN), Media-Oriented System Transport (MOST), and FlexRay. The LIN protocol was introduced to complement the CAN bus. It is a low speed bus and supports various applications including door locks, and seat belts. The CAN bus has a maximum speed of 1 Mbps. Higher speed is supported by MOST, a standard multimedia and infotainment networking in automobiles. FlexRay was designed to be the next-generation and fault-tolerant protocol to support high-bandwidth and safety-critical applications [1]-[3]. Modern-day vehicles typically deploy more than one of these protocols. CAN is currently dominant, and vehicles include two or three CAN buses providing two to three different speeds.

Modern vehicles are equipped with 50-70 embedded electronic control units (ECUs), which supervise a great deal of their functionality [4]. This functionality has a broad set of tasks including overseeing door looks, climate, sunroof, body systems, transmission, advanced safety and collision avoidance systems, and pressure monitoring systems. On each ECU, a specialized and independent firmware is executed, and upgraded versions of the firmware are introduced as errors are identified or new functionality is added [5]. ECUs receive signals sent by sensors located at various parts and in different components of the vehicle. Based on these signals, ECUs control various key units in the vehicle [6].

The entire network, including the buses and the ECUs, need to be protected against security attacks. Various analyses of the buses, especially the CAN bus; have revealed various vulnerabilities in the available in-vehicle network protocols [7] [8]. The in-vehicle networks connecting the ECUs to the buses are not deemed closed network but an open network attracting many cyber-attacks. The fact that some ECUs, such as the immobilizer, are equipped with specific security capabilities does not rule out the reality that the security requirements; confidentiality, authenticity, availability, integrity, and nonrepudiation; are not satisfied [9]. A security analysis, which was carried out recently on a production vehicle, showed that an adversary might tamper with the brakes when the car is running once access to the in-vehicle network via the Bluetooth is assured [10] [11]. Other attacks are made possibly through the On Board diagnostics (OBD-II) port. Compromising one ECU allows the attacker full access and control of all other ECUs since the in-vehicle network is fully connected [12]. Security needs to be considered in the early stages of the development process of vehicle electronics systems by demanding firmware standards that avoid firmware defects that giving rise to cyberattacks, and by incorporating security mechanisms, such as authentication and cryptology, to enable the verification of the identity of the sender to prevent bogus and potentially harmful messages to be replayed/transmitted across the communication network [13].

All ECUs' firmware needs to be updated. Updates include urgent firmware fixes through recalls, feature upgrade, security patches, and customer complaints fixes. It is also possible to replace the whole firmware with a brand new one. Currently, all firmware updates are performed at the dealership. When the work is completed, the technician checks the targeted ECU to ensure it is functioning correctly. Assessment of the traditional approach signified that such updates are time and resource consuming, result in higher cost of labor and customer dissatisfaction, and prevent parallel updates as a result of physical equipment connection [14]. A future trend in auto industry is to adopt Firmware Over-The-Air (FOTA) updates. FOTA refers to the process of wireless firmware transfer to the ECUs [15]. Mobile phone companies have been successfully updating their software Over-The-Air. It is anticipated that FOTA will gain wide acceptance in automotive industry following the great success in mobile phone industry. With FOTA, updates will be performed at the customer (any) location and not at the dealership site. This will mean fast, effective, and cost efficient approach of firmware updating.

Firmware Over-The-Air (FOTA) definitely implies wireless communications. This will widely open the door for many cyberattacks. Many of the current wireless security attacks will take advantage of the FOTA approach. The consequences will be disastrous as safety is involved. Therefore, there should be a serious and imminent move by auto industry to protect their vehicles' ECUs against all the possible attacks. To cope with such vital attacks, few researchers introduced their analysis and possible solutions to such challenges. Phung and Nilsson [16] proposed a threat model for the vehicle software architecture to pinpoint possible threats and suggested countermeasures for some improper conduct caused by malicious or poorly designed applications. Their approach is based on modifying the application at the wireless gateway of the vehicle before installation to guarantee safety and security of the vehicle through spotting likely attacks. The approach relied on the reference monitor component to decide whether to grant requests for resources based on security policy [17]. The vast majority of attacks take place when the software is being transferred from the manufacturer site and before reaching the gateway. In addition, setting a security policy for the arrived software is hard to achieve when many vendors provide different software and firmware to auto manufacturers.

Idrees et al [18] proposed on-board security architecture to facilitate the firmware update processes using both hardware and software modules. This was followed by a protocol to demonstration how their security architecture was employed to accomplish secure firmware updates for electronic control units (ECUs). Their approach is mainly based on a hardware security process to safeguard critical parts, such as secure key storage and the functioning of the cryptographic algorithms, of their architecture during the firmware update. The introduction of hardware is definitely valuable. However, from a security point of view, this will introduce the additional problem of hardware attacks in addition to software attacks. Furthermore, the paper indicated the use of a public key but no private key was specified.

Miller and Valasek [19] introduced possible attacks on various vehicles through the CAN bus and the Electronic Control Units (ECUs). They investigated a remote attack on an unaltered vehicle model and similar vehicles that causes a physical control of some parts of the vehicle. They hoped that their work on this further remote attack will help in enhancing the security of connected vehicles in the future by avoiding the vulnerabilities that result in compromising the CAN and ECUs.

This paper presents security architecture for Over-The-Air update of ECUs. It covers the update of firmware at the production site, dealer site, and customer location. A security protocol to implement this architecture is introduced. Both symmetric and asymmetric cryptology will be used. The suggested architecture and protocol will ensure that the security requirements; confidentiality, integrity, authentication, and non-repudiation will be satisfied. The remainder of the paper is organized as follows: Section II will discuss the FOTA security architecture. Section III will introduce the implementation of the architecture via a security protocol. The approach is extended in Section IV to cover application software in addition to firmware. The paper is concluded in Section V.

II. FOTA SECURITY ARCHITECTURE

The FOTA security architecture is depicted in Fig. 1, which uses two different colors to highlight the connections between the components. It is composed of seven components: Certificate Authority (CA), Firmware Repository (FR), Firmware Distribution Authority (FDA), Vendor Firmware Packaging Manager (VFPM), Production Site Manager (PSM), Dealer Stock Manager (DSM), and Master ECU (MECU). All the components are connected to both CA and FDA. In addition, FDA is connected to CA.

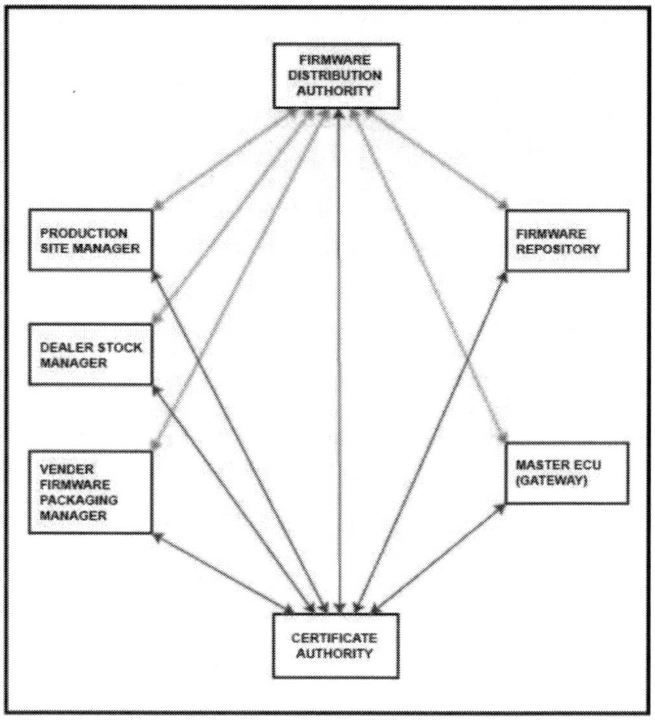

Figure 1. FOTA security architecture

The Certificate Authority (CA) is in charge of issuing certificates to all components including the Firmware Distribution Authority (FDA). The CA can be part of the manufacturing site or an independent party. The most important component is the Firmware Distribution Authority. The FDA is responsible for firmware updates to all vehicles at the dealership, production lines, and customer locations (garages, parking lots, streets, etc.). It receives the packaged firmware updates from vendors and stores them in the firmware repository prior to sending it to vehicles. Further responsibilities include ensuring all vehicles of that type and model have been updated and the updated ECUs are functioning properly. Updates include improving the ECU's functionality, firmware bug fixes, and brand new firmware to completely replace the old version. It is assumed that the manufacturer site has the capability to verify the update is functioning correctly. The FDA is also in charge of issuing the session keys and the Message Authentication Code (MAC) keys.

The Firmware Repository (FR) is the firmware storage at the manufacturer's site. It is in charge of storing the firmware received from the FDA and providing the FDA with the needed firmware when requested. For each firmware, additional information including update version number, update type (full, bug fix, and enhancement), ECU type, date it was received, size of updates in bytes, vehicle model, vendor ID, and checksum. The Vendor Firmware Packaging Manager (VFPM) is responsible for preparing the firmware update and securely forwarding it to the Firmware Distribution Authority at the manufacturer's site to be stored in the Firmware Repository.

The Production Site Manager (PSM) is charge of updating all the vehicles in the production lines before sending them to dealerships. Updating all the used and new cars at the dealership is the responsibility of the Dealer Stock Manager (DSM).

The Master ECU (MECU) plays a major role in the firmware update. It is a gateway equipped with the needed hardware, software, and memory. MECU may be closed to disable interfaces like Universal serial Bus (USB), Universal Asynchronous Receiver/Transmitter (UART), and Joint Test Action Group (JTAG). For this purpose, the Telematics Control Unit (TCU) can also be used. The MECU receives the firmware updates from the Firmware Distribution Authority and updates the ECUs in question in addition to updating its own. It warns the FDA when the firmware update is completed. Note that both DSM and PSM communicate with MECU of their vehicles. They behave like brokers. The direct secure communication between the MECU of the customer and the FDA will be discussed in the next section. The behavior of the MECUs connected to the Dealership Stock Manger and Production Site Manager is similar. Therefore, it will be explained once. To elucidate the participating parties in the architecture, Table 1 should be relied on.

TABLE I. PARTICIPATING PARTIES

Symbol	Role
CA	Certificate Authority
FDA	Firmware Distribution Authority
FR	Firmware Repository
DSM	Dealership Stock Manager
PSM	Production Site Manager
VFPM	Vendor Firmware Packaging Manager
MECU	Master ECU
SDM	Software Download Manager
SCM	Software Charge Manager
RDM	Remote Diagnosis Manager

III. SECURING THE FOTA

Securing the FOTA updates will include securing the communication between the seven components of the above security architecture. For this purpose, cryptographic protocols are used. The protocol notations are introduced in Table 2 to illustrate the role they play in the protocol.

TABLE II. PROTOCOL NOTATIONS

Symbol	Meaning
PU_{FDA}, PR_{FDA}	Public & private key of FDA
PU_{FR} , PR_{FR}	Public & private key of FR
PU_{CA} , PR_{CA}	Public & private key of CA
PU_{DSM}, PR_{DSM}	Public & private key of DSM
PU_{PSM}, PR_{PSM}	Public & private key of PSM
PU_{VFPM}, PR_{VFPM}	Public & private key of VFPM
PU_{MECU}, PR_{MECU}	Public & private key of MECU
KS_{FR}	Session Key shared between FDA and FR
KS_{DSM}	Session Key shared between FDA and DSM
KS_{PSM}	Session Key shared between FDA and PSM
KS_{VFPM}	Session Key shared between FDA and VFPM
KS_{MECU}	Session Key shared between FDA and MECU
KM_{FR}	MAC Key shared between FDA and FR
KM_{DSM}	MAC Key shared between FDA and DSM
KM_{PSM}	MAC Key shared between FDA and PSM
KM_{VFPM}	MAC Key shared between FDA and VFPM
KM_{MECU}	MAC Key shared between FDA and MECU
$C(KM_X, F)$	MAC function
X	Refers to FDA, FR, DSM, PSM, VFPM, or MECU
T_{Si} $i=1$-12	Time stamps
T_1	Time stamp
T_2	Certificate validity period
N_X	Nonce for X
CR_X	Certificate of X
ID_U	Update ID
F	Firmware
ID_{ECU}	ID of the ECU to be updated
ID_V	Vendor ID
$H(B)$, $H(I)$	Hash function of bug and improvement messages
L	List of vehicles VIN numbers
E	Encryption
VIN	Vehicle identification number

A. Certificate Authority

The Certificate Authority (CA) is in charge of issuing certificates to all the other components. The CA shares its public key (PU_{CA}) with the components. The component requests its certificate by sending its public key (PU_X), its ID (ID_X) and a nonce (N_X) all encrypted with the public key of the CA. Here, X is used to denote any of the six components. Upon receiving the request, the CA decrypts it with its private key (PR_{CA}) and sends X its certificate encrypted with PR_{CA}. The certificate of the component (CR_X) will have the format below:

$$CR_X = E\,[PR_{CA}, (PU_X \,||\, ID_X \,||\, T_1 \,||\, T_2)]$$

The certificate and the nonce will be concatenated and then encrypted with the public key (PU_X) of the requesting component and sent to the component. Assuming the private key of the component (PR_X) is not compromised, this will assure no one but the requester can access the certificate.

$$CA \rightarrow X: E\ [PU_X, CR_X \,||\, N_X]$$

In addition to the public key and ID, the certificates include a timestamp, T_1, and a certificate validity period (expiration date), T_2. Both T1 and N_X are attached for additional assurance that the message involving the certificate is not a replay. The parties (components) receiving this message will decrypt it with its private key, verify T_1 and N_X and get its certificate (CR_X). Note that X will be replaced with FDA, FR, VFPM, PSM, DSM, or MECU in the next sections to denote the different components.

B. Firmare Distribution Authority

The Firmware Distribution Authority exchanges its certificate (CR_{FDA}) with all other components. It will decrypt the received certificates to obtain the public key and ID of each component.

FDA creates the session keys; KS_{FR}, KS_{VFPM}, KS_{PSM}, KS_{DSM}, and KS_{MECU}, to be shared with each component, encrypts them with the corresponding public keys; PU_{FR}, PU_{VFPM}, PU_{PSM}, PU_{DSM}, and PU_{MECU}, and sends them to FR, VFPM, PSM, DSM, and MECM respectively. In a similar fashion, the FDA creates the MAC keys KM_{FR}, KM_{VFPM}, KM_{PSM}, KM_{DSM}, and KM_{MECU}, and sends them to the respective components.

When the Vendor Firmware Packaging Manager informs the FDA about the packaging of a firmware update via a secret message, it acknowledges the message. This step is then followed by the actual transfer of the firmware update. Once the update is received, the FDA sends a notification message to the Firmware Repository. After this message is acknowledged, the firmware update is forwarded to the FR as follows:

$$X_1 = E\ [PR_{FDA}, C\ (KM_{FR}, F) \,||\, Info \,||\, ID_U \,||\, T_{S1}]$$
$$FDA \rightarrow FR: E\ [KS_{FR}, F \,||\, E\ (PU_{FR}, X_1)]$$

The term C (KM_{FR}, F) refers to the MAC of the firmware; F. Info represents additional information, such as update version, update ID (ID_U), date received, ECU ID, vendor ID, vendor name, and type of update. T_{S1} is the time stamp. Note that both public key and symmetric key cryptology is used. Public key cryptology is used for small messages because it is slow, and the symmetric cryptology is used with possibly large messages, *F* in this case.

The MAC is signed with the private key (PR_{FDA}) of FDA. The expression X_1 is encrypted with the public key (PU_{FR}) of FR to provide confidentiality as only FR can decrypt this message with its private key (PR_{FR}). The MAC, C (KM_{FR}, F) provides the message authentication. In addition, the encryption with the symmetric key, KS_{FR}, designates further confidentiality and authentication.

Similar messages will be sent to the other parties with the exception of *info*.

$$X_2 = E\ [PR_{FDA}, C\ (KM_{VFPM}, F) \,||\, ID_{ECU} \,||\, ID_U \,||\, T_{S2}]$$
$$FDA \rightarrow VFPM: E\ [KS_{VFPM}, F \,||\, E\ (PU_{VFPM}, X_2)]$$

$$X_3 = E\ [PR_{FDA}, C\ (KM_{PSM}, F) \,||\, ID_{ECU} \,||\, ID_U \,||\, T_{S3}]$$
$$FDA \rightarrow PSM: E\ [KS_{PSM}, F \,||\, E\ (PU_{PSM}, X_3)]$$

$$X_4 = E\ [PR_{FDA}, C\ (KM_{DSM}, F) \,||\, ID_{ECU} \,||\, ID_U \,||\, T_{S4}]$$
$$FDA \rightarrow DSM: E\ [KS_{DSM}, F \,||\, E\ (PU_{DSM}, X_4)]$$

$$X_5 = E\ [PR_{FDA}, C\ (KM_{MECU}, F) \,||\, ID_{ECU} \,||\, ID_U \,||\, T_{S5}]$$
$$FDA \rightarrow MECU: E\ [KS_{MECU}, F \,||\, E\ (PU_{MECU}, X_5)]$$

C. Firmware Repository

After performing the required decryptions on the received message, E [KS_{FR}, F || E (PU_{FR}, X_1)], calculating and verifying the MAC, and ensuring T_{S1} is current, the FR stores the firmware, F, together with *Info* and any other data needed for indexing. Upon receiving a request from the FDA, it retrieves the firmware in question and sends it to FDA within the following message:

$$X_6 = E\ [PR_{FR}, C\ (KM_{FR}, F) \,||\, ID_{ECU} \,||\, ID_U \,||\, T_{S6}]$$
$$FR \rightarrow FDA: E\ [KS_{FR}, F \,||\, E\ (PU_{FDA}, X_6)]$$

The FR stores the date the request was received and the date the firmware, F, was sent for auditing purposes.

D. Vendor Firmware Packaging Manager

Auto manufacturers deal with several vendors. The security architecture above contains only one box for the Vendor. Therefore, the message sent here will include the vendor ID.

$$X_7 = E\ [PR_{VFPM}, C\ (KM_{VFPM}, F) \,||\, ID_V \,||\,||\, ID_{ECU} \,||\, ID_U \,||\, T_{S7}]$$
$$VFPM \rightarrow FDA: E\ [KS_{VFPM}, F \,||\, E\ (PU_{FDA}, X_7)]$$

Note that ID_V is the ID of the vender. ID_{ECU} represents the ID of the affected ECU. The message above is preceded by a notification message (of new update) sent and an acknowledgement message received.

In addition to the vendor initiating updates and packaging them, the FDA can request updates when a bug is discovered or an improvement is needed. A message containing the bug or the improvement will be sent to that specific dealer:

$$X_8 = E\ [PU_{VFPM}, B \,||\, E\ (PR_{FDA}, H\ (B) \,||\, ID_V \,||\, ID_{ECU} \,||\, T_{S8})]$$
$$FDA \rightarrow VFPM: X_8$$

Or,

$$X_9 = E\,[PU_{VFPM},\, I \,||\, E\,(PR_{FDA},\, H\,(I) \,||\, ID_V \,||\, ID_{ECU} \,||\, T_{S9})]$$
$$FDA \rightarrow VFPM:\, X_9$$

Here, B is the bug detail, I the improvement detail, H (B) and H (I) represent the hash function of B and I respectively, and ID_{ECU} is the ID of the ECU that has a bug or needs improvement. The VFPM will decrypt the message, calculate the hash and verifies it is the same as the received hash. When the verification is successful, the update process will take place. Note that only public key cryptology was used here because the message is not large.

E. Production Site Manager

The PSM is responsible for the updates of the ECUs in all the vehicles in the production lines. After receiving the message X_3 from the FDA and executing the required decryptions and verifications, PSM has to send the firmware to the MECU of the vehicles in that line. For this purpose, it will act like the FDA and communicate similar encrypted messages with the MECU of each vehicle. Once the update is received by the MECUs, the update will be implemented in parallel as they all received it. The approach used by the MECUs of production line's vehicles is the same as in (G) below. The MECUs will inform the PSM when the updates are completed for that update ID (ID_U). The PSM will then inform the FDA of all the vehicles that has their firmware updated by sending a message containing the list of vehicles VIN numbers, L. This is needed for ensuring that all vehicles are updated and for reporting purposes.

$$X_{10} = E\,[PR_{PSM},\, C\,(KM_{PSM},\, L) \,||\, U_{ID} \,||\, T_{S10}]$$
$$PSM \rightarrow FDA:\, E\,[KS_{PSM},\, L \,||\, E\,(PU_{FDA},\, X_{10})]$$

F. Dealer Stock Manager

The firmware updates at the dealership site are controlled by the DSM. The task of the DSM is similar to that of the PSM. The work will be completed by the MECUs in parallel here too.

G. Master ECU

The Master ECU is responsible for managing the updates of the firmware of the ECUS. For customers' vehicles, the MECU will communicate with the driver through the vehicle screen or via email to warn about a new update and request the vehicle to be turned off as soon it is possible. Vehicles in the production lines and at the dealerships are assumed to be not running since they are under control.

The MECU will fulfill the required decryptions and verification of the MAC. Once successful, it will extract the firmware F, ID_{ECU}, and ID_U. The MECU will then communicate with the desired ECU based on the ID_{ECU} to start the updating process. For busses where there is limitation on the size of the data packets, such as eight bytes for the CAN bus, the protocol can use the Counter Mode (CTR) to divide the plain/cipher text (firmware) to be encrypted/decrypted into blocks of eight bytes each.

Upon completing the update using any secure process, the MECU of customer's vehicle will inform the FDA by sending the following message:

$$X_{11} = E\,[PR_{MECU},\, ||\, ID_{ECU} \,||\, ID_U \,||\, VIN \,||\, T_{S11}]$$

$$MECU \rightarrow FDA:\, E\,(PU_{FDA},\, X_{11}]$$

For firmware update at the dealership and production sites, the MECU will send a similar message to DSM and PSM respectively. As, mentioned above, DSM and PSM will send a list of all the vehicles' VINs that are updated by collecting the information from all the MECUs within their site.

IV. EXTENDING THE SECURITY ARCHITECTURE

The above security architecture can be enhanced to deal with software apps in addition to firmware. In general, software is not free. To accommodate software download and software update, two components need to be added to the architecture; Software Download Manager (SDM) and Software Charge Manager (SCM). The latter is needed when the software is not free. Both SDM and SCM will be connected to FDA and CA. All the security measures used above will still apply here. With these two new components, the auto manufacturer will be able to implement Software On-The-Air (SOTA) in addition to FOTA.

An important component that could further be added in the future is the Remote Diagnosis Manager (RDM). Software companies, such as Microsoft, can remotely connect to our computers with our permission to diagnose problems. Upon customer request, it is anticipated that RDM will connect to the vehicle and diagnose problems. Once the problem is diagnosed, a message requesting firmware update for the particular ECUs will be sent to FDA. Another task that the RDM will be responsible for would be testing the update to certify the ECU is functioning as expected. The FDA will initiate the needed firmware update following the cryptographic protocol above. Certainly, RDM will be connected to both FDA and CA.

In the aforementioned protocol, it was assumed that one MECU will take care of updating all the ECUs. It is suggested adding more MECUs and dividing the ECUs among them. In other words, each MECU will be in charge of some ECUs. The added MECUs can play a backup role too in case an MECU is not functioning. Furthermore, if an MECU is compromised, it will not impact other MECUs (other ECUs).

A further extension will be replacing the Master ECU with the Telematics Control Unit (TCU). The TCU is a small computer that listens in on the communications of other electronic systems (ECUs) in the vehicle, then construes and disseminates that information as necessary. The TCU connects to the external server. This server could well be the

FDA. All that is needed is to make the TCU more powerful in terms of processing and memory.

V. CONCLUSION AND FUTURE WORK

With the FOTA gaining increasing popularity among auto manufacturers as a future trend, security measures need to be enforced to ensure the firmware travelling on the air will not be attacked. To account for possible security attacks, this paper presented a security architecture and protocol to protect the updating of firmware of various ECUs at the customer location, the dealership site, and the production lines. Both symmetric and asymmetric cryptology techniques were adopted. The suggested security architecture and protocol can be further extended to include Software On-The-Air (SOTA). Future work will also concentrate on the most suitable algorithms for symmetric and asymmetric cryptography, MAC and hash functions, and the length of the various keys.

REFERENCES

[1] Freescale Semiconductors, "In-Vehicle Networking," https://cache.freescale.com/files/microcontrollers/doc/brochure/BRINVEHICLENET.pdf, 2006, pp. 1-11, [retrieved: March, 2016].

[2] On Semiconductor, "Basics of In-Vehicle Networking (INV) Protocols," http://www.onsemi.com/pub_link/Collateral/TND6015-D.PDF, pp. 1-27, [retrieved: March, 2016].

[3] K. Parnell, "Put the Right Bus in Your Car," Xcell Journal, Available: http://www.rpi.edu/dept/ecse/mps/xc_autobus48(CAN).pdf, [retrieved: March, 2016].

[4] D. K. Nilsson, P. H. Phung, U. E. Larson, "Vehicle ECU Classification Based on Safety-Security Characteristics," in Proc. the 13th International Conference on Road Tarnsport Information and Control (RTIC'08), Manchester, England, UK, 2008, pp. 1-7.

[5] D. K. Nilsson, and U. E. Larson, "A Defense-in-Depth Approach to Securing the Wireless Vehicle Infrastructure," Journal of Networks, vol. 4, no. 7, 2009, pp. 552-564.

[6] National Instruments, "ECU Designing and Testing Using National Instruments Products," http://www.ni.com/white-paper/3312/en, 2009, [retrieved: March, 2016].

[7] T. Hoppe, S. Kiltz, J. Dittmann, "Automotive IT-Security as a Challenge: Basic Attacks from the Black Box Perspective on the Example of Privacy Threats," Computer Safety, Reliability, and Security, 2009, pp. 145-158.

[8] M. Wolf, A. Weimerskirch, C. Paar, "Security in Automotive Bus Systems," in Proc. the 2nd Embedded Security in Cars Workshop (ESCAR 2004), Bochum, Germany, 2004, pp. 11-12.

[9] I. Studnia, V. Nicomette, E. Alata, Y. Deswarte, M. Kaaniche, Y. Laarouchi, "Survey on Security Threats and Protection Mechanisms in Embedded Automotive Networks," in Proc. the 43rd Annual IEEE/IFIP Conference on Dependable Systems and Networks Workshop (DSN-W), Budapest, Hungary, 2013, pp. 1-12.

[10] S. Checkoway, D. McCoy, B. Kantor, D. Anderson, H. Shacham, S. Savage, K. Koscher, A. Czeskis, F. Roesner, T. Kohno, "Comprehensive Experimental Analyses of Automotive Attack Surfaces," in Proc. the 20th USENIX Symposium on Security (SEC'11), San Francisco, CA, USA, 2011, pp. 77-92.

[11] K. Koscher, A. Czeskis, F. Roesner, S. Patel, T. Kohno, S. Checkoway, D. Mccoy, B. Kantor, D. Anderson, H. Shacham, S. Savage, "Experimental Security Analysis of a Modern Automobile," in Proc. IEEE Symposium on Security and Privacy (SP), Oakland, CA, USA, 2010, pp. 447–462.

[12] F. Sagstetter, M. Lukasiewycz, S. Steinhorst, M. Wolf, A. Bouard, W. Harris, S. Jha, T. Peyrin, A. Poschmann, and S. Chakraborty, "Security Challenges in Automotive Hardware/Software Architecture Design," in Proc. Design, Automation & Test in Europe Conference & Exhibition (DATE), Grenoble, France, 2013, pp. 458-463.

[13] C. Lin, and A. Sangiovanni-Vincentelli, "Cyber-Security for the Controller Area Network (CAN) Communication Protocol," in Proc. International Conference on Cyber Security, Washington, DC, USA, 2012, pp. 1-7.

[14] Red Bend Software, "Updating Car ECUs Over-The-Air (FOTA)," www.redbend.com/data/upl/whitepapers/red_bend_update_car_ecu.pdf, 2011, pp. 1-14, [retrieved: March, 2016].

[15] Novero, "Automatic Over-The-Air Software Update," 2012, http://novero.com/wp-content/uploads/2014/12/Novero_Automotive_Software_Over_the_Air_Handout1.pdf, [retrieved: March 2016].

[16] P. H. Phung, and D. K. Nilsson, "A Model for Safe and Secure Execution of Downloaded Vehicle Applications," in Proc. Road Transport Information and Control Conference (RTIC 2010), London, UK, 2010, pp. 1-6.

[17] J. P. Anderson, "Computer Security Technology Planning Study," Deputy for Command and Management System, USA, Tech. Rep., 1972, http://csrc.nist.gov/publications/history/ande72.pdf, [retrieved: March, 2016].

[18] M. S. Idrees, H. Schweppe, Y. Roudier, M. Wolf, D. Scheuermann, O. Henniger, "Secure Automotive On-Board Protocols: A Case of Over-The-Air Firmware Updates," in Proc. the 3rd International Workshop Nets4Cars/Nets4Trains, Oberpfaffenhofen, Germany, 2011, pp. 224-238.

[19] C. Miller and C. Valasek, "Remote Exploitation of an Unaltered Passenger Vehicle," 2015, http://illmatics.com/Remote%20Car%20Hacking.pdf, [retrieved: March, 2016].

A Regenerative Relay Transmission in Linearly Precoded MU-MIMO Downlink

Yasunori Iwanami
Dept. of Computer Science and Engineering
Nagoya Institute of Technology
Nagoya, Japan
E-mail: iwanami@nitech.ac.jp

Kentaro Iida
Dept. of Computer Science and Engineering
Nagoya Institute of Technology
Nagoya, Japan
E-mail: cke17506@stn.nitech.ac.jp

Abstract—**Recently, Muti-User MIMO (MU-MIMO) downlink system which uses multiple antennas at base station and accommodates multiple users with multiple receive antennas attracts much attention. In MU-MIMO downlink system, by knowing the Channel State Information (CSI) at the base station, Inter User Interferences (IUI's) among users are pre-excluded at the base station. By increasing the number of transmit antennas assigned to each user, the transmission quality of each user is improved. In MU-MIMO, there exists linear precoding or nonlinear precoding method, but linear precoding is considered more easily implemented and adjusted than nonlinear precoding. In this paper, we aim the coverage extension and the transmission quality improvement by using a regenerative Detect & Forward (DF) relay in MU-MIMO downlink system. We use Block Diagonalization (BD) + Eigen mode transmission (E-SDM) for linear MU-MIMO scheme. By sharing the BD matrix at both base station and relay, the relay can demodulate the receive signal only with receive CSI and can forward the signal to each user. With this system configuration, we have shown the effectiveness of regenerative relay through simulations.**

Keywords-MU-MIMO; Block Diagonalization; Eigen mode transmission; Regenerative relay; Detect & Forward.

I. INTRODUCTION

Recently, Multi-User MIMO down link communication systems in which base station can transmit spatially multiplexed signals to multiple users without Inter-User Interference (IUI) are well investigated [1]-[7]. In MU-MIMO downlink system, in order to remove the IUI at base station, the channel state information (CSI) of downlink has to be known at the base station. By increasing the number of transmit antennas at base station, the channel quality to each user can be arbitrary improved. As representative methods, there exist BD (Block Diagonalization) [2] and Channel Inversion (CI) [3] categorized as linear methods, and DPC (Dirty Paper Coding) [4], THP (Tomlinson-Harashima Precoding) [5] and Vector Perturbation (VP) [6][7] as nonlinear methods. Although nonlinear methods can achieve greater channel capacity than linear methods, its complexity is higher and the design method is more difficult. As for the linear methods, the CI method has the problems of increasing transmit power and limited sum-rate. The BD method consumes a lot of degree of freedom to make the nulls, but it can remove the IUI completely. Also, the BD method matches the Eigen mode transmission (E-SDM; Eigenbeam -Space Division Multiplexing) [8] well and is considered a practical design method. On the other hand, concerning the use of relay in MU-MIMO downlink, increasing the channel capacity by using the relay has been discussed [9][10]. On the relay transmission in MU-MIMO downlink system, the BD methods are used to remove the IUI at base station [11]-[15]. In [11], during the 1st time slot transmission from base station to relay, MU-MIMO is not employed, but during the 2nd time slot from relay to each user, it is used. In [12]-[15], the transmission from base station to relay is done during the 1st time slot, but the direct link from base station to each user during the 1st time slot is not considered.

In this paper, on the DF relay in MU-MIMO downlink system, we employed the BD+E-SDM method for the transmission from base station to each user during the 1st time slot. We assume that the DF relay which locates between base station and each user already knows the precoding matrix of the base station. By knowing the precoding matrix, the relay can demodulate the receive signal only by using receive CSI. Accordingly, the base station does not need to assign the transmit antennas to the relay and the transmission from base station to relay becomes SU (Single-User)-MIMO. During the 2nd time slot, the DF relay transmits the signals to each user also using the BD+E-SDM method. At each user, the received signals during the 1st and the 2nd time slots are combined using the symbol LLR (Log Likelihood Ratio) addition and the combined signal is demodulated. We show the effectiveness of the proposed novel DF relaying system in MU-MIMO downlink through computer simulations.

The paper is organized as follows. In Section II, the DF relay model in MU-MIMO downlink is introduced. In Section III, we design the downlink transmission during the 1st time slot. In Section IV, we design the downlink during the 2nd time slot. In Section V, we present the symbol LLR combining method of received signals at each user terminal. In Section VI, we clarify the BER characteristics through computer simulations. The paper is concluded with Section VII with the most important results and future work.

II. DF RELAY MODEL IN MU-MIMO DOWNLINK

The proposed DF relaying model in MU-MIMO downlink system is shown in Figure1. The base station is equipped with N_s transmit antennas. There exist total N_u users and the user $i\,(=1,\cdots,N_u)$ has m_i receive antennas. Thus, there are total $N_d=\sum_{i=1}^{N_u} m_i$ receive antennas at users.

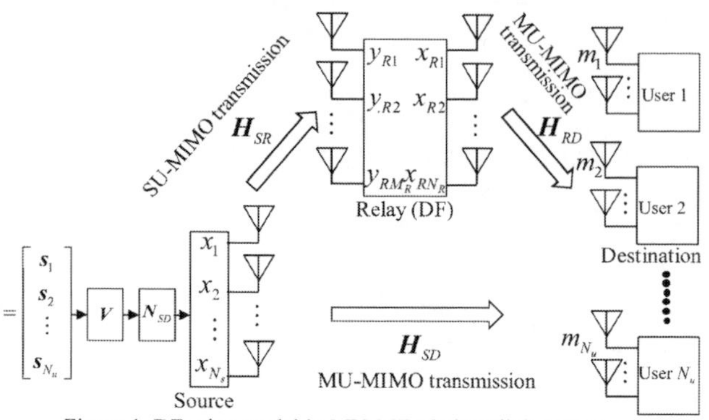

Figure 1. DF relay model in MU-MIMO downlink system

The DF relay, which locates between base station and user terminals, has M_R receive and N_R transmit antennas. At base station, the transmit signal $s = [s_1 \ \cdots \ s_i \ \cdots \ s_{N_u}]^T$ to each user is firstly multiplied by the precoding matrix V for making the multiple stream transmission using E-SDM. The transmit signal to user i is expressed as $s_i = [s_i^{(1)} \ \cdots \ s_i^{(S_i)}]$ where S_i is the number of signal streams of user i. The matrix V is expressed as

$$V = \begin{bmatrix} V_1 & 0 & 0 \\ 0 & \ddots & 0 \\ 0 & 0 & V_{N_u} \end{bmatrix} \tag{1}$$

where the diagonal element matrix of V is the precoding matrix of E-SDM for each user. Secondary, the precoding matrix N_{SD} for BD is multiplied by Vs. The transmit signal from the base station antenna is then given by $x = N_{SD}Vs = [x_1 \ x_2 \ \cdots \ x_{N_s}]^T$. During the 1st time slot, the transmit signal x is broadcasted both to user terminals and the DF relay. The precoding matrix N_{SD} makes the channel matrix H_{SD} from base station to each user block diagonal. The receive signal vector y_{SD} at destination (users) is expressed as

$$\begin{cases} y_{SD} = H_{SD}N_{SD}Vs + n_{SD} = B_{SD}Vs + n_{SD} = H_{SD}x + n_{SD} \\ B_{SD} = H_{SD}N_{SD}, \quad x = N_{SD}Vs \end{cases} \tag{2}$$

B_{SD} in (2) is the block diagonalized channel matrix and is expressed as

$$B_{SD} = \begin{bmatrix} B_{sd1} & 0 & \cdots & 0 \\ 0 & B_{sd2} & \cdots & \vdots \\ \vdots & \cdots & \ddots & 0 \\ 0 & \cdots & 0 & B_{sdN_u} \end{bmatrix} \tag{3}$$

where $B_{sdi}, i = 1, \cdots, N_u$ is the block channel matrix for user i and $n_{SD} = [n_{sd1} \ n_{sd2} \ \cdots \ n_{sdN_u}]$ in (2) is the receive noise vector for each user. The size of block channel matrix B_{sdi} for user i in (3) is given by $m_i \times n\ell_i$, $i = 1, \cdots, N_u$, where $n\ell_i$ is the nullity of matrix $\tilde{H}_{sdi}$ $(N_d - m_i \times N_s)$ [16] with $\tilde{H}_{sdi}$ being the matrix in which the channel matrix H_{sdi} $(m_i \times N_s)$ for user i is subtracted from the entire channel matrix H_{SD} $(N_d \times N_s)$. The nullity $n\ell_i$ of the matrix $\tilde{H}_{sdi}$ is defined by

$$n\ell_i = nullity(\tilde{H}_{sdi}) = N_s - rank(\tilde{H}_{sdi}) \tag{4}$$

As the rank of $\tilde{H}_{sdi}$ is given by

$$rank(\tilde{H}_{sdi}) = \min(N_D - m_i, N_s) \tag{5}$$

the nullity $n\ell_i$ is expressed as

$$n\ell_i = N_s - rank(\tilde{H}_{sdi}) = N_s - N_d + m_i > 0 \tag{6}$$

We assume that the DF relay knows the precoding matrix $N_{SD}V$ of the base station. Therefore, the base station has to inform $N_{SD}V$ to the relay before the data transmission starts. The transmission from base station to relay during the 1st time slot is done by Single User-MIMO (SU-MIMO). The receive signal $y_{SR} = [y_{r1} \ y_{r2} \ \cdots \ y_{rM_R}]$ at relay is expressed as

$$y_{SR} = H_{SR}x + n_{SR} = (H_{SR}N_{SD}V)s + n_{SR} \tag{7}$$

where n_{SR} ($M_R \times 1$) is the receive noise vector at relay. The effective channel matrix $(H_{SR}N_{SD}V)$ in (7) is assumed to be known at the relay and the demodulation of transmit signal s is done by MMSE nulling or MLD (Maximum Likelihood Detection). This means that the base station does not need to inform the channel matrix H_{SR} between base station and relay to the relay. The demodulated signal $\hat{s}$ at relay is transmitted to each user during the 2nd time slot using MU-MIMO with BD which is the same transmission scheme as in Source-Relay (SR) link. As in the Source-Destination (SD) link in the 1st time slot, the E-SDM is employed for the multiple stream transmission from relay to each user. At each user terminal, the received multiple stream signals during the 1st and the 2nd time slots are combined using symbol LLR addition and demodulated. When the errors are detected at relay through the CRC (Cyclic Redundancy Check) code for example, the transmission from relay to each user during the 2nd time slot may not be utilized. Because it causes the error propagation. That is, only when errors are not detected at relay, the demodulated signals at relay can be transmitted to the users. In this case, the 2nd time slot is not utilized between relay and each user, thus the vacant time slot can be used as the repeated transmission from base station to each user with BD+E-SDM as in the 1st time slot.

III. DESIGN OF DOWNLINK TRANSMISSION

A. Transmission during the 1st time slot

1) Design of SD Link

The SD transmission during the 1st time slot is done by using BD+E-SDM. The size of block channel matrix B_{sdi} is given by $m_{N_i} \times n\ell_i$ and the number of streams of eigen mode becomes $\min(m_{N_i} \times n\ell_i)$. When the number of streams is one, BD+E-SDM is referred to as BD+MRT (Maximum Ratio Transmission) [17]. From (6), the nullity $n\ell_i$ of user i can be arbitrary chosen by increasing or decreasing the number of transmit antennas N_s at base station. If the elements of channel matrix H_{SD} follow the i.i.d. complex Gaussian random variables, i.e., H_{SD} is the MIMO channel matrix of quasi-static flat Rayleigh fading, the diversity order of the first eigen mode stream in E-SDM for the block channel matrix $\boldsymbol{B}_{sdi}$ is given by $m_i \cdot n\ell_i$ [18]. When the minimum number of receive antennas among users is $m_{\min}$, from (6) the nullity $n\ell_{\min}$ of minimum antenna user is given by

$$n\ell_{\min} = N_s - N_d + m_{\min} > 0 \tag{8}$$

Hence, the number N_s of transmit antennas at base station is expressed as

$$N_s = n\ell_{\min} + N_d - m_{\min} \tag{9}$$

When the number of transmit antenna is N_s, the nullity $n\ell_i$ of user i other than the minimum antenna user becomes

$$n\ell_i = N_s - N_d + m_i > n\ell_{\min} \tag{10}$$

The size of block channel matrix $\boldsymbol{B}_{sdi}$ of user i is determined as $m_i \times n\ell_i$. In this design method, firstly the nullity $n\ell_{\min}$ of the user which has the minimum number of receive antennas $m_{\min}$ is determined and secondary the nullity $n\ell_i$ of the other user i is derived. The diversity orders of the first eigen mode stream of minimum antenna user and other user i are given by $m_{\min} \cdot n\ell_{\min}$ and $m_i \cdot n\ell_i \geq m_{\min} \cdot n\ell_{\min}$ respectively.

For example, we consider the case where the number of total users is $N_u = 3$, the numbers of receive antennas of users are $m_1 = 3$, $m_2 = 2$, $m_3 = 1$, and the total number of receive antennas is $N_d = m_1 + m_2 + m_3 = 6$. In this case, $m_3 = 1$ is minimum and it holds $m_{min} = m_3 = 1$. If the expected diversity order of the first eigen mode stream of user 3 is set to 3 for example, then we obtain $n\ell_{min} = 3/m_{min} = 3/1 = 3$. With those parameters, the total number of transmit antennas at base station N_s is determined as $N_s = n\ell_{min} + N_d - m_{min} = 3 + 6 - 1 = 8$ and the size of block matrix $\boldsymbol{D}_3$ of user 3 becomes $m_{min} \times n\ell_{min}$ $= 1 \times 3$. Thus, the nullity of user 2 is determined as $n\ell_2 =$ $N_s - N_d + m_2 = 8 - 6 + 2 = 4$, the size of $\boldsymbol{D}_2$ becomes $m_2 \times n\ell_2 = 2 \times 4$, and the diversity order of the first eigen mode stream of user 2 is given as $m_2 \cdot n\ell_2 = 2 \cdot 4 = 8$. Likewise, the nullity $n\ell_1$ of user 1 is given by $n\ell_1 =$ $= N_s - N_d + m_1 = 8 - 6 + 3 = 5$, $\boldsymbol{D}_1$ becomes $m_1 \times n\ell_1 = 3 \times 5$, the diversity order of the first eigen mode stream of user 1 is determined as $m_1 \cdot n\ell_1 = 3 \cdot 5 = 15$.

2) Design of SR Link

For the SD link from base station to DF relay, the precoding at base station is not used. This means no degree of freedom of transmit antennas (number of transmit antennas) at base station is consumed for the SR link. This is because if the transmit antennas at base station are assigned to the DF relay also for BD, in the absence of relay the assigned transmit antennas to relay are of no use. Therefore the extra transmit antennas are then used for the users to enhance the SD link quality. In this case, the effect of using relay becomes not obvious compared with the enhanced SD link. That is, the DF relay should be employed when the SD link quality is poor and the additional relay brings great effect to the overall performance. As the demodulation at DF relay is done by only using receive CSI, the precoding matrix $\boldsymbol{N}_{SD}\boldsymbol{V}$ at base station needs to be informed to the relay in advance before the data transmission starts. The DF relay demodulates the receive signal with MMSE nulling or MLD by using equivalent channel matrix of $\boldsymbol{H}_{SR}\boldsymbol{N}_{SD}\boldsymbol{V}$. So, the SR link transmission is done by SU-MIMO and not by MU-MIMO. As the SR link quality directly affects the subsequent Relay-Destination (RD) link quality, we must raise the SR link quality as much as we can. Because the poor SR link quality causes error propagation to the RD link. To solve this problem, increasing the number of receive antennas at relay is considered. Also at relay, MLD with better BER characteristic than MMSE nulling is considered. But when the number of transmit streams of $\boldsymbol{s}$ from base station is large, the exponential increase of complexity in MLD becomes a problem. In such case, we can resort the problem to employ the Sphere Decoding (SD) with less complexity or to use the MMSE nulling with far less complexity for demodulating SU-MIMO signals. Even though the elements of $\boldsymbol{H}_{SR}$ are i.i.d. complex Gaussian random variables, the row elements of equivalent SR link channel matrix $\boldsymbol{H}_{SR}\boldsymbol{N}_{SD}\boldsymbol{V}$ do not always become i.i.d. complex Gaussian random variables. This channel element correlation deteriorates the BER characteristic of MMSE nulling, MLD or SD compared with i.i.d. random variable case. Also if errors are detected at the DF relay by using CRC code etc., we can consider the protocol in which the demodulated data at relay are not forwarded to users in the 2nd time slot. In this case, as the RD link in the 2nd time slot becomes vacant, in order to utilize the vacant time slot effectively, we can repeat the SD link transmission from the base station again in the 2nd time slot.

B. Transmission during the 2nd time slot

For the RD link transmission during the 2nd time slot, we use BD+MRT or BD+E-SDM the same as in the 1st time slot. In this case, the number of streams to each user of SD link should coincide with the one of RD link. This is because the symbol LLR combining for each user stream is done at each user. We can design the RD link quality like the SD link. Thus, we can improve the RD link quality by increasing the number of transmit antennas at relay N_R. In order to prevent the error propagation in the RD link, we adopt the protocol in which the data from relay are only forwarded to each user in case of no error detected at the DF relay. When the error is detected at the relay and the RD link is not used during the 2nd time slot, in order to prevent the degradation of receive signal quality, we repeat the SD transmission using the vacant 2nd time slot. The signals received in the 1st and the 2nd time slots are symbol LLR combined and demodulated at each user.

At each user terminal, each stream of MRT or E-SDM is equivalently represented as the AWGN channel with the complex gain h. When the received signal in each stream is denoted as r and the corresponding transmitted signal $s_l, l=0,\cdots,Q-1$ has Q modulation levels, the equivalent AWGN channel of each stream is expressed as

$$r = hs_l + n,\ l = 0,1,\cdots,Q-1 \tag{11}$$

The symbol LLR is the extension of bit LLR and defined as

$$LLR_l = \log_e \frac{p(r \mid s_l)}{p(r \mid s_0)} \tag{12}$$

where the transition probability density function $p(r \mid s_l)$ is expressed as

$$p(r \mid s_l) = \frac{1}{\sqrt{2\pi}\sigma}\exp\left[-\frac{(r-s_l)^2}{2\sigma^2}\right] \tag{13}$$

and $\sigma^2 = (1/2)E\{|n|^2\}$. From (12) and (13), it holds

$$LLR_l = \frac{2r(s_l - s_0) - (s_l^2 - s_0^2)}{2\sigma^2} \tag{14}$$

When the modulation level is $Q=2$, the symbol LLR coincides with the bit LLR. The symbol LLR combining (or addition) of two independent LLR's is equivalent to the MRC (Maximum Ratio Combining) and they give the same BER characteristics.

IV. INVESTIGATION OF BER CHARACTERISTICS THROUGH COMPUTER SIMULATIONS

We have checked the BER characteristics of the proposed MU-MIMO downlink transmission using DF relay. The abscissa of BER characteristic is taken as the transmit SNR [19], which is defined as the ratio of total transmit power P from the base station to the receive noise power σ^2 at each user receive antenna and is given as

$$\left(\frac{S}{N}\right)_{\text{transmit}} = \frac{P}{\sigma^2} \tag{15}$$

The channel from base station to each user, the channel from base station to relay and the channel from relay to each user are all assumed to be quasi-static Rayleigh fading channel. That is, the element h_{ij} of channel matrix $\boldsymbol{H}$ $(\boldsymbol{H}_{SD}, \boldsymbol{H}_{SR}, \boldsymbol{H}_{RD})$ is an i.i.d. complex Gaussian random variable with the variance of $E\{|h_{ij}|^2\}=1$. We consider the distance from base station to each user is equal among users and the DF relay locates at the middle point between the base station and users. We also set the power decaying exponent as $\alpha = 3.5$ on the different distances from the base station to relay and users.

First, we investigate the case where the number of transmit antennas of base station is $N_s = 2$, the number of user terminal $N_u = 2$, the number of receive antennas of each user $m_1 = m_2 = 1$, the number of receive antennas of relay $M_R = 4$, and the number of transmit antennas of relay $N_R = 2$. We call this as $2\times(4,2)\times(1,1)$ model. In this model, for the SD link during the 1st time slot, BD+MRT scheme is used as the MU-MIMO transmission. QPSK modulation is used for each user stream. The BER characteristic is shown in Figure2. In Figure2, "SD link 2 times w/o relay" means the scheme in which the MU-MIMO transmission on SD link is repeated twice without using the relay. "$2\times(4,2)\times(1,1)$ MMSE" and "$2\times(4,2)\times(1,1)$ MLD" mean the schemes in which the receive signal at DF relay is demodulated using MMSE nulling and the one in which the receive signal at DF relay is demodulated using MLD, respectively.

We see from Figure2 that, by using the DF relay and combining the symbol LLR's of SD link and SRD link signals, the BER characteristic with using relay is very much improved compared with 2 times transmission on SD link without using relay. The SD link transmission without relay shows the diversity order of 1 $(\text{BER} = 10^{-1}/10\text{ dB})$. As stated in III.B, as the row elements of channel matrix $\boldsymbol{H}_{SR}\boldsymbol{N}_{SD}\boldsymbol{V}$ on the SR link do not always become independent, the SR link quality is degraded. Accordingly, the diversity order of 2 at each user is not achieved especially when the MMSE nulling is used at relay. However, by using the MLD at relay, the SR link quality is improved and we can get the diversity order of almost 2.

Next, we consider the case where the number of transmit antenna at base station is $N_T = 4$, the number of users $N_u = 2$ and the numbers of receive antennas of each user are $m_1 = m_2 = 1$. Compared with the previous case of $N_T = 2$, more transmit antennas are assigned to each user. The numbers of receive antenna and transmit antenna at relay are $M_R = 4$ and $N_R = 4$ respectively. We call this as $4\times(4,4)\times(1,1)$ model. The transmission protocols of SD, SR and RD links are the same as the previous $2\times(4,2)\times(1,1)$ model. The modulation format is QPSK. We show the simulation results in Figure3. In Figure3, the channel matrix $\boldsymbol{H}_{SD}$ on SD link is 2×4 and the channel matrix $\tilde{\boldsymbol{H}}_{sdi}$ in which the channel matrix for user i is excluded from $\boldsymbol{H}_{SD}$ becomes 1×4.

From (10), the nullity of $\tilde{\boldsymbol{H}}_{sdi}$ is calculated as $n\ell_i = 4-2+1=3, (i=1,2)$. The size of block matrix $\boldsymbol{D}_i$ of each user becomes $m_i \times n\ell_i = 1\times 3, (i=1,2)$ and the diversity

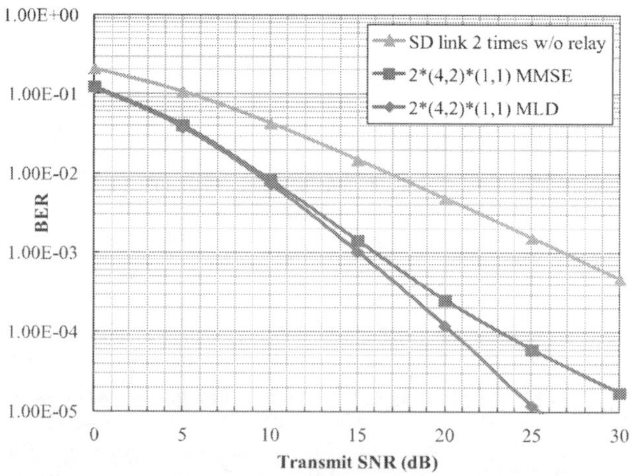

Figure 2. BER characteristics of $2\times(4,2)\times(1,1)$ model (Transmission rate to each user is 2(bps/Hz).)

order of each user stream is given by $m_i \cdot n\ell_i = 3, (i = 1,2)$. From Figure3, "SD link 2 times w/o relay" shows the BER slope of about $10^{-3}/10\,(\text{dB})$ for the transmit SNR=5~15(dB) and we see that the diversity order of 3 is almost obtained. When using relay, we can also expect the diversity order of 3 on the RD link as in the SD link. Thus, if there is no error on the SR link, then we can say the diversity order of 6 is obtained on the BER after the symbol LLR addition at each user. As the transmit SNR becomes higher, the errors on SR link decrease and the diversity order of 6 is more easily achievable at high SNR region. But in Figure3, we see the BER falls by $10^{-1}/2\,(\text{dB})$ for SNR=7~9(dB) and we know the diversity order of 5 is achieved in this SNR region.

Next, we consider the case where the number of transmit antenna at base station is $N_T = 4$, the number of users $N_u = 2$ and the numbers of receive antennas of each user are $m_1 = m_2 = 2$. The numbers of receive and transmit antennas at relay are $N_R = 4$ respectively. We call this as $4\times(4,4)\times(2,2)$ model. In this case, the optimum modulation formats which minimize the BER characteristics are selected under the constant transmission rate of 4(bps/Hz) on the SD link. This means one stream transmission with BD+MRT+16QAM or two stream transmission with BD+E-SDM+QPSK is adaptively selected for given $\boldsymbol{H}_{SD}$ [8]. Also in case of two stream transmission using two QPSK's, the optimum power assignment to the 1st and 2nd eigen mode channels which minimizes the BER is made [8]. In this two stream transmission, the DF relay needs to know in advance the precoding matrix $\boldsymbol{N}_{SD}$ for BD, the matrix $\boldsymbol{V}$ for the eigen mode transmission in E-SDM and the power allocation factor to the 1st and 2nd eigen mode channels. Also in order to make the symbol LLR addition at each user, the number of streams on the RD link must coincide with the one on the SR link. Hence, the BD+E-SDM transmission on RD link adopts the same number of streams as in the SD link. The simulation results are shown in Figure4. In Figure4, BD+E-SDM scheme is employed on the SD link and the size of block channel matrix for each user becomes $\boldsymbol{D}_i = 2\times 2\ (i = 1,2)$. The transmission to each user is done by one stream transmission with the maximum eigen value using 16QAM or two stream transmission with two different eigen values using two QPSK's. Figure4 shows the average BER characteristics. In this $4\times(4,4)\times(2,2)$ model, like in Figure2 and Figure3, the use of DF relay and the symbol LLR addition at each user during the 1st and 2nd time slots improve the diversity order and the BER characteristic when compared with the 2 times transmission on the SD link without using relay.

Next, we consider the case where the number of transmit antenna at base station is $N_T = 8$, the number of users $N_u = 4$ and numbers of receive antennas of each user are $m_1 = m_2 = m_3 = m_4 = 2$. The numbers of receive and transmit antennas at relay is $M_R = 8$ and $N_R = 8$ respectively. We call this as $8\times(8,8)\times(2,2,2,2)$ model. This model is the extension of previous $4\times(4,4)\times(2,2)$ model to $N_u = 4$ users. The transmission protocols are the same as the previous $4\times(4,4)\times(2,2)$ model. On the SD link, the size of

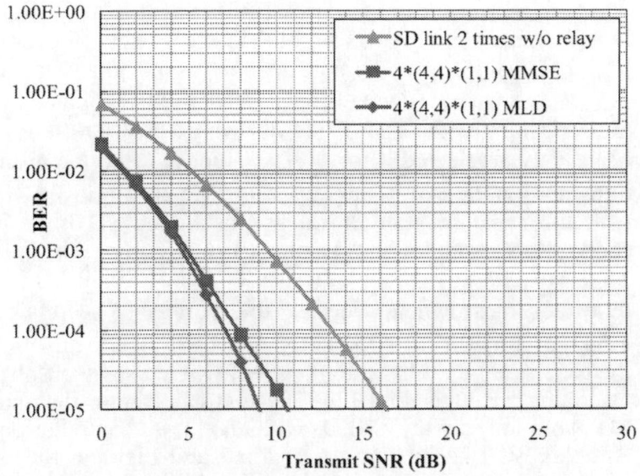

Figure 3. BER characteristics of $4\times(4,4)\times(1,1)$ model (Transmission rate to each user is 2(bps/Hz).)

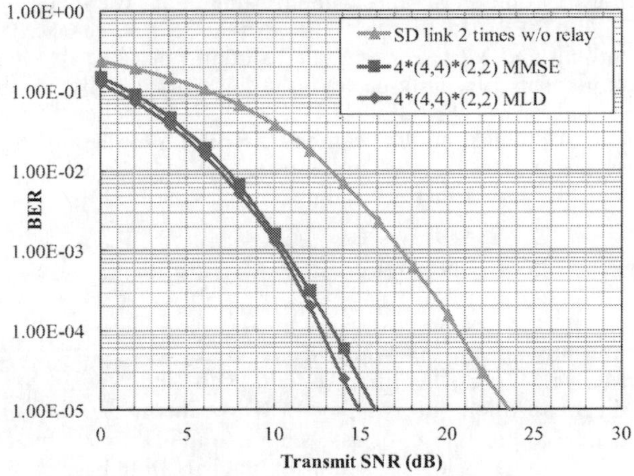

Figure 4. BER characteristics of $4\times(4,4)\times(2,2)$ model (Transmission rate to each user is 4(bps/Hz) and 16QAM or QPSK is optimally selected to minimize the BER.)

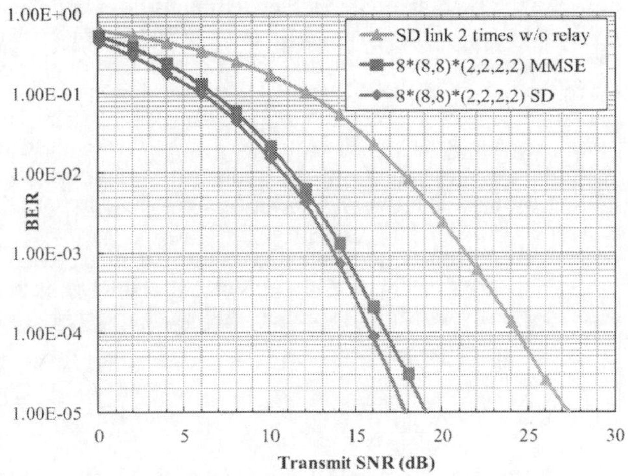

Figure 5. BER characteristics of $8\times(8,8)\times(2,2,2,2)$ model (Transmission rate to each user is 4(bps/Hz) and 16QAM or QPSK is optimally selected to minimize the BER.)

block channel matrix for each user becomes $\boldsymbol{D}_i = 2\times 2$ $(i=1,2,3,4)$. For each user, one stream transmission with BD+MRT using 16QAM or two stream transmission with BD+E-SDM using two QPSK's is adaptively selected for $\boldsymbol{H}_{SD}$ under the constant transmission rate of 4(bps/Hz). The RD link transmission uses the same number of streams as in the SD link. We show the simulation results in Figure5. In this $8\times(8,8)\times(2,2,2,2)$ model, the demodulation using MLD at relay becomes difficult because the number of searches in MLD becomes $4^8 = 65536$ for the total 8 streams from the base station. So instead of the MLD, we used the Sphere Decoding SE algorithm [20][21] that can obtain the same ML solution as the MLD with far less computational complexity. Like in Figure2, Figure3 and Figure4, the use of DF relay and the symbol LLR addition at each user during the 1st and 2nd time slots improve the diversity order and the BER characteristic compared with the 2 times transmission on SD link without using relay. We also see in Figure3~Figure5 that the BER difference between MMSE nulling and MLD (or Sphere Decoding) at relay is not so large. This is mainly because the BER of relay by MMSE nulling or MLD (or Sphere Decoding) is far better than the one of SD link, and the combined BER at destination is not so affected by the BER difference between MMSE nulling and MLD (or Sphere Decoding).

V. CONCLUSION AND FUTURE WORK

In this paper, we discussed the improvement of transmission quality when the DF relay is applied to the MU-MIMO down link system with the linear block diagonalization plus MRT or E-SDM scheme. By knowing the precoding matrix of base station at the DF relay, the DF relay can demodulate the transmit signals from base station only with the receive CSI. As the existence of relay does not affect the design of precoding matrix at the base station, we can add the DF relay only when the cannel quality between the base station and user terminals is insufficient. By adding the DF relay and utilizing the 2nd time slot, we can improve the receive quality of each user terminal. We made the design of SD, SR and RD links during the 1st and the 2nd time slots and verified the effectiveness of using DF relay. Although the SR link quality affects the total BER performance very much, we can utilize the simple MMSE nulling by increasing the number of receive antenna at DF relay to improve the SR link quality.

As future studies, although we handled the case where the numbers of transmission streams on SR and RD link are equal, the case of different numbers will be considered.

ACKNOWLEDGEMENT

This study is supported by the Japanese Grant-in-Aid for Scientific Research of 15K06059 and Sharp cooperation.

REFERENCES

[1] H. S Quentin, B. P. Christian, and A. Lee Swindlehurst, M. Hardt, "An introduction to the multi-user MIMO downlink," IEEE communications Magazine, vol.42, Issue 10, pp.60-67, Oct. 2004.

[2] Q. H. Spencer, A. L. Swindlehurst, and M. Haardt, "Zero forcing methods for downlink spatial multiplexing in multiuser MIMO channels," IEEE Trans. Sig. Processing, vol.52, no.2, pp.461-471, Feb.2004.

[3] T.Haustein, C. von Helmolt, E.Jorswieck, V.Jungnickel, and V.Pohl, "Performance of MIMO systems with channel inversion," IEEE 55th VTC Spring, vol.1, pp. 35 – 39, 2002.

[4] S. Vishwanath, N. Jindal, and A. Goldsmith, "Duality, achievable rates, and sum-rate capacity of MIMO broadcast channels," IEEE Trans. Inform. Theory, vol. 49, no. 10, pp. 2658–2668, Oct. 2003.

[5] Veljko Stankovic and Martin Haardt, "Successive optimization Tomlinson-Harashima precoding (SO THP) for multi-user MIMO systems," IEEE International Conference on Acoustics, Speech, and Signal Processing, Proceedings (ICASSP '05), vol.3, pp.iii/1117-iii/1120, March 2005.

[6] C. B. Peel, B. M. Hochwald, and A. L. Swindlehurst, "A vector-perturbation technique for near-capacity multi antenna multiuser communication-part I: Channel inversion and regularization," IEEE Trans. Commun., vol. 53, pp.195-202, Jan. 2005.

[7] C. B. Peel, B. M. Hochwald, and A. L. Swindlehurst, "A Vector-Perturbation Technique for Near-Capacity Multi antenna Multiuser Communication—Part II: Perturbation," IEEE Trans. Commun., vol. 53, pp. 195–202, Jan. 2005.

[8] K. Miyashita, T. Nishimura, T. Ohgane, Y. Ogawa, Y. Takatori, and K. Cho, "Eigenbeam-Space Division Multiplexing (E-SDM) in a MIMO Channel," IEICE Technical Report, RCS2002−53, pp.13−18, May, 2002.

[9] H. Sun, S. Meng, Y. Wan, and X. You, "Sum-rate evaluation of multi-user MIMO-relay channel," IEICE Trans. Commun., vol.E-92-B, No.2, pp.683-686, Feb. 2009.

[10] K. Nishimori, N. Honma, M. Mizoguchi, "Effectiveness of relay MIMO transmission in an actual outdoor environment," IEICE Technical Report, RCS2008-228, pp.95-100, March 2009.

[11] K. Fujii and T. Fujii, "Adjacent Cell Interference Reduction Using Multiuser MIMO Relay Station," IEICE Technical Report, RCS2010-164, pp.31-36, Dec. 2010.

[12] W. Liu, C. Li, J.-D. Li, L. Hanzo, "Block diagonalization-based multiple input multiple output-aided downlink relaying," IET Commun, Vol.6, Iss.15, pp.2371-2377, 2012.

[13] L. Liang, W. Xu, X. Dong, "Limited feedback-based multi-antenna relay broadcast channels with block diagonalization," IEEE Trans. Wireless Commun., Vol.12, No.8, pp.4092-4101, Aug. 2013.

[14] Y. Tanahashi, Y. Iwanami, R. Yamada, N. Okamoto, "Study on VP Transmission Schemes for Multiuser MIMO Downlink using Non-Regenerative Relay," IEICE Technical Report, RCS2013-371, pp.395-400, March 2014.

[15] T. Taniguchi and Y. Karasawa, "An Elementary Study on Node Pair Selection in Relay-Aided Communication System Based on Stable Marriage Problem," IEICE Technical Report, RCS2014-50, pp.105-108, June 2014.

[16] G. Zhang and Y. Iwanami, "A design of communication quality in linearly precoded MU-MIMO downlink system," IEICE Technical Report, RCS2015, March 2016.

[17] T. K. Y. Lo,"Maximum Ratio Transmission," IEEE Trans. Commun.,vol.47, no.10, pp.1458-1461, Oct. 1999.

[18] Paulraj, R. Nabar and D. Gore, Introduction to Space Time wireless Communication, Cambridge University Press, 2008.

[19] J. K. Cavers, "Single-User and Multiuser Adaptive Maximum Ratio Transmission for Rayleigh Channel," IEEE Trans. On Vehicular Technology, Vol.49, No.6, pp.2043-2050, Nov. 2000.

[20] Z. Guo and P. Nilsson, "Reduced Complexity Schnorr-Euchner Decoding Algorithms for MIMO systems," IEEE communication letters, vol.8, no.5, pp286-288, May 2004.

[21] B. Shim and I. Kang, "Sphere Decoding with a probabilistic tree pruning," IEEE transactions on signal processing, vol.56, no.10, pp4867-4878, Oct. 2008.

Dispersion Characteristics of Anisotropic Coupled Circuits with Arbitrarily Located Metallic Strips in Multilayer Configuration

M. L. Tounsi
Faculty of Electronics and Informatics
U.S.T.H.B University, Algiers, Algeria
email : mltounsi@ieee.org

A. Khodja
Instrumentation Laboratory,
Faculty of Electronics and Informatics
U.S.T.H.B University, Algiers, Algeria

M.C.E. Yagoub
EECS, University of Ottawa,
800 King Edward,
Ottawa, Ontario, Canada

Abstract –**In this paper, a fullwave-mode analysis method is proposed for analyzing the dispersion properties of anisotropic coupled microstrip circuits with arbitrary located metallic strips in multilayer configuration. The numerical procedure is based on a spectral domain approach via an adequate choice of basis functions for current densities on the strips. The proposed model should be useful in computer-aided design of such structures in ultra-wide band (UWB) and millimeter-wave applications. Numerical results are in good agreement with data available in the literature.**

Keywords- multilayer; anisotropy; spectral technique; dispersion.

I. Introduction

In microwave and optical regions, several techniques and technologies have been well developed, leading to various applications in radar, communications and other commercial sectors. The growing interest for coupled structures in microwave integrated circuits applications has considerably increased recently due to their various applications in microwave frequencies including UWB band (3.1-10.6 GHz) to build mixers, modulators, filters and other specific circuits.

Layers of suitable materials may be added to improve the performance of a device or may be required as essential building blocks in the design of a component. For example, in suspended microstrip couplers, extra-layers of dielectrics may be used to improve directivity, very useful in filter design [1]. The analysis of such coupled structures is complicated by the inhomogeneous nature of the problem. The analysis method depends on a number of considerations, such as efficiency, accuracy, memory requirement and versatility.

Anisotropic coupled microstrip-type structures with arbitrary located strips are the most popular circuit elements in microwave integrated circuits (MICs) since they are useful in many practical applications due to their flexibility in the design process and easier matching to external element connections [2]. In such coupled structures, the propagation is described in terms of C- and π-modes [3], which correspond to in-phase and out-of-phase modes, respectively. As mentioned, the analysis of such coupled structures is complex due to the inhomogeneous nature of the problem.

In this paper, the authors propose an original approach that combines speediness and accuracy to efficiently characterize coupled circuits with arbitrary located strips as well as in arbitrary multilayer configuration by the well-known spectral domain approach (SDA) method using the Galerkin's procedure via a suitable choice of basis functions.

This paper is organized as follows. In Section 2 we discuss the hybrid-mode spectral domain approach for asymmetric anisotropic coupled structures in multilayer configuration. Numerical results are presented in Section 3. Finally we summarize our major results and outline our future work.

II. Formulation of The Method

To illustrate the adopted numerical procedure used to evaluate the model dispersion parameters, we considered a shielded coupled microstrip structure with different widths (w_1 not necessary equal to w_2) in multilayer configuration (Figure 1). The number of layers can be arbitrarily set.

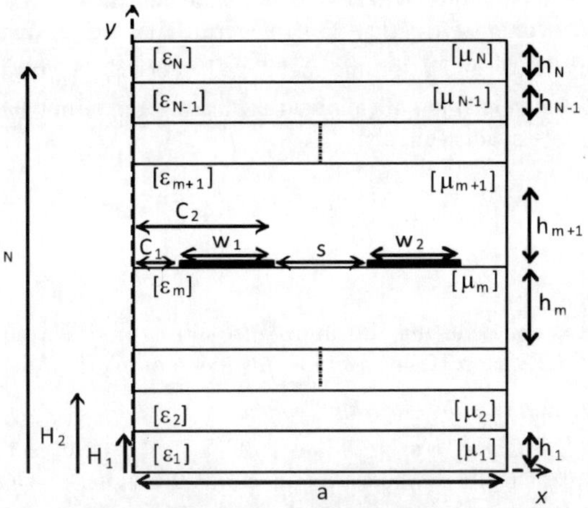

Figure 1. Cross section of an anisotropic microstrip coupler with arbitrary located strips in multilayer configuration

All dielectric layers are assumed anisotropic and lossless. Each layer i (i =1 ... N) is characterized by its own permittivity $[\varepsilon_i]$ and permeability $[\mu_i]$ as

$$[\varepsilon_i] = \begin{bmatrix} \varepsilon_{xi} & 0 & 0 \\ 0 & \varepsilon_{yi} & 0 \\ 0 & 0 & \varepsilon_{zi} \end{bmatrix} \qquad [\mu_i] = \begin{bmatrix} \mu_{xi} & 0 & 0 \\ 0 & \mu_{yi} & 0 \\ 0 & 0 & \mu_{zi} \end{bmatrix}$$

To get the dispersion characteristics, the spectral domain immittance approach technique [4] was used in multilayer configuration [5]. The immittance approach allows obtaining the Green's functions via a recursive process based on the determination of the equivalent admittances at all dielectric interfaces H_i (i=1 ... N).

Because the propagation modes are hybrid in a fullwave analysis, the EM field components have been evaluated in each dielectric layer assuming that the hybrid mode is the superposition of LSE (E_y=0) and LSM (H_y=0) modes. So, the transverse EM field components in the Fourier domain can be expressed as

$$\widetilde{H}_{xi} = -\beta\frac{\omega\varepsilon_{yi}}{(\alpha_n^2+\beta^2)}\widetilde{E}_{yi} - j\alpha_n\frac{\mu_{yi}}{\mu_{ci}(\alpha_n^2+\beta^2)}\frac{\partial\widetilde{H}_{yi}}{\partial y} \quad (1a)$$

$$\widetilde{H}_{zi} = \alpha_n\frac{\omega\varepsilon_{yi}}{(\alpha_n^2+\beta^2)}\widetilde{E}_{yi} - j\beta\frac{\mu_{yi}}{\mu_{ci}(\alpha_n^2+\beta^2)}\frac{\partial\widetilde{H}_{yi}}{\partial y} \quad (1b)$$

$$\widetilde{E}_{xi} = -j\alpha_n\frac{\varepsilon_{yi}}{\varepsilon_{ci}(\alpha_n^2+\beta^2)}\frac{\partial\widetilde{E}_{yi}}{\partial y} + \beta\frac{\omega\mu_{yi}}{(\alpha_n^2+\beta^2)}\widetilde{H}_{yi} \quad (1c)$$

$$\widetilde{E}_{zi} = -j\beta\frac{\varepsilon_{yi}}{\varepsilon_{ci}(\alpha_n^2+\beta^2)}\frac{\partial\widetilde{E}_{yi}}{\partial y} - \alpha_n\frac{\omega\mu_{yi}}{(\alpha_n^2+\beta^2)}\widetilde{H}_{y} \quad (1d)$$

where E_y and H_y are solutions of the field propagation equations [5]. α_n and β are the spectral parameter and the phase constant, respectively, with $\varepsilon_{ci}=\varepsilon_{xi}=\varepsilon_{zi}$ and $\mu_{ci}=\mu_{xi}=\mu_{zi}$. The index ~ represents the Fourier transform following x.

The following step was to use boundary conditions at all dielectric interfaces H_i to express the tangential electric field components (E_z, E_x) in terms of the currents densities J_x and J_z on the metallized interface H_m in the spectral domain. This allowed evaluating the admittance Green's dyadic functions:

$$\begin{bmatrix}\widetilde{J}_x(\alpha_n)\\ \widetilde{J}_z(\alpha_n)\end{bmatrix} = \begin{bmatrix}Y_{11} & Y_{12}\\ Y_{21} & Y_{22}\end{bmatrix}\begin{bmatrix}\widetilde{E}_x\\ \widetilde{E}_z\end{bmatrix} \quad (2)$$

and then, deducing the impedance form of the dyadic Green's matrix [G] by a simple inversion of matrix [Y].

A. Resolution by Galerkin Technique

The Galerkin's procedure is a particular case of the moment method where trial functions are equal to basis functions. In this technique, the tangential components J_x and J_z of the current density on each conductor strip are expanded onto two complete sets of P and Q basis functions, respectively:

$$J_{x,k} = \sum_{p=1}^{P} a_{p,k} J_{xp,k} \quad and \quad J_{z,k} = \sum_{q=1}^{Q} b_{q,k} J_{zq,k} \quad (3)$$

with $a_{p,k}$ and $b_{q,k}$ the real unknown coefficients to evaluate, with k = 1, 2 (left or right strip conductor of the coupler, respectively).

First, the Fourier transforms of (3) are evaluated and substituted into (2). Next, after using the inner product with trial functions, the Parseval's identity as well as the complementarity relations between the current and electric field on the two strips, we obtained an algebraic system of 2(P+Q) homogeneous linear equations in terms of the 2(P+Q) unknown coefficients $a_{p,k}$ et $b_{q,k}$ (k=1, 2).

$$\begin{pmatrix}[C_{11}(\omega,\beta)] & [C_{12}(\omega,\beta)] & [C_{13}(\omega,\beta)] & [C_{14}(\omega,\beta)]\\ [C_{21}(\omega,\beta)] & [C_{22}(\omega,\beta)] & [C_{23}(\omega,\beta)] & [C_{24}(\omega,\beta)]\\ [C_{31}(\omega,\beta)] & [C_{32}(\omega,\beta)] & [C_{33}(\omega,\beta)] & [C_{34}(\omega,\beta)]\\ [C_{41}(\omega,\beta)] & [C_{42}(\omega,\beta)] & [C_{43}(\omega,\beta)] & [C_{44}(\omega,\beta)]\end{pmatrix}\begin{bmatrix}a_{p1}\\ a_{p2}\\ b_{q1}\\ b_{q2}\end{bmatrix} = \vec{0} \quad (4)$$

The above homogeneous system was then solved for the phase constant β at each frequency f by setting the determinant of the matrix $[C_{j,m}(\omega,\beta)]$ (j, m =1... 4) to zero and by seeking the roots of the resulting equation.

B. Basis functions choice criterias

An adequate choice of basis functions is essential to assure a reliable solution with minimum numerical treatments and processing time. Indeed, a suitable choice of basis functions leads to a better configuration of the current density on the strips. This choice must respect several convergence criteria as detailed in [6]. Convergence may be speeded up by using basis functions whose behaviors resemble the physical distribution. Sinusoidal trial functions with metallic edge singularities have been chosen for the general nonsymmetrical case [7]:

$$\begin{cases} J_{px1}(x) = \sin\left(\dfrac{p\,\pi\,(x-C_1)}{w_1}\right) & x \in [\,C_1\,,\,C_1+w_1\,] \\ J_{px2}(x) = \sin\left(\dfrac{p\,\pi\,(x-C_2)}{w_2}\right) & x \in [\,C_2\,,\,C_2+w_2\,] \end{cases}$$

$$\begin{cases} J_{qz1}(x) = \dfrac{\cos\left(\dfrac{(q-1)\,\pi\,(x-C_1)}{w_1}\right)}{\sqrt{(\frac{w_1}{2})^2-(x-C_1-\frac{w_1}{2})^2}} & x \in [\,C_1\,,\,C_1+w_1] \\ J_{qz2}(x) = \dfrac{\cos\left(\dfrac{(q-1)\,\pi\,(x-C_2)}{w_2}\right)}{\sqrt{(\frac{w_2}{2})^2-(x-C_2-\frac{w_2}{2})^2}} & x \in [\,C_2\,,\,C_2+w_2] \end{cases}$$

Note that the solution accuracy for β can be systematically enhanced by increasing the number of basis functions.

III. NUMERICAL RESULTS AND DISCUSSIONS

To confirm the adequate choice of basis functions, we analyzed a bilayer nonsymmetrical shielded coupler. Figures 2 and 3 show the convergence of the effective permittivity versus the total number of basis functions Nfb (equal to 2*(P+Q)) and the total number of Fourier terms Ntf. Note that 100 Fourier terms and about 8 basis functions were sufficient to achieve a good convergence.

Moreover, we note that narrow strips ($w_1 = w_2 = 0.18$mm) require more spectral terms compared to wide ones ($w_1 = w_2 = 0.36$mm). A good compromise was found between accuracy, CPU time and memory storage with regard to differential methods since 4 basis functions per current density components were sufficient to reach convergence. Compared to differential methods which require a very dense mesh for a very good accuracy resulting on a large CPU time (as finite element method or FDTD method), the proposed technique is faster with a minimum memory storage.

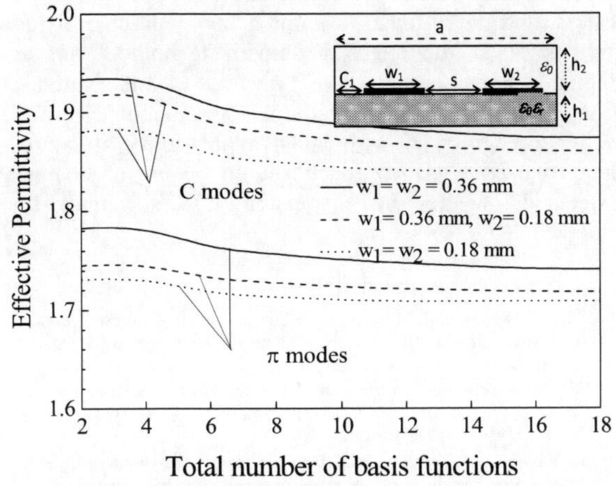

Figure 2. Convergence of the effective permittivity versus Nfb (a=3.556 mm, S=0.45 mm, h_1=0.254 mm, h_2 =6.858 mm, C_1=0.5 mm, ε_r=2.22, f=10 GHz, Ntf=500)

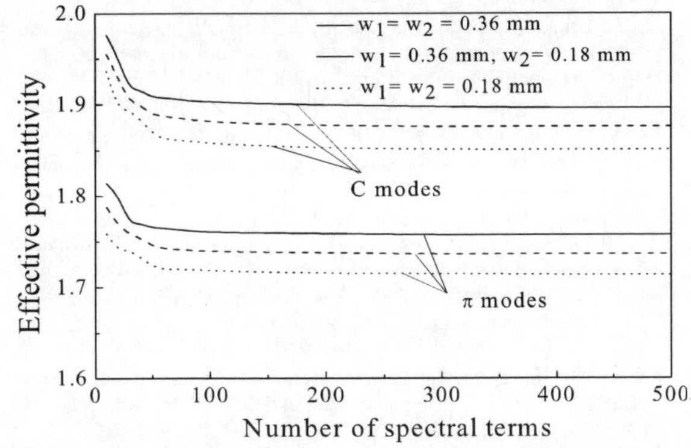

Figure 3. Convergence of the effective permittivity versus Ntf (a=3.556 mm, S=0.45 mm, h_1=0.254 mm, h_2 =6.858 mm, C_1=0.5 mm, ε_r=2.22, f=10 GHz, Nfb=16)

Figure 4, showing the variation of the determinant of $C_{i,j}(\beta)$, demonstrates the simultaneous existence of two distinct solutions for β, very similar to those published in [7]. Note that the authors in [7] used the resonance transverse method (TRM), generally used to get the wave propagation constant in waveguides including dielectric ones. It takes advantage of the fact that a standing wave is present along a certain direction (transverse with respect to the main propagation direction), due to purely reactive loads at both ends of the transmission line (which represents the wave propagation). Compared to TRM which is an integral method, the CPU time was reduced of about 20% depending of spectral terms Ntf and the number of basis functions Nfb

Figure 5 shows the variation of the effective permittivity ε_{eff} for different values of h_1. The results agree well with [7]. The evolution of the effective permittivity is characterized by the existence of three regions: first, ε_{eff} decreases with h_1 for both c and π modes, this can be explained by the high concentration of fields in the thin substrate (near horizontal walls of the shield). Then, ε_{eff} reaches a constant value of about 1.6 corresponding to equal thicknesses between the substrate and the air region.

Finally, ε_{eff} decreases from h_1= 6.6mm, due to the larger thickness of the substrate. The effective permittivity is higher for the lowest values of the substrate thickness.

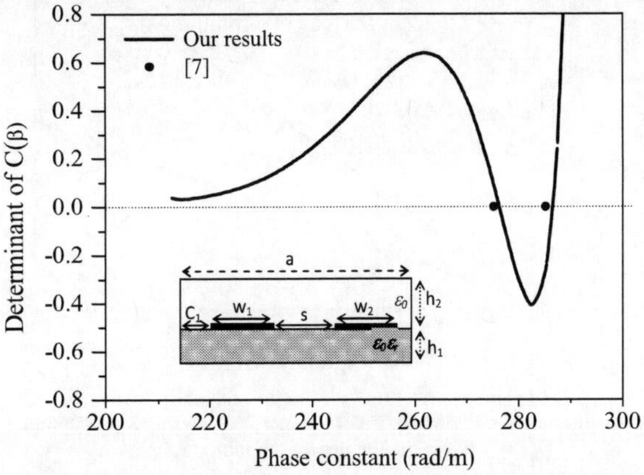

Figure 4. Determinant of C(β) versus phase constant β (a=3.556 mm, S=0.45 mm, h_1=0.254 mm, h_2 =6.858 mm, W_1= W_2=0.36 mm, C_1=0.5 mm, ε_r=2.22, f=10 GHz)

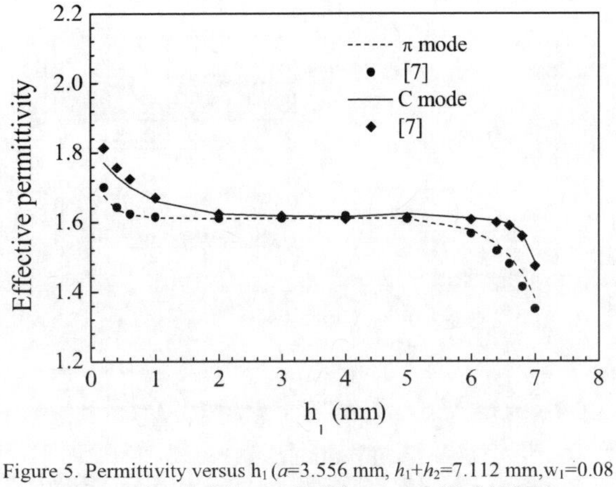

Figure 5. Permittivity versus h_1 (a=3.556 mm, h_1+h_2=7.112 mm,w_1=0.08 mm, w_2=4w_1, S=0.45 mm, C_1=0.9 mm, ε_r=2.22, f=10GHz)

Table I shows the effective permittivity of both even and odd modes for a coupled structure on epsilam 10 substrate. The relative average error is estimated to 1.5% for the odd mode and about 2% for the even mode.

TABLE I. VARIATION OF EFFECTIVE PERMITTIVITY VERSUS w/h_1
(h_1=1mm, h_2=9mm, S=0.1mm, a=50mm, f=100 MHz, ε_c = 13, ε_y = 10.3)

w/h	odd	odd [8]	even	even [8]
0.1	6.29	6.29	7.02	6.83
1	6.49	6.38	7.69	7.57
3	7.01	6.82	7.98	8.13

Figure 6 shows a comparison of dispersion charts between two anisotropic couplers using epsilam 10 substrate (ε_x=ε_z=13, ε_y=10.3) and niobate lithium (ε_x=ε_z=28, ε_y=43), respectively. Note that the phase constant is greater for lithium niobate due to higher field concentration.

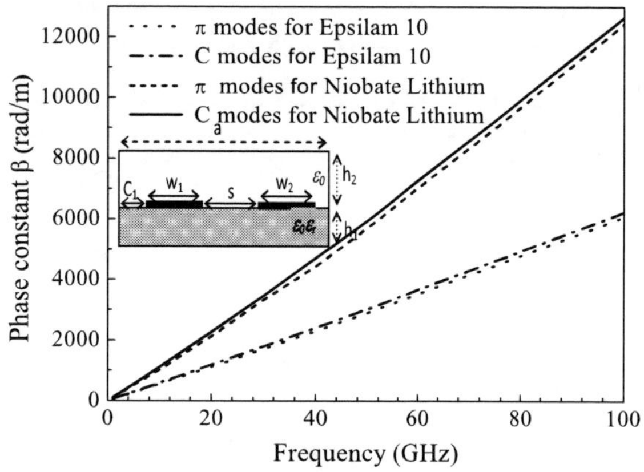

Figure 6. Dispersion chart for two anisotropic materials: Epsilam10 and niobate lithium. (a=3.556 mm, S=0.45 mm, h_1=0.254 mm, h_2=6.858 mm, w_1=w_2=0.36 mm, C_1=0.5 mm).

Figure 7 illustrates the variation of the guided wavelength λ_g versus frequency for a three-layer anisotropic coupler (ε_x=ε_z=28, ε_y=43) and a bilayer isotropic coupler.

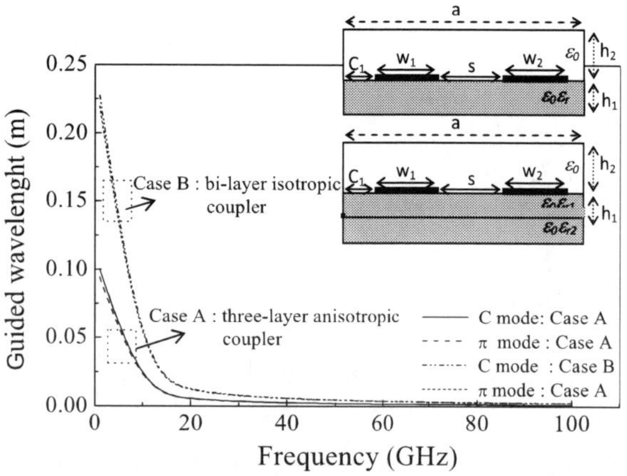

Figure 7. Comparison between a three-layer anisotropic coupler and a bilayer isotropic coupler (a=3.556 mm, S=0.45 mm, h_1=0.254 mm, h_2=6.858 mm, w_1=w_2=0.36 mm, C_1=0.5 mm, isotropic: ε_r=2.22, Sapphire (ε_x=ε_z=9.6, ε_y=11.6) and Epsilam10 (ε_x=ε_z=13, ε_y=10.3).

The curves show that λ_g is always smaller for the three-layer coupler than for the bi-layer, thus allowing reducing the device size.

IV. CONCLUSION

This paper highlights an efficient and fast way to determine the fullwave numerical solutions required in multilayered coupled microstrip line analysis with arbitrary located metallic strips. Such devices are used in various applications in microwave integrated circuits, particularly in wireless communication, multiplexors, shifters, and delay lines, to name a few. To achieve this aim, we used the spectral domain technique via an adequate choice of basis functions for c- and π-modes through the Galerkin's procedure. The computed results are in good agreement with data available in the literature. The proposed CAD approach should be useful in high frequencies where the dispersion effects cannot be neglected.

REFERENCES

[1] T.C. Edwards and M.B. Steer, Foundations of Interconnect and Microstrip Design, Chichester, England: Wiley and Sons, 2000.

[2] K. Wincza and S. Gruszczynsky, "Asymmetric coupled line directional couplers as impedance transformers in balanced and η-way power amplifiers", IEEE Trans. Microwave Theory Tech., vol. 59, Jul. 2011, pp. 1803-1810.

[3] A. Khodja, R. Touhami, M.C.E. Yagoub, and H. Baudrand, "Full-*wave mode analysis of asymmetric coupled microstrip structures: particular case of quasi-symmetric lines", 27th Progress In Electromagnetics Research Symposium, Mar. 2011, pp. 176-180.

[4] T. Itoh, "Spectral domain immitance approach for dispersion characteristics of generalized printed transmission lines", IEEE Trans. Microw. Theory Tech., vol. 28, Jul. 1980, pp.733 -736.

[5] M.L. Tounsi, R. Touhami, and M.C.E. Yagoub, "Generic spectral immittance approach for fast design of multilayered bilateral structures including anisotropic media,", IEEE Microwave and Wireless Components Letters, vol. 17, Jun. 2007, pp. 409-411.

[6] A. Khodja, R. Touhami, M.C.E. Yagoub, and H. Baudrand, "Full-wave modal analysis of asymmetric coupled-lines using the quasi-symmetric approach", Mediterranean Microwave Symp., Sept. 2011, pp. 142-144.

[7] A. Khodja, M.C.E. Yagoub, R. Touhami, and H. Baudrand, "Efficient characterization of millimeter-wave asymmetric coupled microstrip structures using the quasi-symmetric approach", International Journal of RF and Microwave CAE, Ed. Wiley, vol.23, Issue 5, Sept. 2013, pp. 527–538,.

[8] N.G. Alexopoulos, "Integrated circuit structures on anisotropic substrates, IEEE Trans. Microwave Theory Tech., vol. 33, Oct. 1985, pp 847-881.

Testing Technologies to Support Network and Services Testing in a 5G Test Network

Teemu Kanstrén, Jukka Mäkelä, Esa Piri, Jussi Liikka, Atso Hekkala
VTT, Oulu, Finland
email:firstname.lastname@vtt.fi

***Abstract*—Trends such as 5G and Internet of Things are driving modern systems towards increasing complexity in diverse configurations of heterogeneous networks, ubiquitous integration of hardware and software, and complex interactions between the different parts. This paper describes the testing technologies developed and deployed in our 5G test network (5GTN), to support development and testing of such systems, next generation services deployed on them, and the underlying network technologies. We describe the 5GTN testing technologies, including the software architecture enabling distributed test generation, monitoring and data collection from test execution. We also describe the 5GTN integrated data analytics services enabling efficient use of the test data, as well as initial results for the first tests in the network.**

Keywords - ***5G, test network, testing technologies, big data, analytics***

I. Introduction

Internet of Things (IoT), cloud computing, big data processing and fifth generation (5G) networks are all trends currently strongly driving next generation software and service development. They are enabling services such as accurate (indoor) positioning, low latency control, high bandwidth streaming, deep data insights, and large scale computational capacity on demand. However, these are currently fast evolving technologies, and for many actors in the service development space it is difficult to benefit from these opportunities to create such next generation services, due to limited access to suitable environments enabling innovation in this space.

The Finnish national 5G test network (5GTN, [11]) is a joint effort created by VTT, University of Oulu and 15 industry partners. It is designed to support a number of use cases for testing, network management and business development purposes. Some of the main examples include:

- Support testing new applications and services, as well as networking solutions in evolving networks.
- Provide a living lab environment for 3rd party application, service, algorithm, system testing.
- Offer a test network for virtualized services.

Some of the generally identified prime objectives in 5G technologies are increased capacity, increased data rate, lower latencies and higher quality of service [3]. Specific technologies typically associated with 5G are, for example, small cell access points, virtualized network elements/network cloud, and increased IoT traffic and adoption [3]. These provide both opportunities for new types of service development (e.g., higher bandwidth and lower latencies) but also challenges (e.g., different types of traffic profiles in IoT stressing the network in unanticipated ways). Making use of the opportunities and addressing the challenges makes 5G relevant to almost all actors in the software and networking domain.

The 5GTN is an environment intended to enable service innovation in this context by providing a test environment that is constantly incorporating latest technologies available in the 5G networking infrastructure, as well as providing support for different levels of cloud computing (including mobile edge computing [17]), IoT devices and services, and extensive monitoring and big data analytics support. The test network is provided as a service to interested parties working in the area, to provide an environment for developing and testing new innovative next generation services. This both removes the barrier for companies who do not have direct access to such environment themselves, as well as provides a place for network and telecom equipment vendors to test their products with actual end users, customers and next generation services.

The initial version and use cases for 5GTN have been described in [5], and a general overview of its testing technologies was given in [4]. A more recent technical overview of the network elements is given in [9]. In this paper, we focus on describing latest developments in the testing technologies part, as well as in describing the initial use cases/test scenarios.

The rest of the paper is structured as follows. In Section II, we describe related work. In Section III, we present the 5GTN architecture. In Section IV, we briefly illustrate some example scenarios for the 5GTN. In Section V, we discuss these in a broader context. Finally, conclusions sum it all up.

II. Related Work

5G is currently a hot topic and various test networks exist to support different actors in developing 5G products and services. The big players in the field have been running their own specific 5G technology tests already for a long time [2]. However, access to such technology is limited for smaller players. 5G test networks are means for these two types of actors to interact, with the smaller (more software service focused) players having access to a more realistic and state-of-the-art test environment, and the telco actors getting access to real end users to test their products.

We briefly review some of these other 5G networks here to give added context to our 5GTN. Each of these has a specific focus, while we provide a holistic overall test network ranging from 5G devices and virtualized network functionality to software services. 5GTN is also itself part of a broader network of Finnish testbeds related to 5G development, called 5GTNF [12].

The *5G Berlin* [15] is a German test network providing a number of different testbeds for 5G development and testing, such as 5G access technologies, optics, core network technologies and virtualization. Some examples of the 5G Berlin work include the air-interface related topics as described in [8]. The *5G Dresden* [13] another German effort, focusing on research in the area of *Tactile Internet*, which refers to near-realtime interaction of people with physical and virtual objects [1]. The *5G Innovation Centre* [14] is a test network located in Surrey, UK. It focuses especially on new air-interface technologies.

Many test network system issues related to these types of networks are discussed in [21], and with our test network we aim to address also these issues. In comparison to the other 5G test networks such as the ones mentioned above, in 5GTN we provide a unified test network allowing a holistic overview for testing of devices and services, while supporting also linking to a larger nation-wide testbed concept as part of 5GTNF. We also provide integration with an advanced monitoring and data analytics infrastructure to provide means to not just run the tests but also to deeply analyze and understand the results and use them to guide and optimize towards better products and services.

In relation to different types of tests, various approaches for integrating performance and function tests, with e.g., behavioral models and their monitoring against large scale test data have been applied [20]. Currently, we perform this in a more qualitative way, as illustrated by our performance test scenario example in Section IV. However, if needed, our approaches in the test network could be extended to include this type of testing more formally as well.

The complexity of building a test environment supporting big data style data analytics and complex integrations of all required parts in test environments is discussed in [22]. In our test network, we aim to make the application of such techniques possible for all interested parties by providing and managing the complexities of the infrastructure as a service.

In relation to the types of traffic profiles and tests we support, many works have also targeted specific areas of the types of testing that we support in our test network, such as such as video Quality of Service (QoS) ([7]). We combine support for these as a holistic platform in our 5GTN.

III. 5GTN

Figure 1 shows a high-level picture of our test network from the testing technologies viewpoint. The macro cell provides extensive outdoor coverage for the relevant test scenarios. A set of small cells is deployed indoors to provide an indoor test environment. The backend system contains the full Evolved Packet Core (EPC) with all the associated components, along with network monitoring components deployed as Virtualized Network Function (NFV) instances on top of the OpenStack platform.

Supporting various types of actors (developers of infrastructure, services, end user devices, etc.) in their testing needs requires the ability to generate and execute tests at different levels of such a network, to collect extensive data about the performance of different elements in the network, and to be able to perform advanced analytics on them. A related architecture called "Big Data Network Highway", and associated challenges, is described in [10]. Expanding on the three layers presented in [10], we define several layers for the network, the end user device (e.g., phones, sensors, computers) layer, the (wireless) access (point) layer, the basic routing infrastructure, the core network (e.g., EPC, Content Delivery Network (CDN) servers) layer, and the datacenter layer (here test data and analytics architecture).

Not many actors have access to such complex environments, expertise on using all the advanced testing technologies, executing complex test setups, and performing the advanced analytics. We provide support for all these layers in terms of supporting diverse sets of protocols at the end user and access point layer, a full EPC core network, several test enabling application services such as video streaming CDN servers, IoT sensors and servers, and diverse test tools. Different combinations of these can be combined to create different test scenarios. For the more technical parts of these test network infrastructure components, we refer the reader to [9].

The analytics architecture follows the trend of what is commonly referred to as the Lambda architecture in big data processing [6]. This means we support both batch processing as well as stream processing. Using tools such as Apache Spark Core we provide batch processing support to analyze large scale datasets collected through the different test runs. Using tools such as Apache Spark Streaming and Apache Storm we provide support for near real-time stream processing. With batch processing we can provide support for long term-analysis, finding trends and correlations and doing similar analytics. They can be applied at any time, to explore new topics of interest in existing data sets as new things are learned and hypothesis need to be confirmed. With stream processing we provide support for interested parties to test real-time traffic optimization, network management and similar algorithms, as well as means to guide online test generation.

Apache Kafka in our case forms the "Big Data Highway" for the measurement data, allowing us to effectively stream data from numerous distributed locations to several different and concurrent distributed processing systems. We call this in the following sections the data collection layer. For example, data is published from test tools, test targets, test generators, IoT gateways and similar system elements into this layer. Data is consumed (subscribed) from this layer by several analytics tools to perform real-time stream processing or to store the data for long-term historical batch analysis. Real-time stream processing systems can also publish additional data in the form of derived measures to the data collection layer, from which it can be further consumed by other stream processors and stored in long-term storage by batch storage consumers.

To enable execution of extensive test sets on top of this infrastructure, we also need to be able to generate various types of traffic and collect extensive monitoring data. We provide an extensive set of tools available in this environment, enabling monitoring of all deployed network elements, as well as of any test generation components and application servers that have interfaces to query relevant information.

The set of available test and monitoring tools is constantly

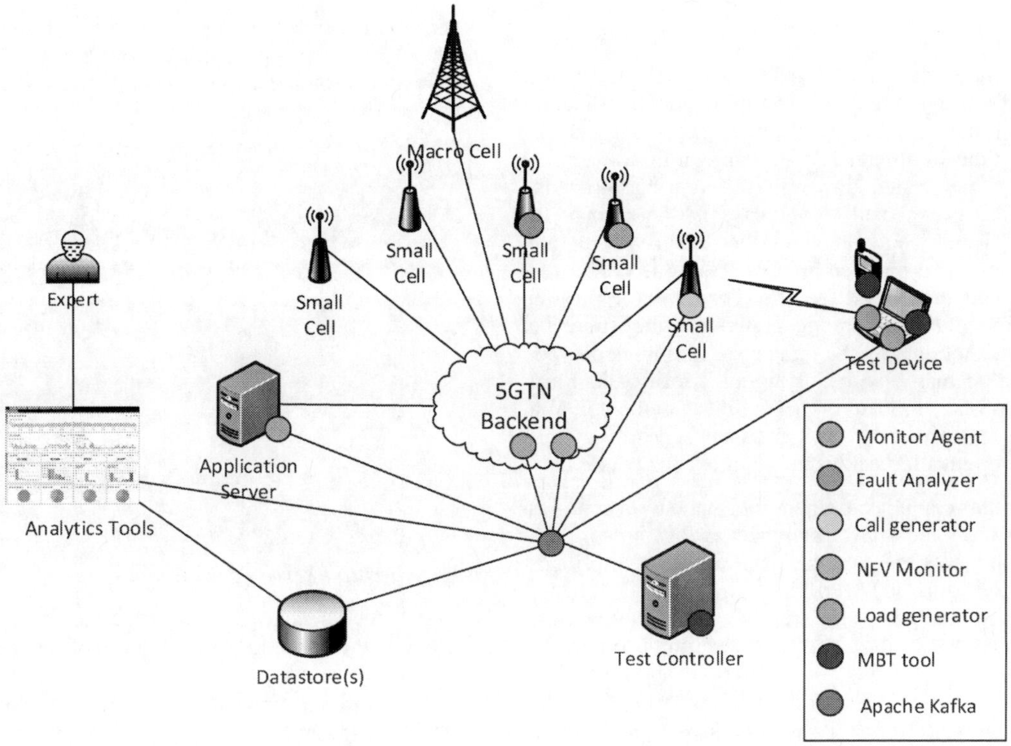

Figure 1. Test and Analytics Architecture overview

evolving, and includes:

- Model-based testing tool: Driving test scenarios to simulate realistic users on test devices, at single device/service as well as overall test scenario level (several devices/services).
- Virtualized (NFV) monitoring tools: Attached to Network Function Virtualization Infrastructure (NFVI) to provide monitoring of network traffic and parameters for the EPC
- IP traffic monitors: Collecting QoS measurements such as packet loss, latencies, ...
- Call generators: Large scale call traffic in the network
- Load generators: Large scale IP traffic in the network
- Test devices: Mobile devices, laptops, IoT devices, ...
- Data store: Used to collect test data such as control information and monitoring statistics
- Analytics tools: Test data analytics, both real-time and long-term historical

For the technical details on these, we again refer the reader to [9].

Our extensive set of monitoring tools enable us to collect data from different parts of the network, and these can be deployed on several network nodes at the same time. For example, QoSMet [18] is a tool capable of measuring detailed QoS network parameters between two endpoints. By deploying this on several of the endpoints at the same time, we can get a detailed view of the QoS for all the different elements. Similar data can be collected from the core network, and its interfaces, using monitoring tools deployed as Virtual Netword Function (VNF) elements with the EPC. Various similar tools can be deployed to monitor different properties as needed, and application specific monitoring interfaces can also be integrated into the data collection layer as needed. The overall data can be accessed through the data analytics layer.

Test traffic can be generated using different devices and services, both with real user equipment (phones, sensors, etc.) and large scale simulators. Specific types of large scale network data and specific service usage sequences can be generated at large scale using general computing resources as part of the network.

Tools such as model-based testing tools are used to generate traffic based on user profiles. These simulate real traffic and user activity in the network and on the service applications deployed on top it. They can be generated either based on recorded real traffic or simulated test models based on a model of the expected behaviour of the end user/sensor in question. The current main test scenarios/user profiles include:

- Video streaming
- Web browsing

- IoT sensors

High quality (e.g., 4k) video streaming is expected to be one of the major usage scenarios for high bandwidth consumption in the future, and provides a baseline for large-scale streaming. This type of stream is high-bandwidth consuming but can typically be scaled down in different QoS levels. IoT sensor traffic is expected to increase at large scale as the current IoT trend continues and the IoT products are increasingly deployed in practice and everything is connected to the network. This provides a specific type of traffic profile, where small burst of traffic are generated but they may be generated in large amounts by the numerous sensors deployed. Some of this traffic may also be of higher priority and must maintain high QoS, such as safety-critical measurements. Web browsing represents a current typical usage scenario that is used to provide a realistic background context for these.

Different profiles can be combined to provide test scenarios for different testing needs. For example, testing network infrastructure components may require generating varying loads of video, browser and IoT traffic, with varying network configurations and analyzing the results using multivariate analysis techniques to identify performance limits, optimization possibilities and problematic configurations and scenarios. From a different viewpoint, testing application services in the test network enables us to see their performance in different network loads, run functional and performance tests across the infrastructure and effectively pinpoint which issues are related to the application server or clients, and which are artefacts of the underlying infrastructure. Also in this context, our test services also enable combining different type of traffic, monitor the overall network, vary the service parameters, and observe and analyze all the results in depth. For end user devices, we can support a number of different protocols (as detailed in [9]), and their co-existence with various other devices and services in the network. In all these cases our aim is to provide a holistic view of the test environment, system under test, its environmental context, and broad analytics support.

IV. USE CASES AND TEST SCENARIOS

In this section, we give examples of the current usage scenarios we are running on the network, and using these to further develop it to be constantly more widely applicable for industrial testing and provide new testing services.

A. *IoT testing*

In this IoT test scenario, we have a Constrained application Protocol application (CoAP [16]) server deployed withing the network. Various actual sensor nodes available in the test laboratory are used to produce test traffic representing real IoT traffic in the network. This is passed through customized service gateway instances in the network edge (which also include the ability to calculate traffic statistics and publish them on the data layer), which forward the data over the test network to the CoAP application server. Several client instances are used over the network to scale up the test traffic over the gateways and other interfaces. More detailed test results for this case are available in [9], where they are shown as examples of measurements in the network, and we do not repeat them here. The important thing to note is how we can provide extensive support for various types of IoT sensor traffic and related protocols. Figure 2 illustrates the base concept of this type of a test case.

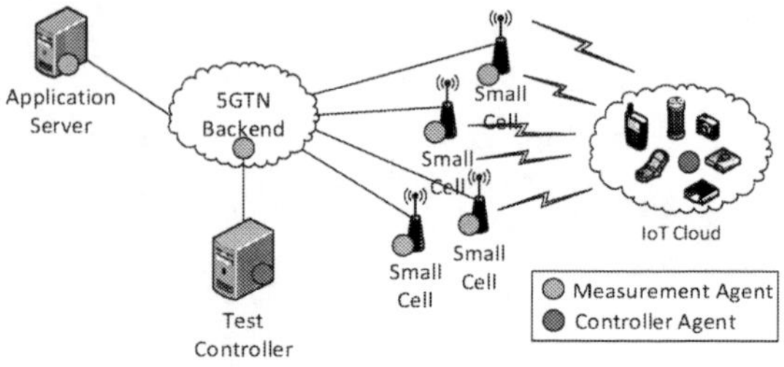

Figure 2. IoT case.

B. *Application server performance*

This test scenario is an example of a mobile service deployed with both mobile clients and an application server as part of the test network. The application server provides location tracking services for several moving nodes that it receives location data for. Any number of clients can be expected to connect to it at any time, and receive continuous streaming updates for sessions of different length. The data is provided as binary streams of protocol buffers messages over SSL encrypted sockets. The application server can be run either as part of the test network or as its own external cloud service (e.g., on Amazon EC2).

Figure 3 illustrates the beginning of one execution for this test scenario. The top row shows the frequency of updates as recorded by the application server (and directly reported to the data layer) in orange, and the average of the receiving frequencies observed at the clients (reported by the tester clients to the data layer) in green. The middle row graph shows the number of SSL errors observed by the clients when connecting to the server (orange for cumulative, green for per frame). The bottom row graph shows the combined number of live sessions by the tester clients during the test execution.

From Figure 3, we can see how at around 1500 concurrent sessions the service quality starts to degrade, with client average latencies starting to fluctuate, and how this fluctuation and number of errors increases as more sessions are initiated. In this case, a single error is an SSL handshake failure, where the client fails to establish a connection to the server, and these are recorded by the customized test client and also reported to the data layer. Running this test causes the system to fail practically all new sessions at around 4000 active sessions, showing a hard limit, where the test system stops after reaching an error threshold for number of failures in a continued sequence.

To better investigate the cause for the issues, we need to understand what is the status with the different system elements. Figure 4 shows the load on the application server, indicating that the server has no issues handing the traffic. This is also visible in top row graph in Figure 3, where the server (orange line) observes a constant result of providing the

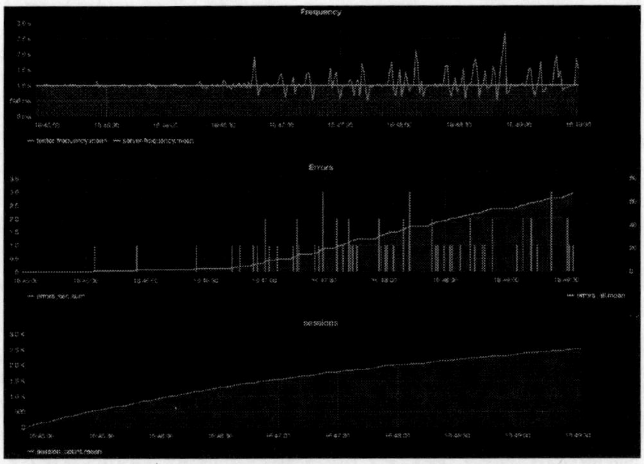

Figure 3. Errors observed in the performance test.

data to the clients on average at 1 second intervals as expected (while the clients show increasing fluctuation). The multiple multi-colored lines on the left side of Figure 4 are load per core, and the single green line on the right is overall load.

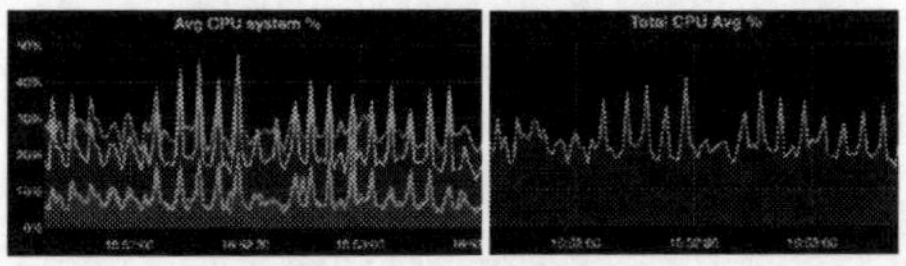

Figure 4. Server load.

We find further insight by looking at the router that is used to connect all the devices together in this case. This load is shown in Figure 5. This is the CPU load on the router collected using Simple Network Management Protocol (SNMP) probes, which again feed the measurements into the data layer. In relation to the server load shown in Figure 4, this has a 5 second resolution as it is the best resolution that the router can provide. This provides some added data analytics challenge due to different granularities of measurements, and automated correlation of failure thresholds to hitting specific limits. However, looking at these, we made the evaluation that the router overload is causing the errors in the test case.

We had high-confidence in this result from looking at the detailed resource use measurements and performance indicators we collected for all the system elements, including the application servers, test clients and router(s). The only one experiencing constant load issues towards the end is the router. For further investigations in this type of scenario we could modify the network configuration to alleviate such bottlenecks but in this scenario the result was enough to provide the needed results for this application server.

Figure 5 shows actually the end of one of these test sequence executions, where the sharp drop indicates the stopping of the test clients. A notable piece of information here is how the load in the router at the the end does not drop to zero but stays at around 25%. This is due to a set of baseline traffic providing a specific traffic profile for a combined test scenario. In this case it is a set of real users streaming YouTube video

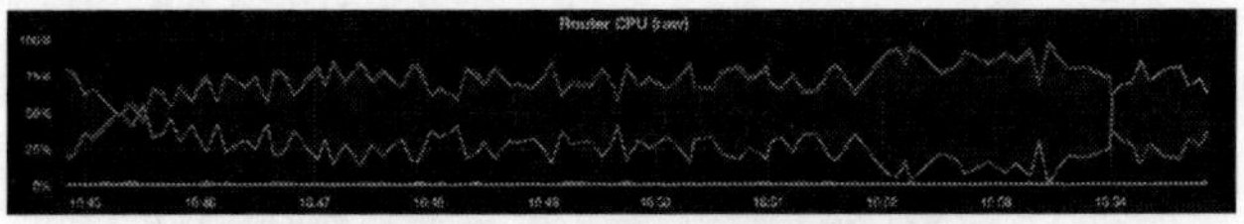

Figure 5. Router load.

traffic on the same network, continuing throughout the test scenario and after.

Thus we can say that the server can handle larger numbers of concurrent clients but the network in this case would need additional resources. We see testing this type of a scenario as useful for scenarios such as large-scale IoT and mobile service deployments, or large events and similar locations where large crowds are gathering. The next iteration in this type of testing would be to add additional network elements, more distribution and continue to investigate the system limits in different configurations. However, we use this example here illustrate our point of using the test network to also provide a holistic view on the test network and system under test, and we leave these topics for future work.

C. *QoS mapping*

Figure 6 illustrates one of our executed test cases for measuring and mapping the QoS for some of our network devices. This one shows the outdoor area surrounding the test network site, with green parts showing where the observed streaming QoS is above a specified threshold value. Red indicates values where the value is below the threshold. The values can be collected using our tools (e.g., QoSMet [18]) for QoS measurement and mapping these to a map of the area of interest.

Similar measurements can also be provided for indoor areas (e.g., indoor small cell coverage). This is a service we can perform as part of our test environment to provide insight into and compare, what is the strength of the signal using various equipment under different configurations. It also gives us insight into how we might expect the QoS to behave for different services being tested in the network when they are mobile through the network. Such QoS values can further be incorporated into the analytics results.

V. DISCUSSION

The examples we have provided here are only intended to illustrate potential use cases for the test network and the benefits of a holistic tests and analytics architecture. As mentioned in the architecture section, in addition to these basic test execution scenarios described above, The overall testing process with the test network is intended to start with the visual data exploration phase described in the previous section, followed by tuning the testing as new things are learned about the system and its performance in the network, and proceeding to deeper analytics enabled by more advanced algorithms that can be implemented on top of the big data analytics platforms.

As mentioned in Section III, we have also integrated support for these big data analytics platforms in the form of tools such as Apache Spark and Storm. In addition to large-scale historical analysis, output from these tools can be used

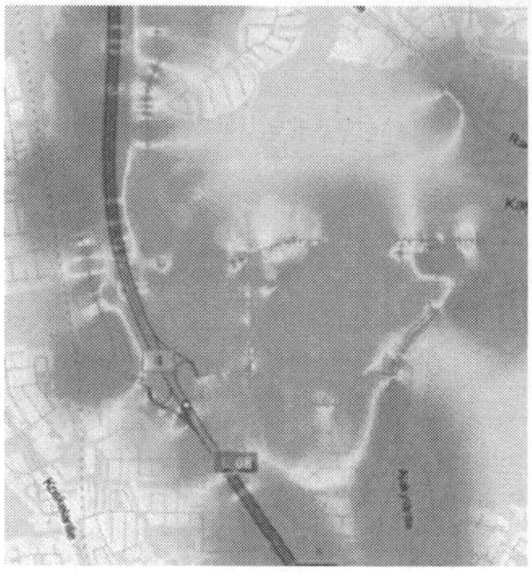

Figure 6. QoS map.

to provide real-time input for algorithms in different domains such as network management or to guide test generation towards interesting goals when specific statistical effects or impacts are observed. Properties of interest to study this way include varying parameters in the test network elements, varying the traffic profiles in relation to these, and analyzing the measurement data to find relations. Besides this current level of integration, one of our long term goals in this relation is the ability to to further link this with more advanced test automation support to enable automated variation, collection and analytics. As our test network constantly evolves and we execute increasingly complex test scenarios we plan to address these as part of our future work.

The application service performance test example given in Section IV focused on the overall performance aspect. In addition to such non-functional properties, we find such tests can also support functional testing through our broad data collection and analytics support. In our performance test example we illustrated how we can integrate any types of service specific measures into the system. In this case they were the application server session counts, and test client and server internal processing latencies. Besides the performance measure, these were also used during testing to identify lingering sessions causing resource leaks in different execution and load scenarios (visible as the live session count not dropping after the tests and high error rates).

In relation to our goals for the test network set in Section III, the architecture and example test scenarios show how we can use this type of a test architecture to support various test goals such as the ones described at the beginning of this paper. We can introduce network elements, including both actual hardware and virtualized (NFV) software appliances, into the network, test their functionality and impact separately and as part of the larger network. Similarly, we can provide a testing platform for next-generation software-based services making use of the features enabled by these fifth generation (5G) networks, and provide a holistic view on their functionality and performance in relation to different elements. All together, we see the 5G test network as providing a holistic innovation platform for next generation services.

Integration of big data monitoring and analytics provides some specific issues to be addressed. Fast reactions and real-time analytics need special attention as telecommunications systems are real-time systems where situations happen quickly and need fast reactions also from analytics and the operations it can trigger. Building such a heterogeneous test network as described here also requires integrating multitude of heterogeneous devices and services, as well as all of the data they produce. This requires extensive integration over different interfaces, and means to combine them.

It also requires integrating the diverse data formats to the diverse set of analytics tools. In our case, we have used data ingestion components collecting the data from different sources and transforming them to the shared binary protocol format. However, besides this basic transformation, the type of data and its meaning requires extensive experience on multitude of domains both within the telecommunications domain and application domains (each different). Within the telecommunications domain alone, specific components alone (e.g., EPC or base stations) can produce hundreds or thousands of parameters. Identifying the relevant elements and their combinations from all this requires diverse expertise from numerous players and takes a lot of time, as well continuous evolution. Our set of diverse project partners is one of the enablers for addressing these needs.

VI. Conclusions and Future Work

In this paper, we described the testing technologies in the 5G test network. The 5GTN is an ongoing project focused on building a platform for next generation services. With a comprehensive test generation, monitoring, and analytics architecture it enables extensive testing of both related devices and software, as well as provides a platform for building innovative services targeting next generations of networks. We continue our work and expand the network and its services, including addressing the issues identified and discussed in this paper.

In the future we will continue evolving the network as new 5G technologies become available and as we learn new things from the testing performed on the network. We will also investigate additional real application services as part of the network and how to evolve the services to support added use cases. For the analytics part, emerging technologies such as edge computing provide interesting options to distribute and optimize the overall analytics architecture.

Acknowledgment

This paper is carried out in a 5GTN project, which is partially funded by Tekes, Finnish funding agency for innovation. The authors would like to thank the whole consortium for all the help and cooperation.

References

[1] G. P. Fettweis, "The Tactile Internet: Applications and Challenges,", IEEE Vehicular Technology Magazine, vol. 9, no. 1, March 2014, pp. 64-70.

[2] J. Gozalvez, "5G Tests and Demonstrations [Mobile Radio],", IEEE Vehicular Technology Magazine, vol. 10, no. 2, June 2015, pp. 16-25.

[3] A. Gupta and R. K. Jha, "A Survey of 5G Network: Architecture and Emerging Technologies,", IEEE Access, vol. 3, 2015, pp. 1206-1232.

[4] T. Kanstrén and J. Perälä, "Testing Technologies in Finnish 5G Test Network", ETSI User Conf. on Advanced Automated Testing (UCAAT), 20-22, October, 2015.

[5] M. Latva-Aho, A. Pouttu, A. Hekkala, I. Harjula, and J. Mäkelä, Small Cell Based 5G Test Network (5GTN), 12th Intl. Symp. on Wireless Comm. Systems, Brussels, Belgium, 25-28, August, 2015.

[6] N. Marz and J. Warren, "Big Data: Principles and Best Practices of Scalable Realtime Data Systems", Manning publications, 2015.

[7] S. Moon, J. Yoo, and S. Kim, "Exploiting Adaptive Multi-interface Selection to Improve QoS and Cost-Efficiency of Mobile Video Streaming", IEEE Int'l. Conf. on Mobile Services, June/July, 2015, pp. 134 - 141.

[8] T. Wirth, et al., "An Advanced Hardware Platform to verify 5G Wireless Communication concepts", IEEE 81st Vehicular Technology Conf. (VTC Spring), May, 2015, pp. 1-5.

[9] E. Piri, et al., "5GTN: A Test Network for 5G Application Development and Testing", European Conf. on Networks and Communications (EuCNC), Athens, Greece, 2016.

[10] X. Yi, F. Liu, and H. Jin, "Building a Network Highway for Big Data: Architecture and Challenges", IEEE Network, July/August, 2014, pp. 5-13.

[11] http://5gtn.fi/, "5GTN - 5G Test Network", Oulu, Finland, [retrieved: April, 2016].

[12] http://5gtnf.fi/, "5G Test Network Finland", Finland, [retrieved: April, 2016].

[13] http://5glab.de/, "5G Lab Germany", Dresden, Germany, [retrieved: April, 2016].

[14] http://www.surrey.ac.uk/5gic, "5G Innovation Centre", Surrey, UK, [retrieved: April, 2016].

[15] http://www.5g-berlin.org/, "5G Berlin", Berlin, Germany, [retrieved: April, 2016].

[16] Z. Shelby, K. Hartke, and C. Bormann, "The Constrained Application Protocol (CoAP)", IETF Request for Comments: 7252, 2014.

[17] ETSI,"Mobile-Edge Computing (MEC); Service Scenarios", GS MEC-IEG 004, rev. V1.1.1, Nov., 2015.

[18] J. Prokkola, "Qosmet Enabling passive QoS measurements", [Online], Available: http://www.cnl.fi/qosmet.html, 2016, [retrieved: April, 2016].

[19] P. Gimenez, B. Molina, C. E. Palau, and M. Esteve, "SWE Simulation and Testing for the IoT", IEEE Int'l. Conf. on Systems, Man, and Cybernetics (SMC), October, 2013, pp. 356 - 361.

[20] X. Che and S. Maag, "A Passive Testing Approach for Protocols in Internet of Things", IEEE GreenCom & iThings/CPSCom, August, 2013, pp. 678 - 684.

[21] P. Rosenkranz, M. Wählisch, E. Baccelli, and L. Ortmann, "A Distributed Test System Architecture for Open-source IoT Software", Workshop on IoT Challenges in Mobile and Industrial Systems, May, 2015, pp. 43-48.

[22] M. Yesudas, G. Menon, and S. Nair, "High-Volume Performance Test Framework using Big Data", 4th Int'l. Workshop on Large-Scale Testing, January/February, 2015, pp. 13-16.

How Facilitating Conditions Impact Students' Intention to Use Virtual Lectures? An Empirical Evidence

Ahmed Shuhaiber
Management Information Systems
Al-Zaytoonah University of Jordan
Amman, Jordan
Email: ahmed.shuhaiber@zuj.edu.jo

***Abstract*—Virtual lectures are popular live delivery of lectures via the Internet, which have been adopted recently as alternative or adjunct to traditional lectures worldwide. Whereas the adoption and usage of virtual lectures have been studied extensively, we do not know how facilitating conditions influence students' intention to use this technology. Therefore, this research aimed to fill this knowledge gap by studying the dimensions of the facilitating conditions that could influence students' intention to use virtual lectures. A quantitative approach was followed, by obtaining 204 survey responses at a Jordanian university, and statistically testing the dimensions of the 'facilitating conditions' construct adapted from the Unified Theory of Acceptance and Use of Technology (UTAUT) models. Results revealed that students' familiarity, online support, course fee and course nature suitability can significantly influence students' intention to use virtual lectures, whereas technical resources availability and system compatibility showed insignificant impact on usage intention. Research implications and future work were specified afterwards.**

Keywords—Facilitating Conditions; Intention to use; Virtual Learning; Virtual Lectures; Synchronous Student Learning Systems

I. INTRODUCTION

In today's dynamic tertiary education systems, web-based applications are playing an increasingly significant role in supporting the learning process. For instance, utilizing blackboards, e-learning classroom systems, online exams, web-based learning systems and virtual lectures could change education significantly [1]. University virtual lectures, specifically, continue to grow increasingly and are expected to become a more general learning trend in many developing countries worldwide.

A lecture is traditionally defined as "a process in which information passes from the notes of the lecturer to the notes of the student without passing through the minds of either" [2, P.640]. In general, lectures have been remaining the popular approach of undergraduate teaching since universities were founded, for several reasons. Firstly, lectures are effective in delivering big amounts of information by one person to a flexible numbers of students (lecturer-centered approach). Secondly, lectures can be easily combined with other teaching methods [2][3]. Additionally, lectures are considered cost-effective instruction methods, especially for big classes. However, the emerging web technologies have transformed the university learning styles to become more learner-centered, which has popularized the live delivery of internet and virtual lectures as alternative or adjunct to traditional lectures [4]. Virtual lectures (also called synchronous classes or digital live lectures) are playing an increasingly significant role in delivering today's lectures at many universities and educational institutes globally.

It is worth mentioning that virtual lectures are not equivalent to e-learning or online learning. Specifically, e-learning is considered the umbrella of all mentioned terms that indicates utilizing electronic means to support the learning process, whereas online learning comprises the utilization of the internet and web-based application for education purposes, where material could be stored on storage devices for anytime use. Virtual lectures, however, means attending live lectures synchronously and by digital means without students' physical attendance to classes.

There are several advantages afforded by the usage of virtual lectures in comparison to traditional lectures:

1) Students have the opportunity to take the lecture in the place of their own choice, resulting in more spatial learning flexibility [4][5].
2) Virtual lectures are highly useful for students who live in rural areas or in a region far from the university campus. They are also suitable for students who find some kind of trouble with transportation to attend university lectures on campus in a daily basis.
3) By using virtual lectures, students can learn at their most attractive mode of learning, such as having the most appropriate setup and convenience [3][4].
4) Virtual lectures provide a better alternative to traditional lectures in large classes with 50 or more students, in which the former are more practical way for every student to take advantage of an instructor's teachings, and the instructional material presented [3].
5) Virtual lectures have environmental and social advantages, such as decreasing pollution rate and road traffic, and saving time in getting on campus of universities or colleges. These advantages benefit students as well as lecturers and people in the society.

Despite its popularity and potential, virtual lectures are currently having very limited adoption rates in Jordanian universities and colleges. In addition, little research in the literature is found to address the factors that influence students' usage of virtual lectures in this country. For instance, students' willingness to accept and take virtual lectures was empirically examined by applying the whole UTAUT model [4]; the findings revealed that facilitating conditions (as one variable) and attitudes towards virtual lectures were exclusively found to have significant direct influence on students' intention to take virtual lectures. Whereas 'attitudes' construct is an original variable in the UTAUT model, and well defined in huge bundle of research, the construct 'facilitating conditions' has been usually included as an optional extension, and has not been clearly measured as the 'attitude' construct. Furthermore, there might be many facilitating conditions that could influence students' intention to use virtual lectures, which varies in its significance and influence power. Whereas the paper [4] fully utilized the UTAUT in an empirical study, the current study extends the previous one by focusing on 'Facilitating conditions' as a focal construct of 6 variables to empirically test and valid them separately, as no previous studies have yet paid any attention to them. Therefore, this study aimed to investigate these dimensions of the facilitating conditions, and to understand which of them could have a significant influence on students' intention to use virtual lectures. Accordingly, this paper reviews the relevant literature in Section II, and then demonstrates research model and hypotheses in section III. In Section IV, the methodology of this research is presented, followed by the findings and analysis in Section V. Finally, a discussion and conclusion are given in the Section VI.

II. LITERATURE REVIEW

Facilitating conditions are originally defined as the objective factors in the environment that observers agree that they make an act easy to accomplish [6][7]. Those objective factors are theorized to have a direct effect on intention to use information technology resources. In the context of virtual lectures, facilitating conditions can be relating to the people directly involved in the process (students and faculty members), the technical infrastructure, and the technical support for the use of the virtual lecturing system [8][9]. Facilitating conditions could act as an adoption enabler if available resources and facilities are adequate, and accordingly individuals may exhibit positive attitudes toward the use of virtual lectures [7]. Conversely, facilitating conditions could lead to negative attitudes towards virtual lectures should those conditions are not found satisfying to users.

As mentioned earlier, facilitating conditions have been extensively used as an extension of the (UTAUT) and its next version (UTAUT2), which are widely used in the field of information and communication technology acceptance modeling [6][7]. In relevance to this study, 'facilitating conditions' has been studied in the fields of electronic learning [8]-[16], online learning [17][18], virtual learning and virtual lectures [19]-[23], and mobile learning [24]. It is noteworthy that most of the studies found in the literature focused on the acceptance and usage of e-learning tools and technologies, whereas very scant research particularly concentrated on the adoption of virtual lectures. In addition, the construct 'facilitated conditions' has been measured by different items, and thus we do not understand precisely how facilitating conditions influence e-learning technologies in general, and virtual lectures specifically. Moreover, this construct is most often studied as one variable while its items differ from one study to another, resulting in low clarity of the nature of this construct, and a little understanding about how it affects intention to use virtual lectures. Importantly, no previous studies have been found yet in the literature that discuss the factors that compose the 'facilitated conditions' variable, and how these components influence students' intention to use virtual lectures specifically, and e-learning technologies in general.

Therefore, this study proposes and tests some variables that are associated with the 'facilitating conditions' construct, and discover its influence on intention to use virtual lectures. This original endeavor has not been seen in the literature, to date. Next section discusses the factors in details.

III. RESEARCH MODEL AND HYPOTHESES

Based on the literature of the 'facilitating conditions' construct and its associated items, six variables were developed to measure their impact on students' intention to use virtual lectures. These variables are: students' familiarity, technical resources availability, system compatibility, online technical support, course fee and course nature suitability. The proposed research model is shown in Fig. 1.

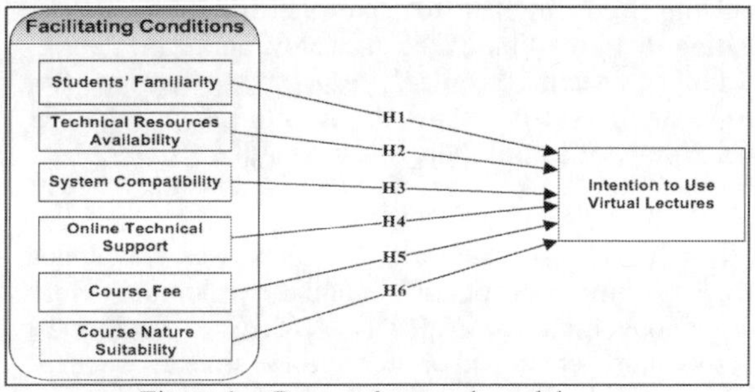

Figure 1 Proposed research model

The research hypotheses associated with the research model are seven, presented in Table I.

TABLE I SET OF RESEARCH HYPOTHESES

H#	Statement
H1	Students' familiarity significantly influences their intention to use virtual lectures
H2	The availability of technical resources significantly influences students' intention to use virtual lectures
H3	System compatibility significantly influences students' intention to use virtual lectures
H4	Online technical support significantly influences students' intention to use virtual lectures
H5	Course fee significantly influences students' intention to have it via virtual lectures
H6	Course nature suitability significantly influences students' intention to use virtual lectures

IV. Methodology

This study followed a quantitative approach to address the research aim. The targeted population was all undergraduate students at the Faculty of Economics and Administration, at Al-Zaytoonah University of Jordan (in Amman, Jordan). This faculty is considered the largest in the university in terms of students and resources, and includes six departments: business administration, accounting, finance, marketing, management information systems, and tourism management. Details about the data gathering, instrument development, and instrument validity are presented in the subsequent subsections.

A. Data Gathering

The research data were gathered through a random sampling approach via an online self-administered survey. In total, 218 respondents completed the survey in two-week duration, but 14 of those responses were discarded due to incompletion, and thus, a net sample of 204 usable questionnaires remained. This sample size is considered statistically sufficient, given the 95% confidence interval and the population size of the Jordanian undergraduate students locally (around 55,000). This sample size is also consistent with the often-cited 10 times rule, which states that the sample size should be equal or larger than 10 times the largest number of structural paths at a particular construct in the model [25][26]. The survey was mainly promoted online and hosted by the e-learning system at the faculty. Students were invited to take the questionnaire by sending them the link of the survey webpage on their e-learning system profiles. As an incentive for participation, respondents were given the chance to enter a prize draw of a bookshop voucher valued 30JDs.

B. Instrument Development

A survey instrument of 29 items was developed based upon the conceptualization and development work of previous literature [6][7][17]-[23]. Specifically, the questionnaire contained 4 items for variables such as 'familiarity', 'system compatibility' and 'course nature', whereas the constructs 'course fee', 'online technical support', 'technical resources', and 'intention to use' had 3 items each. Items are shown in Appendix A. In addition, five items were developed to measure demographic variables, such as gender, age, academic year (on 1st, 2nd, 3rd, or 4th year), major, study program (matinee, or evening), having work (part time, full time, or casual). A 7-point Likert scale was used to measure the constructs presented in the proposed model (scores were ranged from 1 = "strongly agree" to 7 = "strongly disagree", with "neutral" score = 4). This scale could effectively allow respondents to express their opinions in this research, as it offers a wider range of agreements to statements than the 5- point.

The survey was available in two languages (Arabic and English). When translating the questionnaires, the researcher ensured that the meaning of the source language statement was preserved in the translation (called semantic equivalence) [4]. The questionnaire was originally designed in English, and was then translated into Arabic. The back translation method was used after the Arabic version had been translated back into English by another bilingual person.

The survey instrument was refined during the pre-test phase to ensure the internal consistency of the measured instrument, with the involvement of 18 respondent students. Consequently, the wording of some questions was modified. Afterwards, a pilot study was conducted by 29 students to assure the reliability and validity of the instrument. As a result, two items which were assigned to measure the constructs 'technical resources' and 'Online technical support' were removed from the questionnaire due to their very low reliability scores (alpha coefficients of .34 and .27 respectively). Consequently, the questionnaire included 27 validated items in total.

C. Instrument Validity and Reliability

It is essential to check that the questionnaire will measure what it is supposed to measure, which is its validity [25]. Most of the items in the survey instruments were adapted from the items developed by [6][7] to estimate the facilitating conditions employed in UTAUTs, and from other studies in the virtual lectures literature [9][11][12][14][23]. Thus, the face validity of the survey instrument has been already established for most of the items. The internal consistency (reliability) of the instrument was also assessed. Reliability is the extent to which the items measure the same way each time they are used, under the same conditions, with the same sample [25][26]. Instrument's reliability was maximized by using clear conceptualization of the factors and ensuring accurate measurements, in addition to operationalizing each group of factors with multiple indicators [26]. Furthermore, the questionnaire was pre-tested and modified to ensure that it was easily understood. Additionally, the validity and reliability of the constructs and their associated items were statistically assessed in the data analysis phase.

D. Data analysis

Firstly, Descriptive statistics were performed to overview the research sample profile, by using IBM SPSS statistics18.0 software. Secondly, Structural Equation Modeling – Partial Least Squares (SEM-PLS) analysis were conducted, in order to check the effect power among various constructs, by using the SmartPLS2.0 software. SEM-PLS is a second-generation comprehensive statistical data analysis approach, which is more powerful than other first-generation multivariate techniques in measuring multiple relationships at the same time [27]. The findings are shown in the scenario below.

V. FINDINGS AND ANALYSIS

Based on the demographics and other background characteristics of the participants in the research, around 58% of the samples were male students, whereas female students accounted for around 41% of the targeted population. In addition, around two thirds of the sampled students were in their middle academic years (either sophomores or juniors). Students with accounting, Management Information Systems (MIS) and marketing majors accounted for the majority of the study sample. Additionally, more than two thirds of the students had some sort of work (part time 41.7%, full time 19%, or casual 4.4%). Not all of them agreed to share their Grade Point Averages (GPAs), however, many of the respondents had Good or Very Good GPAs (45.6% and 23.5% respectively). Further demographic details are shown in Table II.

TABLE II DEMOGRAPHIC PROFILE OF PARTICIPANTS

Demographic variables	Categories	Response information (N=204)
Gender	Male Female	119 (58.3%) 85 (41.7%)
Academic year	Freshman (1st year) Sophomore (2nd year) Junior (3rd year) Senior (4th year) Other	27 (13.3%) 71 (34.8%) 67 (32.8%) 39 (19.1%) 15 (6.9%)
Major	Business administration Accounting Finance MIS Marketing Tourism management	34 (16.7%) 56 (27.5%) 18 (8.8%) 49 (24.0%) 29 (14.2%) 18 (8.8%)
Work	No work Yes, full time Yes, part time Yes, casual work	71 (34.8%) 39 (19.1%) 85 (41.7%) 9 (4.4%)
Grade Point Average	Excellent Very Good Good Satisfactory Poor	17 (8.3%) 48 (23.5%) 69 (43.6%) 16 (18.5%) 4 (6.8%)

The PLS method is usually analyzed and interpreted in two stages: firstly, by assessing the reliability and validity of the measurement model (constructs and items), and secondly, by assessing the structural model through interpreting the path coefficients and identifying the adequacy of the research model [27]. The subsequent section discusses the results of these two stages.

E. Measurement (Outer) Model Results

In order to view the correlations between the latent variable and the reflective indicators in their outer model, the values of the outer loadings were examined. Indicators with an outer loading above 0.7 were retained, whereas indicators with outer loadings between 0.4 and 0.7 were considered for removal from the scale only when deleting the indicator leads to an increase in the composite reliability (or the average variance extracted) above the suggest threshold value [27]. Indicators with very low outer loadings (below 0.4) were eliminated from the scale.

As a result, the majority of the items were above the acceptable level of (0.4), and thus demonstrating reliable items. However, two items, CN4 and SC2, were found with low loadings: (0.3815) and (0.3156) respectively. Therefore, as recommended by [27][28], these items were eliminated from this study and were not involved in further analysis. All item loadings are shown in Appendix B. In order to examine the discriminant validity across the items, the pattern of item loadings across constructs in the model was also examined. The rule of thumb for demonstrating discriminant validity is to keep the difference between an item loading on its intended construct and its next highest loading at least .10 [27]. In this research, the discriminant validity of all items was demonstrated, as all cross loadings among different constructs were not less than the determined cut off point, as shown in the same appendix (Appendix B).

Construct validity assesses whether the measures chosen are true measures of the constructs describing the event, and that these measures are actual tools for representing or measuring the construct being investigated [27][29]. For the current study, construct validity was established, including both convergent and discriminant validity. Convergent validity refers to the extent to which a measure correlates, or converges, with other measures of the same construct [27]. Convergent validity is demonstrated when the Average Variance Explained (AVE) value between the constructs is equal to, or exceeds, 0.5 [27][28]. As presented in Table III, the AVE scores for all constructs in the model were greater than .50, which meets the first requirement of achieving convergent validity. Consequently, all constructs demonstrated convergent validity. Another approach to assess the convergent validity of the constructs is to examine the composite reliability of the constructs [26][27]. All constructs exhibited acceptable to high scores of composite reliability, exceeding the .70 threshold recommended by [25]-[29]. All validity scores are demonstrated in Table III.

TABLE III VALIDITY AND RELIABILITY ESTIMATES OF THE CONSTRUCTS

Construct	AVE	Composite Reliability	Cronbach's alpha
Course Fee	0.684	0.871	0.782
Course Nature Suitability	0.699	0.864	0.796
Familiarity	0.720	0.870	0.818
Online technical Support	0.672	0.896	0.824
Intention to Use	0.761	0.910	0.853
System Compatibility	0.655	0.899	0.835
Technical Resources	0.697	0.901	0.845

In order to assess the internal consistency, Cronbach's alpha measures need to be examined. Internal consistency is achieved when reliability estimates are greater than .70 [25]-[27]. The .07 threshold is regarded in the social sciences and Information Systems reported data to be the most commonly accepted cut off point [25][28]. As presented in Table III, all reliability scores exhibited acceptable to high reliabilities, with Cronbach's coefficient alpha exceeding the .70 threshold recommended by [25]-[28], thereby, satisfying the second requirement of convergent validity. Having provided evidence of the convergent validity of the constructs, the discriminant validity was also assessed.

Discriminant validity examines the extent to which an independent variable is truly distinct from other independent variables in predicting the dependent variable [27]. One popular approach to assess the discriminant validity followed in the current research is through examining the cross-loadings comparisons between constructs. Specifically, the AVE of each latent construct should be higher than the construct's highest squared correlation with any other latent construct [27]. The square roots of the AVE values of all constructs are calculated, and compared with correlations between constructs, as shown in Appendix C. The results indicated that all constructs in the research model achieved this criterion as none of the off-diagonal elements exceeded the respective diagonal element. Thus, discriminant validity was demonstrated.

B. Structural (inner) model results.

An assessment of the structural model was undertaken to determine the significance of the paths and the predictive power of the model through the PLS algorithm, then by considering a bootstrapping process that involved 5,000 random re-samples from the original data set to determine the significant levels of path coefficients [27]. Firstly, a systematic assessment of the structural model was conducted to assess the significance of path coefficients by examining the standard error, T-statistics, R squared value and confidence interval [28]. The amount of variance explained by R^2 provides an indication of the model fit [27] as well as the predictive ability of the endogenous variables [28]. It is suggested that the minimum level for an individual R^2 should be greater than a minimum acceptable level of .10 [27].

Table IV highlights the hypotheses of the study, and shows the path coefficient between the exogenous and endogenous variables, the Average Variance Accounted for, R^2 and bootstrap critical ratios. The bootstrap critical ratios (T-Statistics) determined the stability of the estimates and were acceptable above the value of 1.96 on 0.05 significant level [27]. The R^2 value of 'intention to use' construct was found equal to 0.427, which was greater than the recommended level of .15; indicating that this endogenous variable is explained by 42.7% of the given exogenous variables. Therefore, it was appropriate to examine the significance of the paths associated with these variables. All of the paths and all variables had bootstrap critical ratios as shown in Table IV.

TABLE IV INFLUENCE PATHS AND HYPOTHESES RESULTS

(Endogenous variables) → Intention to Use	**H#**	**Path Coefficient (β)**	**T-Statistics (|O/STERR|)**
Students' Familiarity	H1	0.1657	2.2239*
Technical Resources	H2	0.0387	0.3922
System Compatibility	H3	0.0626	0.594
Online Technical Support	H4	0.3466	3.2511**
Course Fee	H5	-0.1293	1.9894*
Course Nature Suitability	H6	0.3034	3.4567**
* Sig at .05 / **Sig at .01			

In sum, four hypotheses that were associated with familiarity, system compatibility, online technical support, course fee and course nature were supported (H1, H4, H5 and H6), whereas only two hypotheses expressing the influence of technical resource and system compatibility were not supported (H2 and H3). The results of each path are interpreted in the next section.

VI. DISCUSSION AND CONCLUSION

As shown in Fig. 2, the strongest path in the model was associated with the influence of the online technical support on students' intention to use virtual lectures, followed by the influence of each course nature, students' familiarity and course fee. However, two paths were found insignificant; the influence of the technical resource availability and system compatibility on intention to use. Significant paths are presented in normal arrows, whereas insignificant paths are presented in dotted arrows.

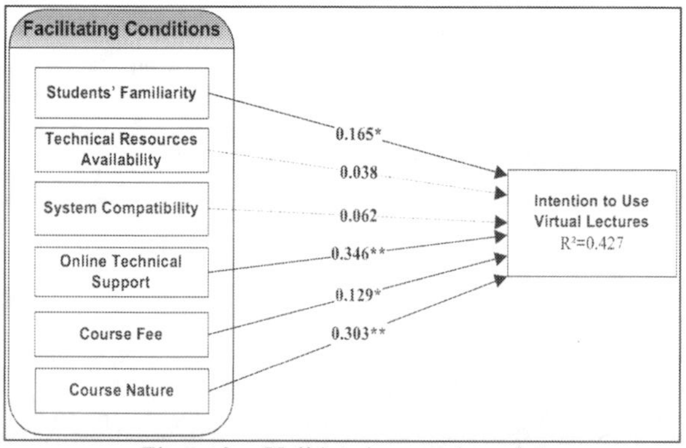

Figure 2 Validated research model

It seems that students were mainly concerned with getting online support to address any potential risk related to virtual lectures, because such a risk, if not handled, may result in losing important information delivered by the lecturer. In addition, the course nature can impact students' intention to use virtual lectures, especially that some practical courses and lab-based lectures require students' attendance in person to get the know-how information directly without intermediaries, to try performing tasks by themselves, or to get involved in some sort of physical class interactions.

Course fee, in turn, can affect students' intention to use a virtual lecture in a reverse way, in that the greater the virtual course fee, the less the intention to use it. Having a low-price option for getting a university course can foster students' opportunities in favor of this option, given that the majority of the students in Jordanian universities are self-funded, and that very few students who receive governmental fund to cover their tuition fees.

Students' familiarity in virtual lectures can also influence their intention to use them. This relationships indicates that the more knowledge in the technology and how to it works the more the intention to use it. However, and due the immaturity of virtual lectures at Jordan universities, students' familiarity about virtual lectures could be described as limited.

This study has several theoretical and practitioner implications. As for theory, the research has explored new constructs and provided new significant factors that influence students' intention to use virtual lectures. As discussed earlier in the literature review, no previous studies have investigated those factors in the virtual lectures arena, which in turn fills an important knowledge gap and significantly contribute to the relevant literature. Practically, it is implied that universities administration should consider the course nature, course cost and the existence of the online support when providing virtual lectures. Specifically, theoretical courses offered in reasonably low prices and supported with online helpdesk, along with educating students about using virtual lecturing systems should contribute to the success of students' usage of virtual lectures. In addition, administrations, in turn, could spread the literacy of using virtual lectures, and may provide training courses and special classes for demonstrations, in order to support students' intention to use virtual lectures. Overall, universities' administration should pay more attention on familiarizing students about virtual lectures; their nature, technicalities, limitations and challenges. In addition, administration should allocate resources for setting up and maintaining the technologies required to operate such a system, and to enable the IT infrastructure to support it. Moreover, a technical support team should be available to provide usage help and directions, especially at the beginning of each virtual course and for newly registered students. Furthermore, virtual courses should be offered in lower prices than traditional courses. By following these recommendations, administration could expect high usage rate of virtual lectures.

Future research directions might include testing the research model, or investigating the newly developed dimensions of 'facilitating conditions' in different yet relevant contexts, such as e-learning and online lectures. It is also suggested to examine the culture factor and to discover its impact on students' intention to use virtual lectures, in Jordan specifically and in the Middle East region in general.

REFERENCES

[1] D. R. Mills, "Integrating educational technology into teaching", 4th ed. Upper Saddle River, New Jersey: Pearson Education, Inc., 2006.

[2] R. Gilstrap, and W. Martin, "Current strategies for teachers". Pacific Palisades, California: Goodyear Publishing Company, Inc., 1975.

[3] J. E. Stephenson, C. Brown, and D. K. Griffin, "Electronic delivery of lectures in the university environment: An empirical comparison of three delivery styles", Computers & Education, vol. 50, no. 3, 2008, pp.640-651.

[4] A. H. Shuhaiber, "Students' Willingness to Accept Virtual Lecturing Systems: An Empirical Study by Extending the UTAUT Model", International Journal of Social, Behavioral, Educational, Economic, Business and Industrial Engineering, vol. 9, no. 4, 2015, pp. 1153-1157.

[5] C. Evans, N. J. Gibbons, K. Shah, and D. K. Griffin, "Virtual learning in the biological sciences: Pitfalls of simply putting notes on the web", Computers & Education, vol. 43, no. 1, 2004, pp. 49–61.

[6] V. Venkatesh, M. G. Morris, F. D. Davis, and G. B. Davis, "User Acceptance of Information Technology: Toward a Unified View", MIS Quarterly, vol. 27, 2003, pp.425-478.

[7] V. Venkatesh, J. Y. L. Thong, and X. Xu, "Consumer acceptance and use of information technology: extending the unified theory of acceptance and use of technology", MIS Quarterly, vol. 36, no. 1, 2012, pp. 157-178.

[8] D. Jong, & T. S. Wang, "Student acceptance of web-based learning system", In Proceedings of the 2009 International Symposium on Web Information Systems and Applications (WISA'09), Nanchang, P. R. China, 2009, pp. 533-536.

[9] F. Akbar, "What affects students' acceptance and use of technology?", 2013, Dietrich College Honors Theses.: http://repository.cmd.edu/hsshonors/179, [Retrieved: Jan, 2016].

[10] J. T. Marchewka, & K. Kostiwa, "An Application of the UTAUT Model for Understanding Student Perceptions Using Course Management Software", Communications of the IIMA, vol. 7, no. 2, 2014, pp. 93-104.

[11] U. Paola Torres Maldonado, G. Khan, J. Moon, and J. Pho, "E-learning motivation and educational portal acceptance in developing countries", Online Information Review, vol. 35, no.1, 2011, pp. 66-85.

[12] J. -L. Chen, "The effects of education compatibility and technological expectancy on e-learning acceptance". Computers & Education, vol. 57, no. 2, 2011, pp. 1501-1511.

[13] Á. F. Agudo-Peregrina, Á. Hernández-García, and F. J. Pascual-Miguel, "Behavioral intention, use behavior and the acceptance of electronic learning systems: Differences between higher education and lifelong learning", Computers in Human Behavior, vol. 34, 2014, pp. 301-314.

[14] C. Keller, S. Hrastinski, and S. A. Carlsson, "Students Acceptance of E-Learning Environments: A Comparative Study in Sweden and Lithuania", European Conference of Information Systems, 2007, pp. 395-406.

[15] C. Nanayakkara, "A model of user acceptance of learning management systems: a study within tertiary institutions in New Zealand", The International Journal of Learning, vol. 13, no. 12, 2007, pp. 223-232.

[16] T. Buchanan, P. Sainter, and G. Saunders, "Factors affecting faculty use of learning technologies: implications for models of technology adoption", Journal of Computing in Higher Education, vol. 25, no. 1, 2013, pp. 1-11.

[17] C.-P. Lin, and A. Bhattacherjee, "Learning Online Social Support: An Investigation of Network Information Technology Based on UTAUT", Cyberpsy., Behavior, and Social Networking, vol. 11, no. 3, 2008, pp. 268-272.

[18] D. Jong, & T.-S. Wang, "Student acceptance of web-based learning system", In Proceedings of the 2009 International Symposium on Web Information Systems and Applications, 2009, pp. 533-536.

[19] B., Sumak, G. Polančič, and M. Heričko, "An empirical study of virtual learning environment adoption using UTAUT", 2010. ELML'10, Second International Conference in Mobile, Hybrid, and On-Line Learning, 2010, pp. 17-22.

[20] E. M. Van Raaij, & J.J.L. Schepers, "The acceptance and use of a virtual learning environment in China", Computers & Education, vol. 50, no. 3, 2008, pp. 838-852.

[21] C. Keller, "Technology acceptance in academic organizations: Implementation of virtual learning environments", in proceedings of the European conference on Information Systems, 2006, pp. 1-8.

[22] C. Keller, "User acceptance of virtual learning environments: A case study from three Northern European Universities", Communications of the Association for Information Systems, vol. 25, no.1, 2009, pp. 465-486.

[23] S. Lakhal, H. Khechine, and D. Pascot, "Student behavioural intentions to use desktop video conferencing in a distance course: integration of autonomy to the UTAUT model", Journal of Computing in Higher Education, vol. 25, no. 2, 2013, pp. 93-121.

[24] K. Jairak, P. Praneetpolgrang, and K. Mekhabunchakij, "An acceptance of mobile learning for higher education students in Thailand", in Sixth International Conference on eLearning for Knowledge-Based Society, Thailand, 2009, pp. 361-368.

[25] D. W. Straub, "Validating instruments in MIS research", MIS Quarterly, vol. 13, no. 2, 1989, pp. 147-169.

[26] J. F. Hair, W. Black, B. Babin, and R. Anderson, "Multivariate data analysis", Pearson Prentice Hall Upper Saddle River, NJ, 2006.

[27] J. F. Hair, G. T. M. Hult, C. M. Ringle, M. Sarctedt, "A primer on partial least squares structural equation modeling (PLS-SEM)", Sage Publications, 2013.

[28] W. W. Chin, B. L. Marcolin, and P. R. Newsted, "A partial least squares latent variable modeling approach for measuring interaction effects: Results from a Monte Carlo simulation study and an electronic-mail emotion/adoption study", Information systems research, vol. 14, no. 2, 2003, pp. 189-217.

[29] D. Gefen, & D. Straub, "A practical guide to factorial validity using PLS-Graph: Tutorial and annotated example", Communications of the Association for Information systems, vol. 16, no. 1, 2005, pp. 91-109.

Appendix A – Measurement Items

Code	Item
FAM1	I have the knowledge necessary to use virtual lectures.
FAM2	I am familiar with virtual lectures.
FAM3	I think I am able to use virtual lectures.
FAM4	Using virtual lectures fits my learning style.
TS1	I have the technical resources necessary to use virtual lectures.
TS2	I think I have the software and hardware required to use virtual lectures.
TS3	I think that using virtual lectures may requires some special technical resources. *(reverse coded)*
SC1	Virtual lecturing system is compatible with other systems I use.
SC2	The virtual lecturing system is compatible with other e-learning systems I use.
SC3	The virtual lecturing system is compatible with other application programs that I use.
SC4	The virtual lecturing system is compatible with hardware and software I have.
OS1	I think I can get help from others when I have difficulties virtual lectures.
OS2	I think a specific person (or group) is available for assistance with system difficulties.
OS3	It is important to me to have an online help while using virtual lectures.
CF1	I have the financial resources necessary to use virtual lectures.
CF2	The cost of virtual lecture courses should be considerable.
CF3	It is important to me that the administration consider lower fees for virtual lectures courses.
CN1	I have applied university courses
CN2	I have theoretical university courses
CN3	I have some courses which are mix of theory and application
CN4	I have lab courses
INT1	I intend to use virtual lectures in the future.
INT2	I will always try to use virtual lectures in my university life.
INT3	I plan to use virtual lectures frequently.

Appendix B – Items loadings and Cross loadings

	C_ fee	C_n ature	Fam iliari	Sup port	Intent ion	Compa tibility	Resour ces

			ty				
CF1	.77	.28	.27	.23	.64	.24	.24

CF2	**.77**	.27	.30	.34	.46	.31	.21
CF3	**.60**	.37	.29	.36	.56	.32	.35
CN1	.04	**.60**	.15	.43	.25	.43	.55
CN2	.05	**.79**	.29	.56	.43	.38	.39
CN3	.08	**.70**	.26	.53	.44	.30	.37
CN4	-.10	**.38**	.32	.51	.32	.36	.40
FAM1	.17	.47	**.86**	.55	.34	.58	.51
FAM2	-.10	.40	**.81**	.46	.39	.26	.53
FAM3	-.13	.31	**.84**	.40	.34	.23	.49
FAM4	.17	.44	**.75**	.37	.30	.41	.45
OS1	.22	.39	.28	**.63**	.34	.47	.36
OS2	.28	.38	.39	**.56**	.35	.54	.37
OS3	.24	.38	.21	**.79**	.25	.48	.37
INT1	-.44	.23	.53	.16	**.88**	.33	.04
INT2	-.40	.25	.50	.14	**.90**	.22	.11
INT3	-.57	.26	.32	.12	**.81**	.30	.03
SC1	.25	.41	.22	.32	.19	**.73**	.37
SC2	-.33	.46	.30	.24	.19	**.31**	.29
SC3	-.32	.43	.21	.26	.16	**.81**	.21
SC4	.24	.56	.32	.50	.34	**.85**	.43
TS1	.35	.39	.63	.35	.32	.31	**.79**
TS2	.40	.28	.58	.35	.39	.22	**.78**
TS3	.29	.32	.52	.41	.24	.25	**.70**

Appendix B – Discriminant Validity

	AVE	C_fee	C_nature	Familiarity	Support	Intention	compatibility	Resources
fee	.68	**.82**						
nature	.69	.30	**.83**					
Familiarity	.72	.56	.36	**.84**				
Support	.67	.17	.50	.36	**.82**			
Intention	.76	.40	.38	.67	.42	**-.87**		
compatibility	.65	.34	.60	.34	.45	.30	**.80**	
Resources	.69	.08	.44	.32	.61	.45	.43	1

Pre-selection Algorithm of Access Points in a Handover Management Scheme

Meriem Kassar*, Souheib Ben Amor†, Brigitte Kervella‡, Daniel Fernandes Macedo§

*Communication Systems Laboratory, ENIT, University of Tunis El Manar, Tunisia
Email: Meriem.Kassar@enit.rnu.tn
†INRS-EMT, Montreal, Canada
Email: ben.amor.souheib@gmail.com
‡LIP6, University Pierre & Marie Curie-Paris6, UMR 7606, France
Email: Brigitte.Kervella@lip6.fr
§Federal University of Minas Gerais, Belo Horizonte, MG, Brazil
Email: damacedo@dcc.ufmg.br

***Abstract*—Recently, wireless networks and mobile terminals are rapidly evolving. Wireless networks are evolving towards heterogeneous overlaying environment, while the mobile terminals evolve towards having multi-interface functionality in order to face seamless service continuity. Traditional horizontal handover management schemes that mainly depend on signal strength for decision making are unable to fulfill ubiquitous and seamless mobility across heterogeneous networks. Vertical handover is more related to convenient criteria such as user preferences or application requirements. The use of location information in decision making would certainly enhance horizontal or vertical handover mechanisms by supporting optimized handover management. For that, using the location information and the mobile terminal movement can participate to a handover decision improving the handover execution procedure. For example, when a mobile terminal is moving with a certain velocity, it can perform handover execution uselessly that affects handover performance. This paper proposes and describes a pre-selecting access points algorithm in a location-aided handover management scheme in order to reduce unnecessary handovers in a moderate mobility scenario. It shows by simulation the feasibility of the proposed algorithm applied to a random mobility and a dense environment.**

Keywords–Handover management ; Location information ; Polar coordinates ; Access Points selection.

I. Introduction

Handover management is the key aspect in the development of solutions supporting mobility scenarios. It is the process by which a Mobile Terminal (MT) maintains its connection active while moving from one point of attachment (access point or base station or access router) to another. Handover management issues include mobility scenarios, metrics, decision algorithms and procedures. Mobility scenarios can be classified into horizontal (between different cells of the same network) and vertical (between different types of networks, for example, Cellular Networks and Wireless Local Area Networks (WLAN)). In homogeneous networks, horizontal handovers are typically required when the serving access point becomes unavailable due to MT's movement. In heterogeneous networks, the need for vertical handovers can be initiated for convenience rather than connectivity reasons (e.g., according to user choice for a particular service).

Conventional handover management techniques consider usually the link quality parameters (received signal level, reliability, etc.) and user parameters. In low mobility scenarios, this solution is quite efficient because MT always selects the best access network according to link and service quality. However, when MT moves at a moderate speed, the frequency of handovers increases, and thus the time of connection to each cell decreases. Despite of the recent improvements in levels 2 and 3 handover technology, packet loss is always performed and therefore, a slight temporary service degradation can be observed in each handover executed. In a moderate mobility scenario, MT should choose the network or the cell that provides the maximum connection time, especially in a dense environment. Such choices would allow MT to remain over time in each cell and reduce the number of unnecessary handovers and thus service degradation. For that, a location-assisted handover can be used in such scenarios. More specifically, the location information can be added to the link quality parameters in the handover decision process performed before selecting the best access network.

In our paper, we propose the use of location information of moving MT and Access Points (APs) in the choice of the target AP for the handover process. According to several measurements of the MT's position over time, it is possible to estimate the direction of its movement. Furthermore, if this information is increased with its context (e.g., the user moves on a highway between two towns), it is possible to predict its future position. In this contribution, we only focus on an outdoor moderate mobility scenario in a way that high mobility has to consider more parameters such as cellular connectivity parameters. The cell type concerned by our proposal covers picocell (range of $\approx$ 200 m or less) or femtocell (range of $\approx$ 10 m) in cellular networks and WiFi hotspots cell (e.g., WiFi range of $\approx$ 100 m). In our scenario, thanks to the location information of each detected AP, it is possible to give more weight to the nearest APs of the MT's future position. These APs will be in the coverage of MT longer than those whose MT rolls away. Then, we can choose among APs in MT movement direction the one that gives the best link quality parameters thanks to a multi-criteria decision method. Each AP knows the position of its neighboring access points. This information can be obtained in two ways: (i) from agreements between operators, which provide the location of their access points; (ii) cooperation between users, which record the APs, their location and their Quality of Service (QoS) parameters. Location information can be collected with other technologies: Global Positioning System (GPS), Radio-Frequency IDentification (RFID), WiFi,

Bluetooth, etc. In our paper, we gather location information from GPS as geographic/cartesian coordinates and we convert it to polar coordinates in order to pre-select the nearest APs in the MT movement direction.

Based on a location-assisted solution, we propose an intelligent handover management scheme. Our solution considers a pre-selection algorithm of access points, an important phase in our handover process in order to reduce unnecessary handovers that can affect handover performance in a moderate mobility scenario. After this phase, an access network selection can be processed based on user preferences. In this paper, we focus on the feasibility of our algorithm in a dense environment and with a random mobility by simulation results. Here, we define a dense environment as an area in which the APs are deployed such that MT always detects the overlapping of more than two APs.

Our paper is organized as follows. Section II presents the related work. Section III describes the whole handover management scheme. Section IV introduces the proposed algorithm for pre-selecting access points in the handover management scheme. Section V gives the simulation results. Finally, Section VI concludes our work.

II. Related Work

The handover management process is described in three phases [1][2][3]:
(1) the handover information gathering: used to collect all the information, through monitoring and measurements, required to identify the need for handover and to apply handover decision policies. It can be called also "handover initiation" phase or "system discovery".
(2) the handover decision: used to determine whether and how to perform the handover by selecting the most suitable access network (taking into account some criteria such as user preferences) and by giving instructions to the execution phase. It is also called "network selection" or "system selection".
(3) the handover execution: used to change channels and addressing conforming to the details resolved during the decision phase.

A handover management process can be enhanced by adding location information. Localization techniques use different technologies. GPS gives a more precise location information in outdoor environments. Signal quality based techniques such as the quality or a mapping of the Signal Strength (SS) received are used to estimate MT position. These techniques give a position with a margin of error of several meters. Otherwise, they can be useful and sufficient to deduce MT direction movement. Connectivity based techniques can also be used in a way that MT can estimate its position using the location of all the APs detected in its vicinity (i.e., intersection of all the APs coverage). Hybrid techniques use GPS and the cellular network (such as Global System for Mobile Communications (GSM)) for Assisted-GPS. Here, the cell coverage information is used to enhance the precision of the estimated location especially in poor satellite signal conditions.

In the literature, many works propose a location-based handover management process [4][5][6][7]. In [4], the authors propose a location-assisted handover (LAH) which is the use of position information to aid and optimize handover and interface selection decisions within the multimode MT. LAH supports more intelligent handover services that ensure optimized MT operation. They have developed a novel multimode MT architecture in order to realize LAH for such terminals. Depending upon velocity, direction and on-going traffic of MTs, it can estimate the time when a handover is needed. The authors proposed an architecture with no evaluation performance results. Otherwise, Yu et al. [5] shows that a proposed 3G-WLAN heterogeneous network handover algorithm based on location information has effectively reduced the number of handovers, limited the ping-pong effect, improved the handover performance compared to a traditional vertical handover. But, the simulation experiments were made only on two cells, one cell of 3G cellular network and one of WiFi hotspot and on an MT moving with a fixed velocity and direction. In the same cellular-WLAN scenario, Nielsen et al. [6] contribution performs two proactive handover decision algorithms by using movement prediction to determine the right time and the right place for a user terminal to handover. But, the authors do not give precision on the positioning system used in their solutions. For more accurate results, Folstad and Helvik [7] proposes a reliability model of a trajectory (defined as the series of APs) based on measurement reports and signaling from networks (i.e., extension of Media Independent Handover (MIH)) in order to find the optimal AP selection and handovers for a dual homed service.

GPS can be used in location-based handover solutions [8][9]. In [8], the handover latency is reduced by reducing the number of APs scanned by MT during the handover process by using GPS. It is a pre-authentication mechanism to the most potential selected AP in order to reduce the scanning delay. In [9], another scheme is based on a GPS pre-selective scanning to reduce the scanning delay which is 90 percent of whole handover delay.

Other works proposed handover algorithms considering MT movement in low to moderate mobility scenario. Jeong et al. [10] exploits a mobility prediction scheme with a relatively low velocity in order to propose an optimized handover decision algorithm in hierarchical femto/macro cell networks. Dam et al. [11] proposes a vertical handover algorithm considering the user movement prediction, energy consumption and QoS parameters for the end-to-end connections. It considers a peer-to-peer scheme in a WLAN connection between devices and a server bounce mechanism. Both works [10][11] use a centralized component such as a server to gather terminal mobility and network related information.

Our proposal is based on a location-aided handover management. It does not use the location information to estimate the right time to handover like in [4] (i.e. that is fulfilled by the handover initiation), but to do the right handover by pre-selecting the candidate APs in MT movement. Our solution collects the location information related to MT trajectory like in [7] and uses it to calculate the speed and the direction. Our experiments were made on a coverage of various cells with a random movement but not only two cells compared to [5] that fixed the speed and the direction values. For that, it uses a GPS like in [8][9] but the location information is integrated in a more sophisticated handover management scheme. We give more intelligence to our handover management scheme like the works in [10] and [11] but without a centralized component to store location information.

III. Our Handover Management Scheme

Our handover management scheme is composed of four phases :

(1) Handover initiation,
(2) Pre-selection of access points,
(3) Multi-criteria handover decision for network selection,
(4) Handover execution.

First of all, we need to collect all the necessary handover criteria such as the phase defined previously (Section II). These latter are required to be context-aware in the sense that it should be conscious of possibilities offered by each access network, MT movement and QoS requirements for the demanding service. In traditional handover decision, only one criteria is used, the Received Signal Strength (RSS). For a vertical handover decision, it is not sufficient. Context information are relevant in a way that they are useful enough to avoid false decisions, therefore, bad performances. They can be relative to the network, the terminal, the service and the user. Here, we group it into two parts as in [12]: all the information related to the network on one side and all the information that may exist at the terminal on the other side. There are: (i) *Network context*: QoS parameters (bandwidth, delay, jitter, packet loss), Coverage, Monetary cost, AP location information ; (ii) *Terminal context*: User preferences, Service capabilities (real-time and non real-time), Terminal Status (battery and network interfaces), Priority given to interfaces, Location information (velocity, direction).
The third phase concerns the selection of the best available network. This phase is aided by the second phase which reduces the number of target access networks in order to avoid the ping-pong effect (i.e., number of unnecessary handovers). These two phases can be defined as the handover decision phase as defined in Section II. The pre-selection phase is more related to the MT movement (slow, moderate or high mobility).

Our handover management process is given in Figure 1, highlighting the pre-selection phase concerned by this paper. Our process begins with the handover initiation (*Phase (1)*). It is mainly based on connectivity criteria in a way that performs if a handover is needed or not. While MT uses a running application and a handover is needed due to connectivity reasons, a phase of pre-selection of access points (*Phase (2)*) is triggered according to the location information (velocity, direction, position). The decision to initiate a handover to the best access point or network among those pre-selected according to user preferences is performed at the *Phase (3)*. Here, we consider a decision in which all the available alternatives (access points or networks) have to be evaluated according to given objectives. For that, the AHP (Analytic Hierarchy Process) method is used to assign scores to these networks (network scores). It carries only the calculation of the final decision, *Decision Making*, when all parameters (scores) are already available. Before applying it directly, two steps must be performed: (i) assigning scores to criteria, *Criteria Scoring*, a pre-configuration step in which the importance of each objective is evaluated according to user preferences; (ii) assigning scores to networks, *Scoring Network*, where available networks are evaluated and compared according to each objective. The last phase is the handover execution (*Phase (4)*) that establishes the IP connectivity through the selected access network. Details on the phases 1, 3 and 4 are given in [12].

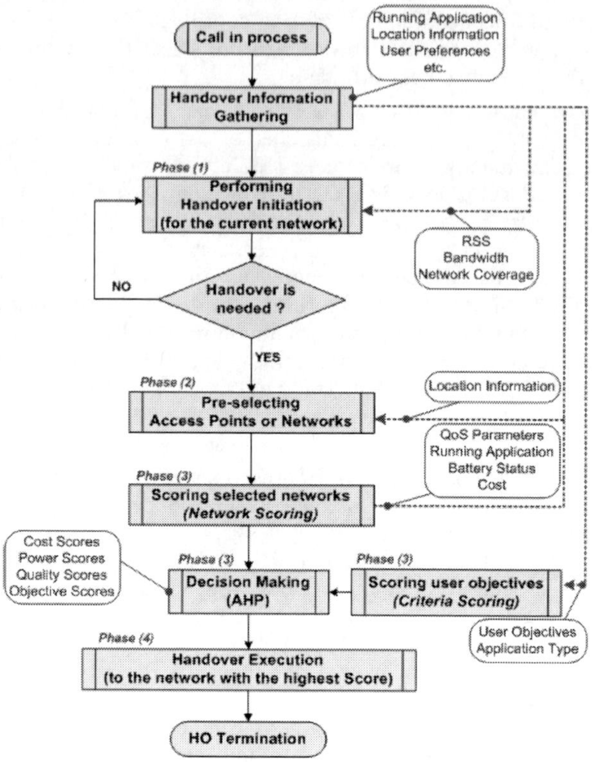

Figure 1. Our Handover Management Scheme

IV. Our AP pre-selection Algorithm

Our pre-selection algorithm has to retrieve the location information given by GPS and to convert the coordinates in order to compute an area of selected APs according to the direction and the velocity of MT movement.

A. Location information gathering and processing

Before any processing, we have to retrieve the MT position. This latter can be obtained via GPS that gives geographic coordinates (longitude, latitude and elevation in degrees). For more simplicity, these coordinates have to be converted to cartesian/geocentric coordinates (x, y, z in meters) such as in [13]. Once MT position obtained, we have to define periodically the MT velocity and direction. These two parameters are computed by the equations 1 and 2.

$$v = \frac{\sqrt{(x_{k-1} - x_k)^2 + (y_{k-1} - y_k)^2 + (z_{k-1} - z_k)^2}}{\Delta t} \quad (1)$$

$$\overrightarrow{\alpha} = arctan\left(\frac{|y_{k-1} - y_k|}{|x_{k-1} - x_k|}\right) \quad (2)$$

Here, the indexes k and $k-1$ are the last two successive samples of location information (the most recent values) between two times t_{k-1} and t_k. Δt is the sampling period. These parameters are computed in order to allow a periodic update of MT velocity and direction. In order to choose Δt value, we have to consider the transmission period of the beacon message. The beacon is a frame transmitted periodically by an AP to announce the presence of a wireless access network containing all the necessary information such as the beacon interval, SSID or the supported data rates. The default value of the beacon interval is $0.1sec$. Because GPS data is updated every second, it is more advisable to choose one second for Δt.

MT receives the location information of all APs that surround it. Once APs localized, the algorithm converts the cartesian coordinates of all detected APs into polar coordinates. Here, each AP can be characterized by a distance (d) and an angle (α). These two parameters allow to localize the APs in a coordinate system whose origin is MT. The distance and the angle between MT and AP are given by the equations 3 and 4.

$$d = \sqrt{(x_{MT} - x_A)^2 + (y_{MT} - y_A)^2 + (z_{MT} - z_A)^2} \quad (3)$$

$$\alpha = arctan\left(\frac{|y_{MT} - y_A|}{|x_{MT} - x_A|}\right) \quad (4)$$

where x_{MT}, y_{MT} and z_{MT} are the cartesian coordinates of MT and x_A, y_A, z_A are those of an access point A.

B. Pre-selection algorithm description

According to the location information as polar coordinates obtained in the previous section, the pre-selection algorithm restricts the set of the available access points to which MT can connect. It selects only the access points in MT's direction (limited by an angle of tolerance X). If we consider A as a set of the available access points, the pre-selection consists of getting a sub-set A^* defined by :

$$A^* = \{(d_i, \alpha_i) \in A | \overrightarrow{\alpha} - X \leq \alpha_i \leq \overrightarrow{\alpha} + X\} \quad (5)$$

where the couple (d_i, α_i) is the distance and the angle of the pre-selected access point i. The vector $\overrightarrow{\alpha}$ represents the MT direction and X is the tolerance angle. An AP is selected if it is in MT proximity, it means that it has to belong to the area limited by the tolerance angle X. The selection is given at the Figure 2 where the stars are the selected access points and the squares are the rejected ones.

We have to consider some criteria in order to determine the tolerance angle in AP selection. The criteria that have to be satisfied are :

- An AP has to be in the coverage area of MT movement.
- The number of candidate APs has to exceed a minimum threshold ($Min\_threshold$). If the number of the candidate APs is under the value 2, our algorithm is not useful. The handover will be executed to the unique available AP.
- The number of selected APs does not exceed a maximum threshold ($Max\_threshold$).

We notice that the conversion to the polar coordinates system can be imprecise in a way that the computing is realized every Δt seconds. The precision can be increased while Δt is decreased. Therefore, we can increase the location information precision by relaxing our method constraints, i.e., by increasing the tolerance angle X in order to select more candidate APs. In this case, the disadvantage of our method will be the time calculation and a high number of possible handovers.

In order to propose a precise AP pre-selection algorithm that fulfills the mentioned criteria, we opt for this process :

(1) A first selection is based on APs position. We choose the APs in the coverage area of MT at the time t_k. It means that we initialize the tolerance angle to $X = 90°$. We choose this X value because we have to consider the maximum value of the available APs that can be detected in MT direction. We obtain a first subset A^* as given in the Figure 2(a).

(2) A second selection has to limit the number of preselected APs in order to be comprised between the two fixed thresholds. For that, we have to eliminate the farthest APs until obtaining a number of APs in the interval $[Min\_Threshold, Max\_Threshold]$

In the second selection of our process, here are the steps to obtain the final number of pre-selected APs.

- X takes the value of the angle of the farthest selected AP from MT. If the number of APs in the set A^* are not included in the $[Min\_Threshold, Max\_Threshold]$, we eliminate this AP. After the change of the set A^*, we affect to X the value of the angle of the farthest AP.
- This first step will be repeated until we obtain a number of APs less or equal to $Max\_Threshold$. We notice that we can face the case in which two APs are symmetric according to MT, i.e., one AP has an angle $\alpha_i = \alpha_T + X$ and the other $\alpha_i = \alpha_T - X$. Here, we have to choose to eliminate one of them and keep the other.
- Finally, we can decrease the value of the $Max\_Threshold$ in order to obtain a more precise pre-selection if MT velocity is very high. As we mentioned previously, the precision is closely related to the final value of the tolerance angle X. In our work, we choose a value of $Max\_Threshold$ equal to 5. This value is sufficient in a way that we will get enough access points to perform a network selection for convenience reasons (i.e., according to user preferences).

Figure 2(b) gives the result of the second pre-selection for an interval $[Min\_Threshold, Max\_Threshold] = [2, 4]$.

The different steps of AP pre-selection are summarized in Algorithm 1.

Algorithm 1 AP Pre-selection algorithm

1. Retrieving MT position (x, y, z)
2. Computing MT direction ($\overrightarrow{\alpha}$) and velocity (v)
3. Converting each available AP $\in A$ coordinates into polar coordinates (d, α)
4. Defining $A^* = \{(d_i, \alpha_i) \in A | \overrightarrow{\alpha} - X \leq \alpha_i \leq \overrightarrow{\alpha} + X\}$
5. First selection: $X = 90°$
selecting the candidate APs in the coverage area of MT direction.
6. Second selection:
repeat Evaluating A^* with $X = X_{farthestAP}$
if $\alpha_{iM} = \alpha_t + X$ of an access point M and $\alpha_{iN} = \alpha_t - X$ of an access point N **then** M or N is eliminated.
until $N_{selectedAPs} \in [Min\_Threshold, Max\_Threshold]$

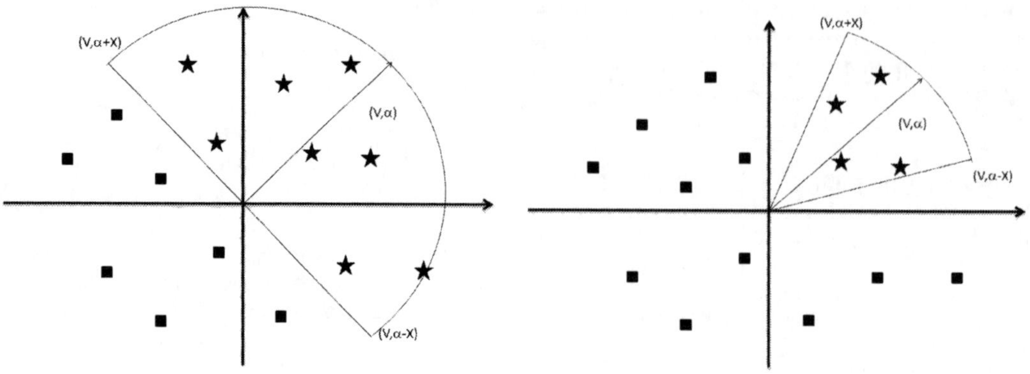

(a) First Selection (b) Second Selection

Figure 2. Our AP pre-selection process results

V. Simulation Results

In this paper, we focus our work on the feasibility of our pre-selection algorithm in a specific scenario. In order to evaluate our proposed algorithm, we use a Java-based event-driven simulator. We choose SIDnet-SWANS (Simulator and Integrated Development Platform for Sensor Networks Applications), a project developed by the Electrical and Computer Engineering department of Northwestern University [14]. SIDnet-SWANS is the GUI (Graphical User Interface) implemented in Java of the network simulator JIST/SWANS. JIST (Java in Simulation Time) is a discrete event-driven simulation environment and SWANS (Scalable Wireless Ad hoc Network Simulator) is the extension to simulate wireless ad hoc networks. JIST/SWANS has the same functionalities as the network simulator NS2 or GloMoSim (Global Mobile Information System Simulator). In our simulation scenario, MT (a node represented by a black point) has a random mobility in which the new position and the velocity are computed using a random direction. The cell coverage used concerns the same type of nodes. We used IEEE 802.11 MAC and PHY layers for each node. The AP/nodes are randomly deployed in a square simulation area of $1000 * 1000$ m.

Our simulation results are presented in the next Figures 3, 4, 5 and 6. In the simulation tests represented by Figure 3 and 4, we use 100 AP/nodes in order to highlight the two selection phases of the proposed AP pre-selection process. Firstly, MT direction and velocity are determined according to its initial position (represented by the black point). The pink point represents the MT current position. Secondly, our implemented algorithm pre-selects the candidate APs in the coverage area of MT movement (represented by the green points) using the tolerance angle $X = 90°$ (see Figure 3). Finally, it selects a fixed number ($Max\_Threshold = 5$) of APs (represented by the yellow points) while reducing the tolerance angle ($X = 15°$) until it answers the second selection criteria (see Figure 4). In Figure 5, we see that when the number of deployed AP/nodes is reduced (equal to 30 nodes), the tolerance angle is adapted to $X = 45°$ to respect the $Max\_Threshold$. If we reduce more the number of deployed AP/nodes until 10 nodes, the first selection criteria are matching the second selection criteria (see Figure 6).

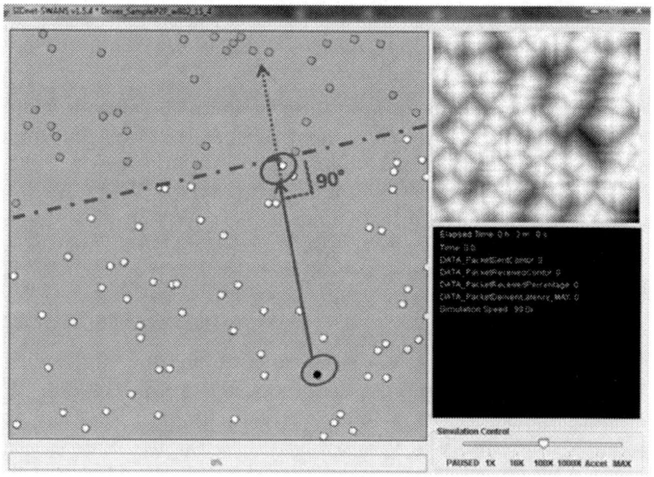

Figure 3. First Selection ($X = 90°$)

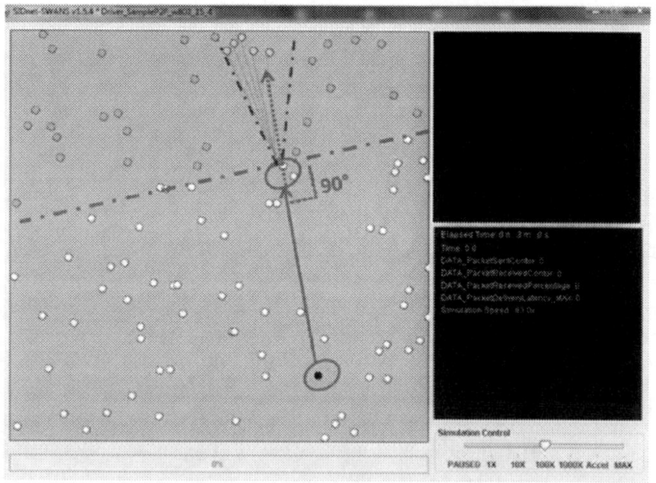

Figure 4. Second Selection ($X = 15°$)

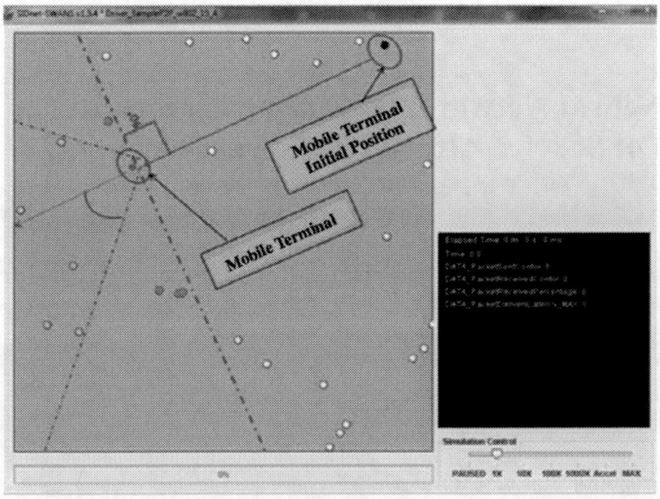

Figure 5. Second Selection ($X = 45°$)

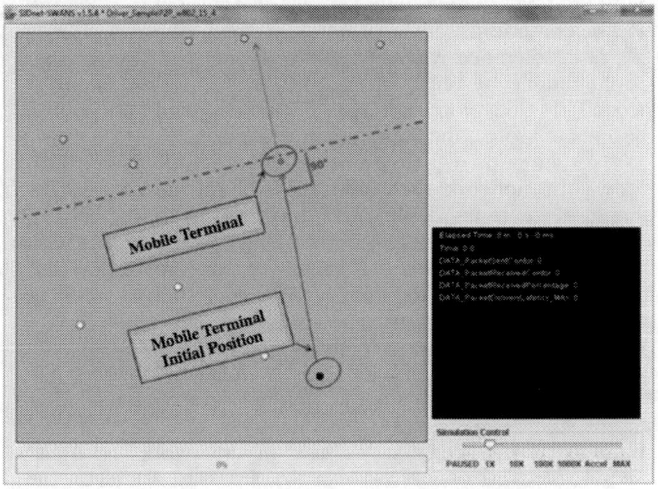

Figure 6. 1^{st}Selection Criteria = 2nd Selection Criteria

VI. Conclusion & Future Work

In this paper, we proposed a pre-selection algorithm of access points in an intelligent handover management scheme. Our proposal converts cartesian coordinates of MT and the APs in MT coverage to polar coordinates in order to retrieve APs position in MT direction. It selects a fixed number of candidate APs according to a tolerance angle that can be reduced until we obtain a minimum value. We showed that our algorithm is feasible in a dense environment and with a random mobility. It will be interesting to test this algorithm with another existing type of mobility, implemented in JIST/SWANS, such as STRAW (STreetRAndom Waypoint) that provides more accurate simulation results by using a vehicular mobility model or GMMM (Gauss-Markov Mobility Model). Here, we can also consider different types of cells (macrocell) for high mobility scenario. Hence, it will be interesting to analyze the mobile speed effect on MT connection time to the network. Our algorithm is involved in a location-assisted handover. It helps the network selection phase in a way that it selects the candidate APs (i.e., access networks) according to MT movement (i.e., direction and velocity). Such a location-assisted handover can reduce the ping-pong effect (i.e., the number of unnecessary handovers) and therefore, a better handover can be performed. More simulation results will be proposed in a near future work that integrates the implemented algorithm to the proposed handover management scheme. Hence, the handover performance of our scheme will be compared to traditional vertical handover management schemes such as RSS or Bandwidth based vertical handover decision schemes. In a future work, we intend to add to our outdoor solution (using GPS) an indoor localization-based solution using WiFi or femtocell coverage.

References

[1] P. Chan, R. Sheriff, Y. Hu, P. Conforto, and C. Tocci, "Mobility Management Incorporating Fuzzy Logic for a Heterogeneous IP Environment," IEEE Communications Magazine., vol. 39, no. 12, December 2001, pp. 42–51.

[2] H. Wang, R. Katz, and J. Giese, "Policy-enabled Handoffs across Heterogeneous Wireless Networks," Second IEEE Workshop on Mobile Computing Systems and Applications, 1999. Proceedings. WMCSA'99., February 1999, pp. 51–60.

[3] M. Kassar, B. Kervella, and G. Pujolle, "An overview of vertical handover decision strategies in heterogeneous wireless networks," Computer Communications, vol. 31, no. 10, 2008, pp. 2607–2620.

[4] T. Ahmed, K. Kyamakya, M. Ludwig, M. Schielein, S. McCann, E. Hepworth, and A. Surtees, "Location-assisted handover for multimode mobile terminals," Proc. of the IEEE/ACM Euro American Conference on Telematics and Information Systems (EATIS), February 2016.

[5] Q. Yu, W. Jiang, and Z. Xiao, "3g and wlan heterogeneous network handover based on the location information," International Conference on Communications, Circuits and Systems (ICCCAS), vol. 2, 2013, pp. 50–54.

[6] J. J. Nielsen, T. K. Madsen, and H.-P. Schwefel, "Location assisted handover optimization for heterogeneous wireless networks," 11th European Wireless Conference 2011-Sustainable Wireless Technologies (European Wireless), 2011, pp. 1–8.

[7] E. L. Folstad and B. E. Helvik, "Reliability modelling of access point selection and handovers in heterogeneous wireless environments," Design of Reliable Communication Networks (DRCN), 2013 9th International Conference on the, 2013, pp. 103–110.

[8] D. Sarddar, J. Banerjee, T. Jana, S. K. Saha, U. Biswas, and M. Naskar, "Minimization of handoff latency by angular displacement method using gps based map," International Journal of Computer Science Issues (IJCSI), vol. 7, no. 3, 2010, pp. 29–37.

[9] D. Sarddar, J. Banerjee, J. G. Chowdhury, R. Jana, K. K. Nundy, U. Biswas, and M. Naskar, "Reducing handover delay by pre-selective scanning using gps," International Journal of Distributed and Parallel systems (IJDPS), vol. 1, no. 2, 2010.

[10] B. Jeong, S. Shin, I. Jang, N. W. Sung, and H. Yoon, "A smart handover decision algorithm using location prediction for hierarchical macro/femto-cell networks," IEEE Vehicular Technology Conference (VTC Fall), 2011, pp. 1–5.

[11] M. S. Dam, S. R. Christensen, L. M. Mikkelsen, and R. L. Olesen, "Location assisted vertical handover algorithm for qos optimization in end-to-end connections," IEEE 11th International Conference on Trust, Security and Privacy in Computing and Communications (TrustCom), 2012, pp. 1632–1640.

[12] M. Kassar, B. Kervella, and G. Pujolle, "An intelligent handover management system for future generation wireless networks," EURASIP Journal on Wireless Communications and Networking, vol. 2008, 2008, p. 6.

[13] "Transformation geographic to geocentric," http://www.ngi.be, last access 14/04/2016.

[14] O. C. Ghica, G. Trajcevski, P. Scheuermann, Z. Bischof, and N. Valtchanov, "Sidnet-swans: A simulator and integrated development platform for sensor networks applications," 2008, pp. 385–386.

Performance Evaluation of an Artificial Neural Network Multilayer Perceptron with Limited Weights for Detecting Denial of Service Attack on Internet of Things

Fernando M. de Almeida, Admilson de R. L. Ribeiro, Edward D. Moreno, Carlos A. E. Montesco
Department of Computing
Federal University of Sergipe – UFS
São Cristóvão, Brazil
email: fernando.m.al.91@gmail.com, admilson@ufs.br, edwdavid@gmail.com, estombelo@gmail.com

***Abstract*—One way to prevent attacks to security in the Internet of Things (IoT) is the adoption of an Intrusion Detection System (IDS). With the use of an Artificial Neural Network (ANN) it is possible to decrease the limitations of the IDS such as false positive that can compromise the system. In this paper, we evaluate the performance of two ANNs to verify which of both is the more adequate to use in an IDS for the IoT environment. We compare the performance of a Multilayer Perceptron (MLP) with Limited Weights with a Multilayer Perceptron with normal weights. The used Multilayer Perceptron presents ten neurons in the hidden layer. The implementation is in C language and run on an embedded platform with an ARM Cortex-M3 micro-controller. It is possible to consider the ANN training in another platform and to permit the embedded platform receives the trained weights. It is also possible to make the training in real time using the received data one time. We conclude that it is viable to use an Artificial Neural Network Multilayer Perceptron in an Intrusion Detection System for the Internet of Things.**

Keywords-IDS System; IoT Internet of Things; Multilayer Perceptron; Neural Network; Limited Weights;

I. INTRODUCTION

The Internet of Things (IoT) is a novel paradigm whose concept is based on the ubiquitous presence of objects, like sensors, actuators, mobile devices and Radio-Frequency Identification (RFID) tags. These objects can interact through single address to achieve common objectives [1].

Anytime, anywhere it will be possible to communicate with anything, a new dimension will be added to communication technologies [2]. The IoT can also be defined as a Wireless Sensor and Actuator Network (WSAN) connected to the Internet, and these sensors and actuators are the atomic components connecting the real world to the digital world [3]. The IoT is extremely vulnerable to attacks, most of the communication is wireless, most of the components have constrained resources and it is possible to physically attack the IoT components [1][4]. Considering that the IoT will have information about almost everything, security and privacy are key concerns in IoT research [5][6].

Xu, He and Li [5] say that the research about security is necessary to the massive adoption of this technology in the industry. Gubbi, Buyya, Marusic and Palaniswami [6] highlight the need of self-protection in domestic applications, arguing that actuators will be connected to the system and they will need protection from intruders.

The IoT, with its potential dimension and attack possibilities, needs a proper feature that allows it to keep safe with minimal human intervention otherwise its scalability will be compromised. According to Roman, Zhou and Lopez [7], fault tolerance will be essential in the IoT. The number of vulnerable systems and attacks will increase, so it is needed to develop intrusion detection and prevention systems to protect the components of the IoT.

The adoption of an Intrusion Detection System (IDS) allows the network to handle attacks. The design of IDS should evaluate the deployment environment. In the case of the Internet, it is important to have a high accuracy rate with a low false positive rate. In Wireless Sensor Network (WSN) should also consider the consumption of resources, such as energy and memory. In the IoT environment, as well as a WSN, there must be concern about the limited resources.

The use of artificial intelligence methods reduces the limitations of IDS [8], such as missing detections and false alarms that can compromise the system. The artificial intelligence method that we use in this work, Artificial Neural Networks (ANN), can be used to indicate the presence of an intruder, from environment features [9]. These features can be: communication duration, source address, destination address, and other information obtained from the environment.

The objective of this work is to implement a Multilayer Perceptron (MLP) optimized in memory and verify the feasibility of using it in IDS system for the IoT environment. The results of the accuracy and false positive rates were compared with related works of IDS that use ANNs. There is also the analysis of memory consumption of the implementation. The MLP was implemented with limited weights and without limited weights, to compare their memory consumption in IDS system using ANNs. The MLP is trained with Quantized Back-Propagation Step-by-Step and with an incremental method, where each input stimulates the ANN once to reduce the need of memory in the training phase.

This paper is organized in five Sections, as can be seen in the following: Section II shows related work, Section III presents the methodology of this work, Section IV shows and discusses the experiments and results and in the Section V there is the conclusion of this work.

II. Related Work

The related works listed in this paper are split into two groups: IDS that uses ANNs and IDS for wireless resource constrained systems. This division was made because as far as we know, there is not an IDS for wireless resources constrained systems that use ANNs.

A. *IDS that uses ANNs*

The IDSs that uses ANNs described in this paper were not related to the resource constrained systems. So there is not any memory consumption evaluation making the comparison of memory consumption impossible.

Lei and Ghorbani [10] present an approach to an intrusion detection system with a neural network with a competitive learning approach. They achieve 4 times more performance in training than Self-Organizing Maps of Kohonen (SOM) with a better accuracy. Their proposal is called Improved Competitive Learning Network (ICLN). The winner neuron weight is updated with a value nearest to the entrance and the weights of the loser neurons are updated with values farthest to the entrance. The training used the KDD99 database, widely used in IDSs.

Eskin, Arnold, Prerau, Portnoy and Stolfo [11] provide a framework for detection of non-labeled anomalies. They perform tests alternating the use of Kernel function in the feature map and three algorithms: Cluster-based estimation, KNN and One Class SVM. Using the KDD99 database, they achieved a detection rate between 91% and 98% with a false positive rate between 8% and 10%.

Amini, Jalili and Shahriari [12] present two solutions related to IDS in unsupervised network. The experiments are made with three types of ANNs: ART-1, ART-2 and SOM. They achieve an accuracy rate between 95.74% and 97.42%, and false positive rate between 1.99% and 3.50%. They also use the KDD99 database.

Yan, Wang and Liu [13] propose a hybrid technique that uses a rule-based decision and an ANN. When rules detect an abnormality, the packet is forwarded to a multilayer perceptron with 50 neurons in the hidden layer and other rule-based decision is made to detect the intrusion or not. Using the KDD99 database, they get an accuracy rate of 99.75% and a false positive rate of 0.57%.

B. *IDS for Wireless Resource Constrained Systems*

Raza, Wallgren and Voigt [14] designed, implemented and evaluated SVELT, an IDS for the IoT. The SVELTE detects sinkhole and selective-forwarding attacks in 6LoWPAN (IPv6 over Low Power Wireless Personal Area Networks) wireless network that uses the RPL routing protocol. The IDS builds the network topology of RPL in the border router and uses algorithms to detect inconsistencies, possible filtered nodes, network topology validity and end-to-end losses.

Salmon *et al.* [15] proposed an anomaly based IDS for WSNs using the Dendritic Cell Algorithm (DCA). The proposed IDS architecture has five elements, distributed between roles in the network. The authors proposed two roles: Dendritic Cells (sensor-dc), responsible for sense the environment's values, managing the monitoring and parameter base, organize the tasks and coordinate the responses and actions to other managers; and the Lymph node (sensor-lymph) responsible to execute the dendritic cell algorithm, detect an attacker, manage the base rules and execute the actions to combat the identified attacks. Several experiments were made, changing configuration, time of jamming attack, number of sensor-dc. Through the tests, the authors concluded that the IDS proposed is efficient for WSNs saving energy from the nodes while there is a jamming attacker.

C. *Related work analysis*

All the related work listed in this paper that uses ANNs, uses the KDD99 database [10][11][12][13]. This database provides a big number of labeled connections that helps supervised training, although it is used in unsupervised training [11][12].

In supervised training, the accuracy rate is bigger than 95% [10][13], and have a small false positive rate. Using unsupervised training, it is possible to achieve an accuracy bigger than 90% with a false positive rate around 9% [11] or decrease the accuracy around 75% with a false positive rate between 2% and 3.5% [12].

The related works of IDS for wireless resource constrained systems do not use the KDD99 database. In Salmon *et al.* [15] work, the network topology focuses on jamming attack, which it is not characterized in the KDD99 database. In SVELTE IDS [14] the attacks are sinkhole and selective forwarding, also they are not characterized in the KDD99 database.

III. Methodology

The ANN that we chose is the MLP with ten neurons in the hidden layer. The choice of ten neurons in the hidden layer was made to minimize the memory consumption. The evaluation of the ANNs was made from a C language implementation, for the MLP and Multilayer Perceptron with Limited Weights (MLPLW). The MLP and MLPLW share the same interface, so the utilization is made with the same steps. The difference between the MLP and MLPLW implementation is in the structure that keeps the trained data and the training algorithm. In the classification phase, there is only need to adapt the value of each weight to represent a float point value. The MLP training algorithm is the Back-Propagation and the MLPLW training algorithm is the QBPSS [16].

The database used was KDD99, which is used in several papers [10][11][12][13] to validate an IDS. This database has connections from the transport layer, like UDP and TCP. Each connection is classified between a normal classification or some kind of attack. The attacks are grouped into four large groups, they are: Denial of Service (DoS), User to Root (U2R), Remote to Local (R2L) and Probe. The database has 4,898,431 data items, each having 41 features.

Unfortunately, the KDD99 database cannot represent an IoT environment. The utilization of KDD99 database is important to check our ANN implementations and see if they can achieve similar results to related works. When the ANN implementation are validated, we can analyze the memory consumption and check if it can be used in an IoT environment.

For this work, it is considered the DoS attacks that can affect 6LoWPAN networks too, making IoT networks that use this protocol stack vulnerable to DoS attacks using ICMP (Internet Control Message Protocol), UDP (User Datagram Protocol or TCP (Transmission Control Protocol).

The training of both networks, MLP and MLPLW, was performed on a PC, called traditional platform, whose features can be seen in Table 1. In a real environment of the IoT, this training can be performed in the cloud, for example, so the metrics of training are not crucial in this work. The third approach of training is using the MLPLW ANN, but performing the training in the constrained resource platform. The training is similar to Back-Propagation, but each input is trained once, considering that the platform will receive numerous packets and does not need to retrain each input, this training removes the need to keep training inputs in the platform, reducing the memory usage.

The first step is to normalize the KDD99 database. The discrete features are quantized, and each possible value represents a number. All the features, discrete or continuous, will have a value between 0 and 1, at the end of the normalization. The sigmoid function was chosen to be the activation function because it has its values between 0 and 1, like the normalized features.

The second step, after the normalization, is to train the ANN. Each input to the database will have an output from the ANN. The output is compared to the desired output and the error is calculated. In (1), it is possible to see the equation to calculate the error E. The desired output is represented by d, the input weight set is represented by $w^{(1)}$, and the hidden weight set is represented by $w^{(2)}$.

$$E=\sum_{j=0}^{n_1} w_j^{(2)}\cdot S\left(\sum_{k=0}^{n} x_k\cdot w_{kj}^{(1)}\right)-d \qquad (1)$$

The neuron weights of the hidden layer are updated by a fraction of the error multiplied by each input feature. In (2) it is possible to see how the hidden weight set is updated, where the hidden weight update is represented by $\Delta w^{(2)}$, the learning rate of hidden layer is represented by η_2, the error is represented by E, and the output set of hidden layer is represented by Y. Equation (3) shows how the input weight set is updated, where the input weight update is represented by $\Delta w^{(1)}$, the output set of the input layer is represented by Y, the hidden weight set is represented by $w^{(2)}$, the learning rate of input layer is represented by η_1, the error is represented by E, and the input is represented by x.

$$\Delta w^{(2)}=-\eta_2\cdot E\cdot Y \qquad (2)$$

$$\Delta w^{(1)}=-(1-Y^2)\cdot w^{(2)}\cdot\eta_1\cdot E\cdot x \qquad (3)$$

Each step of training consists in the update of hidden weights and input weights for an input. The set of steps to train the ANN by each input is called an epoch. The training is finished if the quadratic error, when used a testing set of data, has increased after ten epochs or if it reaches an arbitrary epoch value defined by the designer.

The MLPLW training is similar to the MLP, but after each step, the weight sets are quantized and the previous weight update is added to current weight update. These differences are made in the QBPSS (Quantized Back-Propagation Step-by-Step) [16] to speed up the training phase for a limited weight ANN.

The QBPSS training method is proposed by Bao, Chen and Yu [16] for ANNs with limited weights, reducing training time by up to 7 times. The QBPSS is inspired by Back-Propagation. The algorithm is similar to Back-Propagation, but it is considered a value proportional to previous adjust weight value, also the weight is quantized each step, in the beginning with a soft quantization until reach the quantized value expected.

Equation (4) shows the update of hidden weight set, where the hidden weight update is represented by $\Delta w^{(2)}$, the momentum for the height update is represented by δ, the learning rate for hidden layer is represented by η_2, the error is represented by E, the output set of the input layer is represented by Y, and the last hidden weight update is represented by $\Delta w_{i-1}^{(2)}$. Equation (5) shows the update of input weight set, where the input weight update is represented by $\Delta w^{(1)}$, the momentum for the weight update is represented by δ, the output set of the input layer is represented by Y, the hidden weight set is represented by $w^{(2)}$, the learning rate for the input layer is represented by η_1, the error is represented by E, the input is represented by x, and the last input weight update is represented by $\Delta w_{i-1}^{(1)}$.

$$\Delta w^{(2)}=-(1-\delta)\cdot\eta_2\cdot E\cdot Y+\delta\cdot\Delta w_{i-1}^{(2)} \qquad (4)$$

$$\Delta w^{(1)}=-(1-\delta)\cdot(1-Y^2)\cdot w^{(2)}\cdot\eta_1\cdot E\cdot x+\delta\cdot\Delta w_{i-1}^{(1)} \qquad (5)$$

As the MLP training, the MLPLW training will continue to use all inputs to train the ANN until the quadratic error increases after 10 epochs or an arbitrary value defined by the designer is reached.

The second MLPLW training uses the methods and equations of the QBPSS, but each input stimulates the ANN once. The update of the weights is equal to the first MLPLW training method.

After the training, for both ANNs, the input dataset is used to verify the correct classification and the incorrect classification of each ANN, MLP and MLPLW. With this information it is possible to calculate the accuracy rate and the false positive rate.

IV. Experiments and Results

To perform the test of the two chosen ANNs, two platforms have been selected. One is a personal computer, called traditional platform, and the other is an embedded platform with an ARM Cortex-M3 micro-controller. Both technical features can be seen in Table I.

The choice of Arm Cortex-M3 processor was taken by the highlight of ARM core micro-controllers. The Contiki community, for example, is already adopting the ARM micro-controllers as the focus for the 3.0 version of the operating system [17].

TABLE I. Chosen technical platform features

Technical Feature	Traditional platform	Embedded Platform
Processor	Intel I7-2630 QM	STM32F103VET6 (ARM Cortex-M3 core)
Processor Frequency	2.00 GHZ	72 MHz
Volatile Memory	8 GB	64 KB
Persistent memory	1 TB	512 KB

The measures made for both platforms fit the context of resource-constrained devices: ROM and RAM memory. There is also a measure to prove the efficiency of the ANN: Accuracy and false positive rate. For the incremental training, where each input is used once, it measures the accuracy and false positive rate for each thousand inputs to see the evolution of these measures according to the inputs.

The chosen ANN, MLP or MLPLW, was made as a first test to verify if this ANN configuration can be used in resource-constrained devices. Also, we selected to use ten neurons in the hidden layer to achieve less memory consumption with a greater accuracy rate. The RAM memory consumed by the hidden layer grows linearly proportional to the number of system inputs.

The training phase of both ANN used 90% of KDD99 data as training set and the remaining 10% to test, as the testing set. We used the same proportions of each type of connection in training and testing set to avoid vicious training of testing. After performing the training phase with KDD99 database in MLP and MLPLW ANNs, the trained networks are stimulated with the same input data. The predicted output is compared to the desired output and, if it is equal to the database label, the input is marked as correct, otherwise is marked as incorrect. If a normal connection is classified as an attack, it is marked as a false positive. The sum of correct inputs is compared to the total inputs and is possible to calculate the accuracy rate of the ANN. The sum of false positive inputs is compared to the total inputs and it is possible to calculate the false positive rate of the ANN. In the Table II, it is possible to see the results of the MLP and MLPLW. It is possible to see that the accuracy rate and false positive rate of the MLPLW remained close to the MLP. While average accuracy rate of MLP was 97,75% and the average false positive rate was 2,13%, the average accuracy rate of MLPLW was 97,65%, 0,10% lower than the MLP rate, and the average false positive rate was 2,11%, 0,02% higher than the MLP rate.

The results in Table II, were compared with the results of related works. This comparison is shown in the Table III, the bold lines are the ANNs of this paper. When compared with techniques of unsupervised ANNs, MLP and MLPLW achieve better results, but it should be considered that MLP and MLPLW use labeled data, that help the classification. When compared with the ANNs presented in [10] and [13], the MLP and MLPLW with ten neurons in the hidden layer have similar results.

TABLE II. Accuracy and False Positive rate of Multilayer Perceptron and Multilayer Perceptron with Limited Weights.

ANN	Measure	Average	Standard Deviation
MLP	Accuracy rate	97,75%	0.02
	False Positive rate	2,13%	0.02
MLPLW	Accuracy rate	97,65%	0.01
	False Positive rate	2,11%	0.01

TABLE III. Comparison of results of this paper with results of related works.

ANN	Accuracy	False Positive	Supervised training?
MLP	**97,75%**	**2,13%**	**Yes**
MLPLW	**97,65%**	**2,11%**	**Yes**
ICLN [10]	97.89%	–	Yes
Cluster [11]	93%	10%	No
K-NN [11]	91%	8%	No
SVM [11]	98%	10%	No
RT-UNNID ART-1 [12]	71.17%	1.99%	No
RT-UNNI ART-2 [12]	73.18%	2.30%	No
RT-UNNID SOM [12]	83.44%	3.50%	No
YAN; WANG; LIU [13] (50 neurons in hidden layer)	99.75%	0.57%	Yes

With the results of the MLP and MLPLW training, checking that they have similar results to other related works, both ANNs were trained with a different approach. Each input stimulated the ANN once and, we measured the accuracy after one thousand stimulations. Considering that in the IoT environment the nodes will receive several packets, the ANN can be trained while the node is alive. This experiment checks how fast the ANN can respond to a new type of DoS Attack.

The MLP achieves an accuracy rate of 97% after the seventh thousand connections, considering normal and attack connections, after that the accuracy rate is established around 97,4%. This curve is shown in the Figure 1.

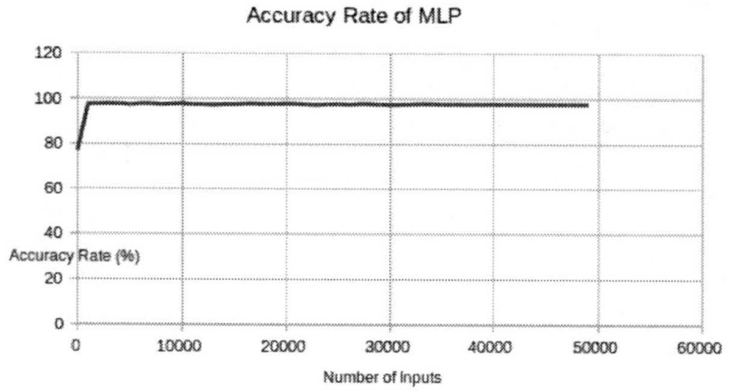

Figure 1. Accuracy rate of MLP after training with each input once

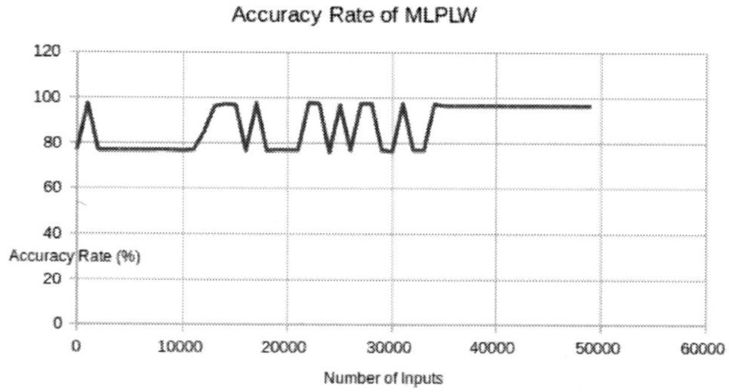

Figure 2. Accuracy rate of MLPLW after training with each input once

In the MLPLW ANN, the accuracy rate achieves 97% in the first thousand connections, but oscillates until the third four thousand connection. This curve is shown in the Figure 2. It is important to highlight that the input data is used in random order, using normal and attack data randomly. We can use a random order input because the KDD99 database is based on connections, and they do not need to be used in a specific order. The part of KDD99 database used has 76% of normal data and 24% of DoS attack data.

The measures related to resources used can be seen in Table IV. It is possible to see that MLPLW consumes more ROM memory than MLP, this is because of some procedures to transform the limited weight into the floating point weight, but when compared to ROM memory available in embedded platform, it is an increase of 0.03%. Besides the RAM memory consumption is smaller in MLPLW and, when compared with RAM memory, available in the embedded platform, it is a decrease of 4.5%. It is possible to see that the MLPLW has a smaller impact in the embedded platform memory.

The ROM memory consumed by MLPLW with training is the biggest, because it needs the code of QBPSS, but analyzing in percentage, the amount of ROM memory consumed is less than 0.5%. The RAM memory consumed is equal to MLPLW and the analysis is the same. It is important to highlight that the MLPLW with training do not need to communicate with a server, reducing the communication and energy consumption, so in the nodes where the energy is a crucial factor, the MLPLW with training presents this advantage.

TABLE IV. MEMORY USED BY MLP AND MLPLW NEURAL NETWORKS WITH REMOTE TRAINING

Resource	MLP	MLPLW	MLPLW with training
ROM memory	214 bytes	354 bytes	1716 bytes
RAM memory	3360 bytes	420 bytes	420 bytes
Related ROM (Embedded Platform)	0.04%	0.07%	0,33%
Related RAM (Embedded Platform)	5.12%	0.64%	0,64%

V. CONCLUSION

In this paper, we presented the performance evaluation of a Multilayer Perceptron with Limited Weights comparing with a Multilayer Perceptron with normal weights. The accuracy and false positive rate decreases 0,10% when the weights are limited to one byte. The ROM memory consumption increases 140 bytes for the weight limitation and 1362 bytes including the training algorithm. The RAM memory, when limiting the weights, decreases eight times.

With this experiment, it was possible to observe the possibility to use a multilayer perceptron in an embedded platform. The consideration of the training in another platform allows the embedded platform in this work to use an ANN trained by 4 million data, with more than 97% of accuracy and using only 354 bytes of ROM and 420 bytes of RAM, less than a kilobyte of memory.

When the ANNs are trained while the platform is running, there is a good response from the MLP, achieving a great accuracy rate for the DoS attacks after the seventh thousand connections. The MLPLW training should be revised to approximate it results to the MLP ANN.

With these results it is possible to achieve better use of ANNs in embedded systems connected to the Internet, using the techniques from the IDSs for the Internet, with high detection rate and low false positive rate, in resource-constrained platforms.

In a future work, it is intended to improve the MLPLW in-node training approximating of MLP in-node training. Also, implement the MLPLW in a 6LoWPAN environment and simulate it with live data.

ACKNOWLEDGMENT

This work was supported by CAPES, CNPq and FAPITEC/SE

REFERENCES

[1] L. Atzori, A. Iera, and G. Morabito, "The internet of things: A survey". Computer Networks, v. 54, n. 15, p. 2787-2805, 2010.

[2] L. Tan and N. Wang, "Future internet: The internet of things". In: Advanced Computer Theory and Engineering (ICACTE), 2010 3rd International Conference on. IEEE, 2010. p. V5-376-V5-380.

[3] M. Presser and A. Gluhak, "The internet of things: connecting the real world with the digital world", EURESCOM mess@ge – The Maganize for Telecom Insiders, vol. 2, 2009. Available: http://archive.eurescom.eu/message/messageSep2009/The-Internet-of-Thing%20-Connecting-the-real-world-with-the-digital-world.asp. Retrieved: December, 2015.

[4] Q. M. Ashraf and M. H. Habaebi, "Autonomic schemes for threat mitigation in Internet of Things." Journal of Network and Computer Applications 49, 2015, pp. 112-127.

[5] L. D. Xu, W. He, and S. Li, "Internet of things in industries: A survey." Industrial Informatics, IEEE Transactions on 10.4, 2014, pp. 2233-2243.

[6] J. Gubbi, R. Buyya, S. Marusic, and M. Palaniswami, "Internet of Things (IoT): A vision, architectural elements, and future directions." Future Generation Computer Systems 29.7, 2013, pp. 1645-1660.

[7] R. Roman, J. Zhou, and J. Lopez, "On the features and challenges of security and privacy in distributed internet of things." Computer Networks 57.10, 2013, 2266-2279.

[8] D. D. Oliveira, R. J. P. B. Salgueiro, and E. D. Moreno, "A Danger Theory Immune-inspired Architecture for the Prediction of Security Attacks in Autonomic Networks". In: Communications Workshop, 2013, Santiago, Chile. Proceedings of 5th IEEE Latin-american Conference on Communications, IEEE LATINCOM, 2013.

[9] H. H. Soliman, N. A. Hikal, and N. A. Sakr, "A comparative performance evaluation of intrusion detection techniques for hierarchical wireless sensor networks". Egyptian Informatics Journal, v. 13, n. 3, 2012, pp. 225-238.

[10] J. Z. Lei and A. Ghorbani, "Network intrusion detection using an improved competitive learning neural network". In: Communication Networks and Services Research, 2004. Proceedings. Second Annual Conference on. IEEE, 2004, pp. 190-197.

[11] E. Eskin, A. Arnold, and M. Prerau, L. Portnoy, S. Stolfo, "A geometric framework for unsupervised anomaly detection". In: Applications of data mining in computer security. Springer US, 2002, pp. 77-101.

[12] M. Amini, R. Jalili, and H. R. Shahriari, "RT-UNNID: A practical solution to real-time network-based intrusion detection using unsupervised neural networks". Computers & Security, v. 25, n. 6, 2006, pp. 459-468.

[13] K. Q. Yan, S. C. Wang, and C. W. Liu, "A hybrid intrusion detection system of cluster-based wireless sensor networks". In: Proceedings of the International MultiConference of Engineers and Computer Scientists, 2009, pp. 18-20.

[14] S. Raza, L. Wallgren, and T. Voigt, "SVELTE: Real-time intrusion detection in the Internet of Things." Ad hoc networks 11.8, 2013, pp. 2661-2674.

[15] H. M. Salmon, et al. "Intrusion detection system for wireless sensor networks using danger theory immune-inspired techniques." International journal of wireless information networks 20.1, 2013, pp. 39-66.

[16] J. Bao, Y. Chen and J. Yu, "An optimized discrete neural network in embedded systems for road recognition". Engineering Applications of Artificial Intelligence, v. 25, n. 4, 2012, pp. 775-782.

[17] Contiki, "Contiki 3.x Roadmap", unpublished. Available: https://github.com/contiki-os/contiki/issues/422. Retrieved: December, 2015.

Quality of Service Parameter Tracking and Transformation in Industrial Applications

György Kálmán

Centre for Cyber and Information Security
Critical Infrastructure Protection Group
Norwegian University of Science and Technology
mnemonic AS
Email: gyorgy.kalman@ntnu.no

Abstract—**Quality of Service (QoS) is a key property to deliver communication services in automation environments. Machine to machine communication offers both an opportunity and poses a challenge for communication networks. In this paper, an overview of typical QoS metrics is given and their relation to automation metrics is analysed. The paper recommends the use of formalized methods from industrial safety to introduce formalized management of communication network requirements in an industrial scenario.**

Keywords–critical infrastructure; QoS; metrics; automation; operational envelope

I. Introduction

Since the introduction of packet switched networks, questions and analyses around the possible service level have been a hot topic. In current networks, the use of best-effort forwarding is dominating. Although it is very efficient, guaranteeing end-to-end connection parameters is a challenge.

The technology landscape is similar in both office or communication and industrial networks: on the Local Area Network (LAN) field, Ethernet is dominating, on the WAN side, standard telecommunication solutions are used also for industrial applications.

Since its introduction in industrial automation, Ethernet's determinism has been a returning concern, mainly because of both outdated information (use of, e.g., 10-Base2) and bus-like topologies [2] with long chains of switches.

Most of the bandwidth-related problems were solved with the introduction of Gigabit Ethernet and for the most demanding applications, technologies like EtherCAT, with intrinsic QoS are available. For traditional switched networks, there are efforts for the inclusion of a resource management plane in the IEEE 802.1 Time-Sensitive Networking Task Group (TSN).

The paper is structured as follows: the second section gives an overview of different QoS metrics. Section 3 provides an overview of Distributed Control System (DCS) structures, Section 4 provides an analysis of how formal methods from safety development could be adapted in QoS requirement specification. Section 5 analyses the need for requirements tracking. The sixth section presents parameters of a control loop and how QoS parameters can be converted between the industrial and communication metrics. Section 7 draws the conclusion and provides an outlook on future work.

II. Quality of Service

QoS is the measure of transmission quality and service availability of a network [3], thus not only limited to actual forwarding parameters like bandwidth and delay, but also, e.g., availability, reconfiguration time and reliability.

Keeping a certain service level was a requirement in telecommunication networks and it was a natural decision to have features to support service level definition when packet switched networks were introduced in the telecom networks.

Providing QoS in Local Area Networks (LANs) networks was focused on services, where at least one of the communicating parties was a human. The services could range from web browsing through VoIP to multi-party video conferencing. The parameters were adopted to the human perception and also tolerance for disturbances was adapted to the human users. The metrics for service quality were not new either at that time; telecommunication networks had service levels defined already and since those were also technical and focused on human users, metrics introduced there were also adapted to computer networks, like Ethernet or more generally, Internet Protocol (IP). In current industrial applications, IPv4 is generally used, if needed, then as IPv4 islands interconnected with tunnels over IPv6 networks. In Internet of Things (IoT) installations, the use of IPv6 is expected as a result of the large number of connected devices.

The evolution of technology showed, that in the vast majority of cases, an over dimensioning of the network resources is both the cheapest and easiest to manage.

A. Telecommunication metrics

As an example, Asynchronous Transfer Mode (ATM) metrics for traffic contracts are composed from traffic parameters such as:

- *Peak Cell Rate (PCR)* The maximum allowable rate at which cells can be transported along a connection in the ATM network. The PCR is the determining factor in how often cells are sent in relation to time in an effort to minimize jitter.
- *Sustainable Cell Rate (SCR)* A calculation of the average allowable, long-term cell transfer rate on a specific connection.
- *Maximum Burst Size (MBS)* The maximum allowable burst size of cells that can be transmitted contiguously on a particular connection.

and QoS parameters,

- *Cell Transfer Delay (CTD)* The delay experienced by a cell between the time it takes for the first bit of the cell to be transmitted by the source and the last bit of the cell to be received by the destination. Maximum Cell Transfer Delay (Max CTD) and Mean Cell Transfer Delay (Mean CTD) are used.

- *Peak-to-peak Cell Delay Variation (CDV)* The difference between the maximum and minimum CTD experienced during the connection. Peak-to-peak CDV and Instantaneous CDV are used.
- *Cell Loss Ratio (CLR)* The percentage of cells that are lost in the network due to error or congestion and are not received by the destination.

The list shows the focus areas of QoS already in the 90s: bandwidth (in bits per second), burstiness and parameters related to disturbances in forwarding.

In addition to these connection-related parameters, the communication network had also network-wide parameters in other relations, like redundancy with, e.g., reconfiguration time in case of link loss or routing alternatives.

ATM is raised as an example, since it offers one of the widest range of possibilities for QoS. It also introduced a couple of concepts, which, although ATM was later deemed as a failure, do a comeback in today's QoS networks.

B. Metrics on packet switched networks

On packet switched networks, initially the focus was on efficient forwarding. Efficiency and simple network operation lead to cheaper devices and ultimately to today's technology landscape with the domination of Ethernet and IP.

While there were different approaches for QoS (integrated and differentiated services), the main QoS metrics were bandwidth, loss, delay and jitter [3]. In future installations with IPv6 it is expected that the use of differentiated services will be more widespread, as after RFC 2460/3697, the properties of Traffic Class and Flow Label can be used to select flows of the aggregated traffic and grant priority. The 20 bit field of Flow Label also allows a large number of flows to be present concurrently which would fit even a large industrial deployment. The impact of this feature however depends on the timing of tasks running on the network and also how this field could be used for other properties important in the automation applications: redundancy and reconfiguration time in case of link loss.

An effort to include some of the traffic engineering possibilities of ATM for LANs is the IEEE Shortest Path Bridging (SPB). This standard is being developed by the TSN working group and allows, amongst others call admission, resource reservation over the whole path. SPB has raised a high interest in the automation field and most of the industry is either contributing directly or closely following the development.

C. Automation

QoS requirements of an automation system tend to be very different than those of an office network. The protocol set used is different and the typical communication inside an automation system runs on Layer 2 [13]. Sources and sinks of traffic streams are typically machines with little tolerance on disturbances, but good predictability in communication.

The network topology of automation networks is often contributing to the challenges around QoS [5]. Networks are built with low port count switches. This typically results in an infrastructure that has more devices than an office network. A bigger refinery can have several hundreds of switches with a typical branching factor of 4-7. The still widely used bus-topology leads to even longer forwarding chain, introducing delay and jitter, which only exists in considerably larger networks in the office/telecommunication scenarios.

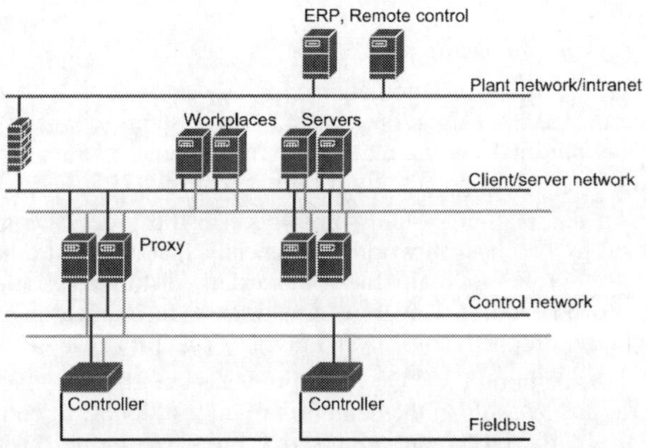

Figure 1. Traditional DCS network architecture

III. DCS ARCHITECTURE

Control systems are traditionally built using a three network levels (Figure 1). The plant, the client-server and the control network. These levels might have different names, but they share the following characteristics:

- *Plant network* is home of the traditional IT systems, like Enterprise Resource Planning (ERP), office services and other support applications. It is typically under the control of the IT department.
- Client-server network is the non-time critical part of the automation system, where the process-related workplaces, servers and other support entities are located. It is firewalled from the plant network and is under the control of Operations.
- Control network includes everything close to the actual process: controllers, sensors, actuators and other automation components. Typically it follows a strict time synchronization regime and contains the parts of the network with time-critical components. It is accessible through proxies from the client-server network and under the control of Operations.

Remote monitoring was introduced to industrial applications decades ago with the different Supervisory Control and Data Acquisition (SCADA) systems. These used various communication technologies (leased lines, radio links, etc.) to feed in status data to a central monitoring entity. Typically remote control was not available.

With current developments in the smart grid and IoT the possibilities for remote operations is being extended by taking current communication solutions in use. The extension of the features also requires a well-defined network infrastructure [9].

A. *QoS in automation*

Traffic flows in automation typically are machine to machine (M2M). This property and the systems connectivity to the physical world require both different tolerances for disturbances and potentially different metrics [7].

An automation system somewhere in the process is connected to the physical world. This means, that amongst others, it has to refer to real time. Forwarding disturbances might lead to potentially dangerous situations with implications far beyond a dropped Voice over Internet Protocol (VoIP) call.

The definition of QoS requirements in the automation world has its roots in the definition of control loops. In control of the early DCSs bus and serial links were used, which typically operated in a slotted or polled way. This allowed the automation engineers to exactly set the communication parameters to meet the requirements of the control system in a deterministic way.

For special applications, technologies with intrinsic QoS are used, e.g., Ethernet for Control Automation Technology (EtherCAT), which allows deterministic communication, but represents a minority of installations. In the following, focus will be on solutions, where no intrinsic QoS is available.

The physical world connection also has an influence on the used QoS metrics. In automation, beside bandwidth, time and availability related metrics are more emphasized, like delay and jitter or availability (redundancy, reconfiguration time). A special aspect is also the quality of time synchronization. The importance and weighting of these metrics is different compared to the telecommunication or other communication operations. One of the most important differences is, that at the moment there is no protocol which would bridge the gap between requirements specification in automation terms and network operations, which results in extended engineering work and challenging life-cycle support. This is in contrast with, e.g., VoIP, where protocols like the Resource Reservation Protocol (RSVP) can be used to reserve resources on the communication path.

IV. Requirements specification

Defining requirements and keeping the original intention in complex systems is a problematic task. In automation, the main challenge is, that the requirements are defined in the automation context, but the bearer network uses by default different metrics for expressing forwarding parameters.

In a control loop, typical parameters are control frequency (how often the data is refreshed or modified), maximum tolerable delay, jitter and availability parameters. One of the most demanding applications, where no technology with intrinsic QoS is used is substation automation with IEC 61850 [6].

IEC 61850 is a standard for communication networks and systems for power utility automation. This protocol is a great step forward for substation automation, as it, amongst others translates all information into data models, which is supported by the application focused architecture. This speeds up the engineering process both in planning and integration [4].

However, also IEC 61850 is not defining exact QoS requirements for the network infrastructure. Although the Specific Communication Service Mapping (SCSM) feature allows the definition of communication links inside the IEC 61850 world, the translation of requirements is not included.

When the control loops are defined, the current process is based on individual mapping of automation requirements to network QoS parameters. This process, although not efficient, can and is working for smaller installations, but suffers from scalability problems.

The lack of direct coupling between the automation and communication parameters typically leads to very pessimistic QoS requirements and over dimensioning the network capacity which leads to excess cost.

In the Internet of Things (IoT) scenario, where the automation networks are extended behind the LAN [8], tracking requirements is becoming more important. Very strict parameters of the automation system on the LAN can be mixed into the WAN requirements, which might lead to prohibitive cost on communication. Validity of requirements for each flow has to be analysed to ensure an efficient fit. The efforts for keeping the QoS parameters as close to the requirements as possible can lead to more efficient and cheaper operation.

A. *Industrial safety*

Conversations on Safety Integrated Systems (SIS) mainly include questions on QoS. The cause is that these installations share the communication network between the automation task and the safety function (as they can also share infrastructure with the fire alarm system). In a safety sense, SIS have no QoS requirements. The safety logic is built in a way, that a communication error is interpreted as a dangerous situation and the safety function will trip. So the system avoids dangerous situations at the expense of lower productivity and availability.

Safety as such is an availability question and through availability, it implies QoS requirements on the automation system as any other communication task. Special treatment is not required.

Although a solution like this does not exists for communication QoS, but the industry has a field, where a similar challenge was solved with structured approach and formal methods: safety. Safety is already considered as a process, which is present for the whole life cycle of the product.

Safety systems are classified into 4 levels, Safety Integrity Level (SIL) 1 to 4. The different levels pose well-defined requirements towards the system. These integrity levels cover all aspects of the system, including hardware, software, communication solution and seen in contrast with the application. A similar approach could be also beneficial for formalizing the relationship between the automation application and the bearer network.

The IEC 61508 standard requires that each risk posed by the components of the safety system is identified and analysed. The result of the risk analysis should be evaluated against tolerability criteria.

Key processes of a safety development are risk analysis and risk reduction. These are executed in an iterative manner until the acceptable risk level is achieved. A possible method for risk classification is shown on figure 2 from the United Kingdom Health and Safety Executive.

Analogue to this, a similar approach could be used for defining an operational envelope for the communication infrastructure. All possible flows of data should be identified (analogue with identifying risk), which is possible with high

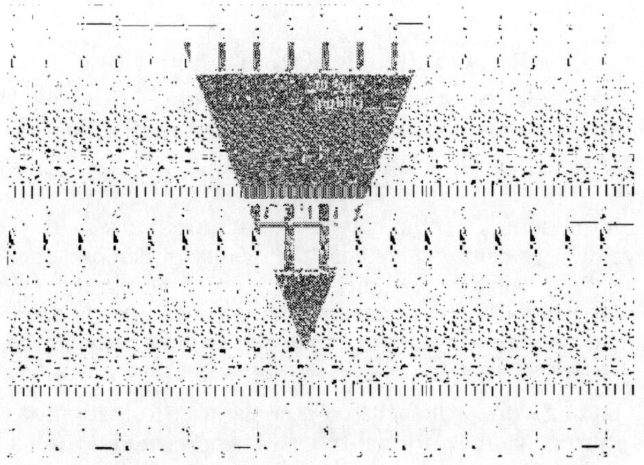

Figure 2. The Health and Safety Executive's Risk criteria

confidence on a mostly machine to machine (M2M) communication system. Then these flows should be analysed and as a result, QoS requirements for the flows should be identified. As these are identified, the aggregated results should be evaluated against the possibilities of the underlying infrastructure [14].

The analysis will result in a range, stating the minimum QoS requirement (with a certain confidence) and the preferred QoS requirement. If the expected QoS after taking communication flows into account is inside the operational envelope, the system can deliver with the defined confidentiality level.

The operational envelope will be larger than zero (not just forming a baseline composed from the single QoS requirements) because of the stochastic nature of best-effort forwarding and large networks. Also, an analogy with the different SIL can be drawn with comparing them to the confidentiality level of keeping the Service Level Agreement (SLA) [11].

The approach taken for safety can be a solution for other properties of the industrial communication system, e.g., QoS for transport or security [15].

V. Requirements Tracking

One of the key aspects missing in engineering work today is the follow-up of requirements stated against the communication infrastructure.

On the LAN level, the lack of tracking only results in minor problems, as network resources are typically not problematic. Even not on the redundancy requirements, since most of the critical network will have approximately the same reliability requirements. As an example, a current IEC 61850 substation will have tens of devices connected to the network.

The local communication of IEC 61850 is composed from horizontal and vertical flows, where horizontal flows tend to use more resources, as Sampled Values (SV) traffic is sent this way. SV is the continuous stream of sampled input or output values, which is sent to a controller for processing. The stream can fill 10s of Mbps. On a network with a gigabit backhaul, conveying traffic in several 100 Mbps range is not problematic. Redundancy is typically covered by either a secondary network or redundant links.

Figure 3. Requirements traceability matrix by the U.S. Department of Transportation

Already in the horizontal-vertical split of flows, different requirements are valid against the network infrastructure. As the automation task gets more far away from the fieldbus level (direct contact with the physical world), so are the deadlines for communication and processing more relaxed.

Requirements tracking is becoming key as the automation system passes the LAN boundary. Costs associated to network communication are becoming more expensive and obeying QoS parameters increasingly problematic.

Several well-known approaches can help the aggregation and validation of the QoS parameters during the life cycle of the project. One of these solutions is the requirements traceability matrix.

In such a matrix, requirements posed by different automation tasks towards the infrastructure can be gathered (figure 3). To allow both aggregation of parameters and identification of the source of a specific requirement.

Source identification is key for long-life installations, where extensions and updates can be expected during the lifetime of the system.

Evaluation if a requirement is still valid in different parts or domains of the system has also a key importance in efficient deployments. It is important to set up an iterative process for QoS parameter evaluation. Here, a possible solution could be to follow the V-model used in, amongst others, software development and safety development. Figure 4 shows the iterative development process. The QoS requirements should be evaluated at each step and their fulfilment validated after each step. With using such a model, the bearer infrastructure would be more integrated into the development process. Integration can lead to more optimized QoS requirements. Current practice results more in a worst-case requirement list.

For Wide Area Network (WAN) situations, tracking requirement validity has key importance. The validity area of the respective QoS parameters has to be limited to cover only the necessary parts. As part of an iterative process, when the communication scope is getting wider (e.g., the data is being passed upward in a hierarchical network architecture), validity of the QoS parameters has to be checked. An example is that if there is a strict time synchronization requirement with IEEE 1588, but there is no such requirement for the WAN section, nor is a loop covering two endpoints in different networks, then the 1588 requirement should not be taken over to the SLA definition of the WAN interface.

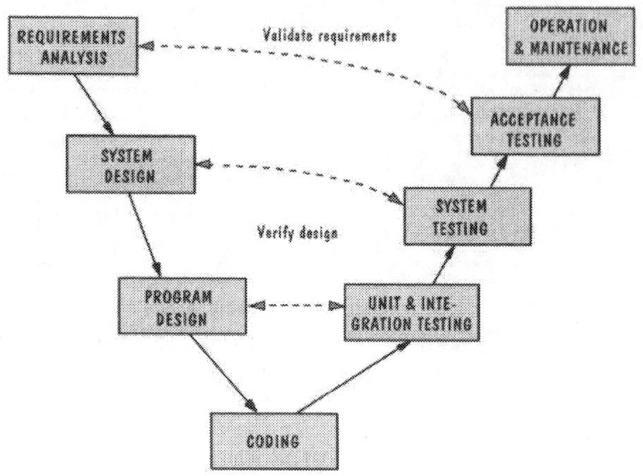

Figure 4. V-model [10]

VI. Control Loop Parameters

Requirements definition for the communication network is one of the actual challenges in automation. The challenge in this task is, that the automation flows are defined using different metrics than the communication links. An example IEC 61850 control loop would be defined as: having a sampling rate of 80 samples per cycle (4800 Hz for 60 Hz networks), with sampling 16 inputs, 16 bit per sample. Event-based traffic is negligible compared to the periodic traffic. If there is a requirement for synchronous operation, time precision (quality) can also be a QoS metric. Redundancy requirements can lead to topologies, which are unusual in a normal network infrastructure: first, the use of Rapid Spanning Tree Protocol (RSTP) to disable redundant links, second the general use of loops (rings) in the network to ensure that all nodes are dual-homed. With dual-homing, the network can survive the loss of one communication link without degradation in the service level. From the network viewpoint, this control loop will introduce a traffic flow, with a net ingress payload stream of approx. 98Mbps. The sampling will generate 2560 bytes of traffic each second, which can be carried by at least two Ethernet frames, thus the system can expect at least approx. 10000 frames per second. The traffic will be forwarded on a horizontal path to the controller. On the ingress port to the backbone, it will enter with approx. 110 Mbps (header+payload). The traffic flow will be consumed at the egress port to the controller.

Due to the stochastic nature of Ethernet, there will be jitter between the frames transmitted over the network. The maximum jitter is defined by the maximum delay variation tolerance of the control loop (typically, every second frame must arrive in good time). This requirement can then be calculated with either the length of the typical frame of the flow or with a maximum length frame. In both cases, the allowed jitter will be considerably longer than the expected disturbances on the LAN. Precision requirement on the time synchronization implies two choices: the choice of protocol and time source. The choice of protocol is generally IEEE 1588v2, which allows high precision time synchronization and GPS as a time source. The choice of GPS is actually an input to the risk analysis of the whole project, as then the time reference will depend on a network controlled by a third party.

VII. Conclusion and Future Work

With communicating automation systems covering large geographical areas and also expanding in logical complexity, current, non-scalable solutions for performance definition and evaluation are getting outdated.

Introduction of the structured approach used in safety development can both enhance the quality of deployments and also allow easier communication between the parties. One of the main advantages of the safety-approach is, that it is widely known and accepted in the industry, so the two worlds of operations and IT could work better together.

Future work will focus on how the transformation of QoS parameters can be formalized and which modifications are needed in the safety processes to suit the QoS process and possibly the security process in an effective manner. Also protocol development or adaptation for resource reservation for automation applications in both LAN and WAN environments is an important field of study, including the use of Software Defined Networking (SDN) in automation [1], [12].

As an outlook, future hot spots of research could be automatic parameter tracking through the design process and real time monitoring of deployments also during their operation. Automation and smart grids are an important field of 5G efforts and it is expected to utilize the existing telecommunication protocols with applying industry-specific profiles. Developing these profiles which will not only define the infrastructure requirements, but also interfaces towards other systems is one of the interesting areas for the success of 5G.

References

[1] Gy. Kálmán, "Applicability of Software Defined Networking in Industrial Ethernet", in Proceedings of IEEE Telfor 2015, pp. 340-343, Belgrade, Serbia

[2] Gy. Kálmán, D. Orfanus, and R. Hussain, "An Overview of Switching Solutions for Wired Industrial Ethernet", The Thirteenth International Conference on Networks ICN 2014, pp. 131-136, Nice

[3] Cisco, "End-to-End QoS Network Design: Quality of Service for Rich-Media & Cloud Networks", Cisco Press, 2013.

[4] M. Rensburg, D. Dolezilek, and J. Dearien, "Case Study: Using IEC 61850 Network Engineering Guideline Test Procedures to Diagnose and Analyze Ethernet Network Installations", in proceedings of PAC World Africa 2015, November 12-13., Johannesburg, South Africa

[5] L. Sheng, "QoS Design and Its Implementation for Intelligent Industrial Ethernet", International Journal of Materials, Mechanics and Manufacturing, Vol. 4, No. 1, 2016., pp. 40-45.

[6] V. Skendzic, I. Ender, and G. Zweigle, "IEC 61850-9-2 Process Bus and Its Impact on Power System Protection and Control Reliability", in proceedings of the 9th Annual Western Power Delivery Automation Conference, April 3-5, 2007, Spokane, USA

[7] J. Bilbao, C. Cruces, and I. Armendariz, "Methodology for the QoS Characterization in High Constraints Industrial Networks", Open Journal of Communications and Software, Volume 1, Number 1, 2014., pp. 30-41

[8] A. Al-Fuqaha, M. Guizani, M. Mohammadi, M. Aledhari, and M. Ayyash, "Internet of Things: A Survey on Enabling Technologies, Protocols, and Applications", IEEE Communication Surveys and Tutorials, Vol. 17, No. 4, 2015., pp. 2347-2376

[9] N. Barkakati and G. C. Wilshusen, "Deficient ICT Controls Jeopardize Systems Supporting the Electric Grid: A Case Study", Securing Electricity Supply in the Cyber Age, Springer, 2009, pp. 129-142

[10] G. Blank, "Object-oriented Software Engineering", http://www.cse.lehigh.edu/~glennb/oose/figs/pfleeger/Vmodel.jpg, Accessed 18.03.2016.

[11] P. Blanco, G. A. Lewis, and P. Merson, "Service Level Agreements in Service-Oriented Architecture Environments", Technical Note, Software Engineering Institute, CMU/SEI-2008-TN-021

[12] D. Cronberger, "The software-defined Industrial Network", The Industrial Ethernet Book, Issue 84, 2014., pp. 8-13

[13] C. Alcaraz, G. Fernandez, and F. Carvajal, "Security Aspects of SCADA and DCS Environments", In Critical Infrastructure Protection: Information Infrastructure Models, Analysis, and Defense, LNCS 7130., Springer, 2012., pp. 120-149

[14] Open Networking Foundation, "Software-Defined Networking: The New Norm for Networks white paper", https://www.opennetworking.org/images/stories/downloads/sdn-resources/white-papers/wp-sdn-newnorm.pdf, Accessed 28.01.2016.

[15] R.C. Parks and E. Rogers, "Best practices in automation security", Security & Privacy, IEEE (Volume:6 , Issue: 6), 2009., pp 37-43

FBT_ARM: A Software Dynamic Translator for the ARM Architecture

Edward David Moreno
DCOMP/PROCC
UFS – Federal University of Sergipe
Aracaju, Brazil
edwdavid@gmail.com

Felipe Oliveira Carvalho, Admilson R.L. Ribeiro
DCOMP/PROCC
UFS - Federal University of Sergipe
Aracaju, Brazil
felipekde@gmail.com, admilson@ufs.br

***Abstract*—Software dynamic translation is a technique that allows code modification and monitoring of program execution. This paper addresses some applications of software dynamic translation (SDT) and the porting of fastBT—a dynamic translator for the IA32 architecture—to the ARM architecture. The result is a dynamic translator called FBT_ARM that works for the ARM and IA32 architectures.**

Keywords-software dynamic translator; ARM architecture; IA32 architecture; fastBT; FBT_ARM

I. INTRODUCTION

Software Dynamic Translation (SDT) is a technique that allows code modification and monitoring of the execution of program instructions at runtime. In the last few years, products using dynamic binary translation have become popular in the areas of virtualization, instrumentation and emulation [8]. SDT can be applied in several forms: dynamic code optimization, hardware architecture simulation, system virtualization, instruction set translation, profilers, debuggers, security constraint checking at runtime, co-designed virtual machines etc.

In the implementation of a SDT system, a software layer acts as virtual machine that manages the execution examining and dynamically translating all or part of the instructions of a program before they get executed by the host CPU.

Software dynamic translators are often written for a single application and/or platform. Besides the lack of portability due to the single application and single architecture approaches, few of the translation or instrumentation systems are open which prevents research in the area making them hard to study requiring the reimplementation of complex and delicate systems. Most of the code of a SDT system depends on the target hardware architecture. Both the data structures and the translated code emission must be designed according to the instruction set architecture.

Unfortunately, robust, general-purpose instrumentation tools are not nearly as common in the embedded arena compared to IA32, for example [3].

The Pin dynamic software translation system [4] provided support for the ARM architecture [3], but the ARM support has been discontinued in early 2007 (a search on http://archive.org indicates that the last version of Pin for ARM was released in January 2007). With the growing relevance of the ARM architecture driven by its adoption on most of the Smartphones, tablets, several embedded systems, and even some network servers (where x86 is commonly used), it makes sense to develop tools that improves the understanding of the ARM architecture, software development and execution in this platform.

As a result of this work, we present a software dynamic translator for the ARM architecture called "FBT_ARM". The translator can be used for program instrumentation in embedded systems based on ARM processors. The designer of a software instrumentation product can provide his own translation table. Such table should contain the routines that must be executed while translating the instructions of the executable code from the original program being instrumented. Such tool can be used to analyze the behavior of a software during its development (searching bugs, performance analysis, exploring ARM extension ideas) or even to run the program in production environment over the dynamic translator (e.g., implementation of a security layer that prevents a program from executing certain functions on a server, execution of a binary that contains non-standard ARM instructions implemented in software, implementation of a software-based transactional memory system).

The rest of the paper is structured as follows. Section II presents main concepts about SDT systems, section III is dedicated to fastBT translator, which is the baseline of our SDT for ARM. Section IV presents the steps for porting fastBT to our FBT_ARM. Finally, section V presents the conclusions and some ideas for future works.

II. THEORY AND IMPLEMENTATION OF SOFTWARE DYNAMIC TRANSLATION SYSTEMS

SDT systems can be divided in two classes according to its implementation approach: based on intermediate representation and table-based. Many SDT systems translate machine code to be executed into an Intermediate Representation (IR) that can be executed by an interpreter or just-in-time compiler. This additional level of indirection simplifies the implementation of the translator that can then represent the state of the translated program (execution stack, registers) in software. Valgrind [5], Strata [7], Pin [4] and QEMU [2] are examples of SDT systems that use an IR (Intermediate Representation) for their translators. An advantage of an IR is that it allows software reuse.

Other approach used in several projects is the Dynamic Binary Recompilation (DBR) [5]. It is similar to the use of IR in compiler projects where the front-ends of several high level programming languages deal with IR code generation that can be compiled by the backend of every supported hardware architecture. Reusing the backend allows compilers of many languages to use most of the compilation optimizations from IR and apply them to all architectures supported by the backend, thus greatly reducing the effort of compiler creation.

A table-based software dynamic translator translates each instruction by executing specified functions from a table for each instruction. In general, this approach generates translators with better performance than IR-based translators. With the gain in performance comes a loss of flexibility, so many restrictions are imposed to the translation of instructions. Branch instructions, for example, should be treated especially so that translated code execution does not escape from translator control.

Finally, SDT can be used in different applications, especially as virtualization, instrumentation and emulation.

Virtualization: SDT is one of the approaches of virtualization of 32-bit x86 systems implemented by VMware [1] in all versions of VMware ESX until version 4.0. VMware ESX is an enterprise level product that provides computer virtualization at the kernel level. The translator used by VMWARE does not map instructions coming from target architecture to another. Instead, it translates the unrestricted x86 code to a subset of itself that can be safely executed. The translator particularly replaces privileged instructions with instruction sequences that perform the same privileged operations in the virtual machine instead of performing them in the physical machine.

Instrumentation: it is a technique that consists in the insertion of code in a program for the data collection and analysis of the instrumented program. One of the instrumentation techniques, Dynamic Binary Instrumentation (DBI), uses SDT to execute the instrumentation code at runtime. One example of the use of this technique is the Valgrind tool set [5].

Emulation: SDT systems are used to implement instruction set emulators. QEMU is an example of architecture emulator that allows, for example, the execution of ARM programs on x86 processors [2].

III. THE FASTBT DYNAMIC TRANSLATOR

The fastBT is a low overhead dynamic translator, it has a low memory footprint, is table-based and provides optimizations for all forms of dynamic control transfer instructions. fastBT presents a novel technique of translated target address prediction for dynamic control instructions combined with adaptive schemes to select the best configuration for each indirect control transfer. These optimizations lead to optimal translation depending on the instruction location in the program and not only in the class of the instruction [6].

The project and implementation of fastBT is neutral in relation to the processor architecture, but the available open source implementation is compatible only with IA-32 and Linux systems. The current implementation provides a table for the IA-32 architecture instructions and uses a thread-local cache for translated code [6]. Although it may increase memory usage, it avoids a complicated and error-prone lock scheme for the translation of multithreaded programs.

Besides that, fastBT authors say that in practice little code is shared between threads during the execution of programs, rendering the translated code cache redundancy even less of a problem.

The translation tables are generated from a high level description and are statically linked to the translator program during compilation. This is a flexibility that is not offered by many translators, see examples on Fig. 1 and Table I.

Finally, we made some experiments with fastBT and studied the performance. We used the programs from the Computer Language Benchmarks Game available in [10]. For most programs the overhead was small except for some cases where the overhead reached 400 % (`revcomp`) or even more than 23000 % (`knucleotide-4`).

IV. FBT_ARM: PORTING FASTBT TO ARM SYSTEMS

In this section we show the steps for porting fastBT to our FBT_ARM software, specific to ARM architectures. We show it using four subsections: How the translator works, the instructions table, the ARM instructions disassembler, implementations of simple calls, and finally, an example how the FBT_ARM works in a real program.

A. *How the Translator Works*

A program can be translated dynamically by preloading the *`libfastbt.so`* library before program execution. This *`libfastbt.so`* defines two symbols that will overwrite the symbols of the same name in the executable: *`_init`* and *`_fini`*. These two symbols are routines responsible for initialization and finalization of the program execution. Thus, this *`libfastbt.so`* defines *`_init`* with code that starts the dynamic translator hijacking control and starting the translation of the program.

The code in *`_fini`* finishes the translator with an error message. This error message is a warning about the loss of control of execution by the translator. If the translator works correctly *`_fini`* should not be executed, for the translator, as the first step, creates a mapping from the code in *`_fini`* to a routine the finishes the translator with no error message. Thus, if the translator is translating the program code, the eventual branch to *`_fini`* will be redirected to the routine that finishes the translator without any error.

The sequence diagram in Figure 2 shows how program control is hijacked by the translator.

At first *`fbt init`* initializes the thread-local storage space and initializes the trampolines. Trampolines are small dynamically generated code blocks that are used when a branch to some specific address in the program is requested and some code must be executed before the branch.

For example, when translating an indirect branch instruction the translator should not simply copy the instruction with the same target in program code as the control of the program would be lost by the translator after the branch to an address in the untranslated original program. This is what happens instead: the branch instruction is translated as a branch to a *`tld->unmanaged_code_trampoline`*.

```
instr_description table_opcode_08[] = {

/*0x0*/ {0, "ADD",    ADD, OPND_REG_SHIFT_BY_IMM, "action_copy", Add_to_register"},
/*0x1*/ {0, "ADD",    ADD, OPND_REG_SHIFT_BY_REG, "action_copy", Add_to_register"},
/*0x2*/ {0, "ADD",    ADD, OPND_REG_SHIFT_BY_IMM, "action_copy", Add_to_register"},
/*0x3*/ {0, "ADD",    ADD, OPND_REG_SHIFT_BY_REG, "action_copy", Add_to_register"},
/*0x4*/ {0, "ADD",    ADD, OPND_REG_SHIFT_BY_IMM, "action_copy", Add_to_register"},
/*0x5*/ {0, "ADD",    ADD, OPND_REG_SHIFT_BY_REG, "action_copy", Add_to_register"},
/*0x6*/ {0, "ADD",    ADD, OPND_REG_SHIFT_BY_IMM, "action_copy", Add_to_register"},
/*0x7*/ {0, "ADD",    ADD, OPND_REG_SHIFT_BY_REG, "action_copy", Add_to_register"},
/*0x8*/ {0, "ADD",    ADD, OPND_REG_SHIFT_BY_IMM, "action_copy", Add_to_register"},
/*0x9*/ {0, "UMULL", UMULL, None "action_copy", Unsigned_long_multiply _(32x32_to_64);
/*0xa*/ {0, "ADD",    ADD, OPND_REG_SHIFT_BY_IMM, "action_copy", Add_to_register"},
/*0xb*/ {0, "STRH",   STRH, OPND_REG_OFFSET | OPND_INCR_OFFSET, "action_copy", Store"},
/*0xc*/ {0, "ADD",    ADD, OPND_REG_SHIFT_BY_IMM, "action_copy", Add_to_register"},
/*0xd*/ {0, "LDRD",   LDRD, OPND_REG_OFFSET | OPND_INCR_OFFSET, "action_copy", Load"},
/*0xe*/ {0, "ADD",    ADD, OPND_REG_SHIFT_BY_IMM, "action_copy", Add_to_register"},
/*0xf*/ {0, "STRD",   STRD, OPND_REG_OFFSET | OPND_INCR_OFFSET, "action_copy", Store"},
};
```

Figure 1. Example of the ARM Instructions Table

The code in this trampoline saves the execution context, calls a function that translates the code in the target of the indirect branch (or finds this code in the translated code cache), modifies `tld->ind_target` to point to the translated code, restores the execution context and finally executes a branch to `tld->ind_target`.

These small code blocks are called trampolines because they are the target of branches and quickly branch to another code region. After initialization, `fbt_start_transaction` gets executed. This function finds out the return address using `_builtin_return_address`. This return address is the address of the first instruction after the branch to `FBT_start_transaction` which is located in the beginning of the program since the call to `fbt_start_transaction` is one of the first things done by the program. It is from this address—`orig_begin`— that code translation starts with the call to `fbt_translate_noexecute`.

Eventually, when `fbt_translate_noexecute` returns a pointer to the translated code block, the return address of the call to `fbt_start_transaction` at the top of the stack is replaced by the pointer to the translated code. Thus, `fbt_start_transaction` does not return execution to the untranslated program code but to the translated code.

The `fbt_translate_noexecute` has a loop that iterates over the program instructions from `orig_begin`, calls `fbt_disasm_instr` for each instruction and executes an action found in the instructions table (see Fig.1 and Table I to generate the translated code equivalent to that instruction. Besides that, `action_copy`, `action_branch`, and `action_branch_and_link`, and others return a value that indicated whether the block translation should be interrupted. Branch instructions (B, BL. ...) for example, interrupt block translation.

Once it happens, a trampoline is added at the end of the translated code block. This trampoline is responsible for starting the translation or execution of the next translation block. When execution reaches the end of the translated code block, control returns to the translator or to the next translated instruction.

B. *The Instructions Table*

To understand the instructions (which operation, arguments ...) and decide how to translate each instruction, the translator queries a table with information about each instruction.

This table is generated from many other tables with a higher level description of the instructions. FBT_ARM supports only the 32-bit ARM instruction set which makes the table-based instruction decoding simpler.

The high level tables in `arm_table_generator/arm_opcode.map.h` are built from the observation that it is possible to define what each instruction is about from the [27:20] and [7:4] bits.

For example, when the 32 bits of an ARM instruction follow the 0x 08 1 format it is already possible to assume that it is an ADD and that the second operand is left-shifted by a length specified in a register. 0x 08 1 is the bi-nary enconding of addf<c>g <Rd>, <Rn>, <Rm>, lsl <Rs> in ARM assembly language.

There is a high level table with 16 entries for each configuration of the [27:20] bits. The index of each entry is the configuration of the [7:4] bits. Fig. 2 shows the table with information about the instructions where the [27:20] bits are 0x80.

These tables are analyzed by the ARM table generator to automate the generation of a table with 4096 (2^{12}) entries. The index used to query this table is the concatenation of the 8 [27:20] bits with the 4 [7:4] bits.

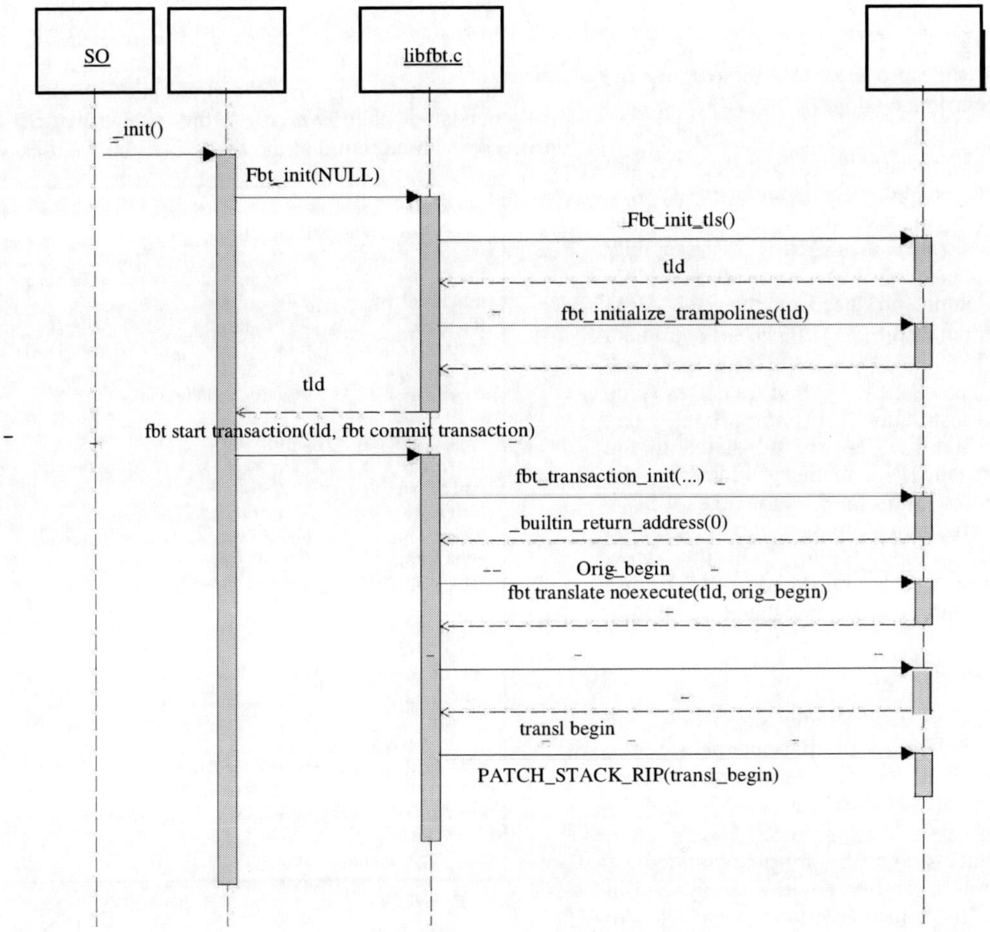

Figure 2. fastBT sequence diagram

TABLE I. COMPARISON OF THE FBT ARM DISASSEMBLER AND OBJDUMP DISASSEMBLER

0x	FBT_ARM	FBT_ARM (--sugar)	objdump -d
e52de004	str lr, [sp, #-4]!	push flrg	push flrg ; (str lr, [sp, #-4]!)
e92d4008	stmdb sp!, fr3, lrg	push fr3, lrg	push fr3, lrg
e59fe004	ldr lr, [pc, #4]	ldr lr, [pc, #4]	ldr lr, [pc, #4] ; 83d4
e8bd8008	ldmia sp!, fr3, pcg	pop fr3, pcg	pop fr3, pcg
eb00002c	bl 8474	bl 8474	bl 8474
012fff1e	bxeq lr	bxeq lr	bxeq lr
e12fff33	blx r3	blx r3	blx r3
e1b010a1	movs r1, r1, lsr #1	lsrs r1, r1, lsr #1	lsrs r1, r1, #1
e1a0c06c	mov ip, ip, rrx	rrx ip, ip	rrx ip, ip
01b0c0a0	movseq ip, r0, r0, lsr #1	lsrseq ip, r0, #1	lsrseq ip, r0, #1
e2844001	add r4, r4, #1 ; 0x1	add r4, r4, #1	add r4, r4, #1
e0a11a04	adc r1, r1, r4, lsl #20	adc r1, r1, r4, lsl #20	adc r1, r1, r4, lsl #20

The tables with the high level description of the ARM instructions for FBT_ARM were created after reading the ARM architecture reference manual.

C. The ARM Instructions Disassembler

To test the instruction table and understand what information is necessary in the tables to decode the instructions, we developed an ARM disassembler (`src/arm/fbt_disassemble.c`).

Table 1 shows the output produced by the FBT-ARM disassembler and the output of the `objdump -d` command that comes from the GNU `binutils` software package. When the *--sugar* flag is passed, FBT_ARM translates some instructions to pseudo-instructions if appropriate. Load instructions like LDR, and LDMIA are translated to the POP pseudo-instruction when the memory address is the register storing the pointer to the base of the stack—SP— and the operands configuration makes the instruction semantically equivalent to the popping from the stack. Similarly, store instructions can be translated to PUSH; and MOVs with shifted-operands can be translated as pseudo shift instructions.

D. Implementation of System Calls

To avoid `libc` as a dependency and allow the interception of system calls we had to implement Linux syscalls in Fbt. The ARM ABI standard defines how system calls should be implemented.

The source file `src/arm/fbt_syscalls_impl.h` has C preprocessor macros and the im-plementation of many syscalls using inline assembly. Besides being used in the translator, this syscalls implementation is also used to implement I/O functions (e.g. `fllwrite`, `fllprintf` ...) and a low-level memory allocator (`fbt lalloc`, `fbt_mem_free` ...) which are used by our FBT_ARM.

E. Translating a Simple Program

Fig. 3 shows the ARM code of the program that will be translated using FBT_ARM. This program sums two 1-digit numbers passed as arguments from the command line (`./prog 3 7`) and terminates with an exit code equals to the sum of the two numbers. It is a simple example without branches consisting of a single translation block. Fig. 4 shows the output of the program of Fig. 3. It is important to observe that the exit code (the *$? shell variable*) is indeed the sum of the two arguments (see Fig. 4).

Fig. 5 shows fragments of the debug output (`debug.txt`) produced by FBT_ARM during the dynamic execution of the program. The debug output fragment produced by FBT_ARM shows the translation of each instruction until SWI, that when found by the translator, concludes the translation of the block (`closing TU upon request, invoking translation function on 0x000088a4`).

It is after the translation of the block that execution con-trol is passed to the translated code (`starting transaction at 0xb5cd6000 (orig. addr: 0x0000885c`)).

The original program code starts at `0x0000885c` and the translated code which is the one executed by the processor can be found at the `0xb5cd6000` address.

```
bl fbt_start_transaction
        // int a = argv[1][0] - '0';

ldr r3, [fp, #-20]    // r3 = argv (argv stored in the stack)
add r3, r3, #4        // r3 = argv + 1
ldr r3, [r3]          // r3 = *(argv + 1) or r3 = argv[1]
ldrb r3, [r3]         // r3 = *(argv[1]) or r3 = argv[1][0]
sub r3, r3, #48       // r3 = argv[1][0] - '0'
str r3, [fp, #-8]     // stores a in the stack

        // int b = argv[2][0] - '0';
ldr r3, [fp, #-20]    // r3 = argv (argv stored in the stack)
add r3, r3, #8        // r3 = argv + 2
ldr r3, [r3]          // r3 *(argv + 2) or r3 = argv[2]
ldrb r3, [r3]         // r3 * (argv[2]) or r3 = argv[2][0]
sub r3, r3, #48       // r3 argv[2][0] - '0'
str r3, [fp, #-12]    // stores b in the stack

        // a + b
ldr r2, [fp, #-8]     // r2= a
ldr r3, [fp, #-12]    // r3= b
add r3, r2, r3        // r3 = a + b

        // exit(a + b)
mov r0, r3            // first argument (a + b)
mov r7, #1            // SYS_exit (syscall code)
swi 0                 // request syscall handling by the kernel

bl fbt_commit_transaction
```

Figure 3. Program code to be dynamically translated

```
$ ./prog 2 3
Starting BT
Stopping BT $
echo $?
5
$ ./prog 8 7
Starting BT
Stopping BT $
echo $?
15
```

Figure 4. Dynamic execution of a simple program

V. CONCLUSIONS

To make this work possible it was necessary to analyze software dynamic translation solutions and the implementation techniques they use. The main target of the analysis was fastBT whose code was extended to support the ARM architecture. FBT_ARM has tables describing 32-bit instructions of the ARMv6 architecture and necessary routines for instruction decoding. To demonstrate how the tables can be used, we have implemented a disassembler that produces the output similar to the output of production disassemblers (`objdump -d`). Although FBT-ARM is not capable of translating full programs, all the infrastructure of fastBT was ported and works on ARM processors.

```
fbt_start_transaction(commit_function = 0x0000dcb8) {

 translate_noexecute(*tld=0xb6f2e000, *orig_address=0x0000885c) {
fbt_ccache_find(*tld=0xb6f2e000, *orig_address=0x0000885c) {

}-> 0x00000000

tld->ts.transl_instr: 0xb5cd6000 fbt_ccache_add_entry(*tld=0xb6f2e000, *orig_address=0x0000885c, *transl_address=0xb5cd6000)
{}
fbt_disasm_instr(*ts=0xb6f2e458) { Disassembling 0xe51b3014 } translating a 'ldr'
action_copy(*addr=0x0000885c, *transl_addr=0xb5cd6000) {}-> NEUTRAL
fbt_disasm_instr(*ts=0xb6f2e458) { Disassembling 0xef000000 } translating a 'swi'
action_copy(*addr=0x000088a0, *transl_addr=0xb5cd6000) {

        Encountered an interrupt - closing TU with some glue code
}-> CLOSE_GLUE

closing TU upon request, invoking translation function on 0 x000088a4
allocated trampolines: 0xb5ccf000, target: 0x000088a4, origin: 0 xb5cd6004
}-> 0xb5cd6000, next_tu=0x000088a4 (len: 0)
starting transaction at 0xb5cd6000 (orig. addr: 0x0000885c)

}
```

Figure 5. Debug output produced by FBT_ARM

FBT_ARM is open source and available in [9]. Since it is a table-based translator which often means better performance than those based on intermediate representation, there are many possibilities of use for FBT_ARM. Its implementation can be extended in the development of several tools that benefit from software dynamic translation like memory profilers, general program analysis tools, secure execution environments, etc.

For future works, we would like to suggest: (i) finish the implementation of our FBT_ARM, adding the translation to ARM´s control instructions, and (ii) execute a final version in real programs and benchmarks, and (iii) compare the performance of FBT_ARM to other systems.

Acknowledgment

This research work received financial support from CNPq, CAPES, FAPITEC (Brazilian Government Institutions for Science and Technology).

References

[1] Agesen, O. Software and hardware techniques for x86 virtualization. 2009. Electronic Publication, www.vmware.com/files/pdf/software_hardware_ tech_x86_virt.pdf. Visited in April 20, 2016.

[2] Bellard, F. Qemu, a fast and portable dynamic translator. In Proceedings of the Annual Conference on USENIX Annual Technical Conference, ATEC '05, pages 41–41, Berkeley, CA, USA, 2005.

[3] Hazelwood, K. and Klauser, A. A dynamic binary instrumentation engine for the arm architecture. In ACM Proc. of the 2006 Intl. Conference on Compilers, Architecture and Synthesis for Embedded Systems (CASES), p. 261–270, USA, 2006.

[4] Luk, C.-K., Cohn, R., Muth, R., Patil, H., Klauser, A., Lowney, G., Wallace, S., Reddi, V. J., and Hazelwood, K. Pin: building customized program analysis tools with dynamic instrumentation. SIGPLAN Not., 40(6):190–200, 2005.

[5] Nethercote, N. and Seward, J. Valgrind: A framework for heavyweight dynamic binary instrumentation. SIGPLAN Notes, 42(6):89–100, 2007.

[6] Payer, M. and Gross, T. R. Generating low-overhead dynamic binary translators. In Proceedings of the 3rd Annual Haifa Experimental Systems Conference, SYSTOR '10, pages 22:1–22:14, New York, NY, USA. ACM, 2010.

[7] Scott, K., Kumar, N., Velusamy, S., Childers, B., Davidson, J. W., and Soffa, M. L. Retargetable and reconfigurable software dynamic translation. In IEEE Proc. of the Intl. Symposium on Code Generation and Optimization (CGO), p. 36–47, USA, 2003.

[8] Wirth, M. Simple pluggable binary translator library in user space. Laboratory for Software Technology, ETH Zurich, 2008. http://www.nebelwelt.net/publications/students/07hs-wirth-fastBT.pdf. Semester thesis. Visited in April 12, 2016.

[9] Moreno, E.D. and Carvalho, F. Electronic Publication: Code of FBT_ARM, available at https://github.com/philix/Fbt, 2015. Accessed in April 30, 2016.

[10] Computer Language Benchmarks Game, Available at https://github.com/philix/c_bench, 2015. Accessed in April 25, 2016.

Active Null Forming: Coordinated MIMO Transmit Precoding for Interference Mitigation in 5th Generation Networks

Abheek Saha
Hughes Systique Corporation,
India
Email: abheek.saha@hsc.com

***Abstract*—3gPP Long Term Evolution (LTE) Advanced and Wireless Local Area Networks (WLAN) are both striding towards the 5th generation wireless networks, with guaranteed cell edge coverage and performance. To achieve this, these networks will have unprecedented density of deployed cells, which will actively work with each other to maximize the link to all possible User Equipments (UEs). In this article, we propose a method by which individual network nodes can use additional antennae so as to transmit data to individual UEs while limiting the interference seen by other UEs on the same frequency and time-slot. Ideally, we should be able to have a dense network of nodes, all transmitting simultaneously on the same resource, without any cross-interference. We show that our proposed algorithm shows substantial performance gains over existing techniques addressing coordinated multipoint transmission between multiple transmitters and receivers.**

***Keywords*—Coordinated Multipoint; Multi-user MIMO; interference pre-cancellation**

I. Introduction

The next generation of wireless networks have several challenging objectives, one of which is to meet target throughput numbers for the cell-edge, i.e., applicable to upto 99% of the UEs within the coverage area [1]. Consequently, it is anticipated that next generation wireless networks will be much denser, to improve coverage. This in turn will lead to significant cross node interference. Interference mitigation is already an active area of research in wireless networks; with the advent of newer techniques such as Inter-Cell Interference Coordination (ICIC), further enhanced as eICIC and feICIC) and Coordinated Multipoint (CoMP), there is an emphasis on inter-node coordination so as to jointly improve UE link conditions. For example, CoMP allows joint coding, where multiple nodeBs coordinate with each other so as to transmit to a single UE, further increasing the diversity (and consequently rank) of the ensemble of Multiple Input Multiple Output (MIMO) channels.

In this paper, we present an idea, first presented in [2] called Active-Null Forming (ANF), which allows network nodes to work together so as to transmit to multiple UEs in the same geographical area, while limiting cross node interference. In ANF, each network node receives feedback from multiple UEs in the neighbourhood, one of which it is transmitting data to (the target UE). It then codes the transmission in such a way that the target UE gets the intended data-stream with no interference, whereas the interference at other UEs (on the same frequency and time-slot) is minimized. The key requirement is that the network node be MIMO capable, with a large number of elements available for transmission. The method is a modification of directed feedback method of broadcast MIMO [3]. In [2], we presented a very simple initial approach to ANF, limited to two UEs and two network nodes, with a fixed template for precoding. In the current work we have extended the problem to multiple UEs and presented the solution of the precoding matrix as a constrained (not necessarily convex) optimization problem. We shall first describe how it can be used stand-alone and then jointly by a cluster of network nodes acting together.

A. Organization of this paper

The rest of this paper is organized as follows. In Section II we describe the problem in more detail, including the previous work done in this area. In Section III we present the ANF algorithm and introduce the underlying principle. In Section IV we formulate the interference nulling problem as an optimization problem, using the conceptual principles introduced in the previous section. Finally, in Section V, we present the simulation results for a simple network node operating on the principles of the ANF algorithm.

II. Coordinated node functions in dense HetNets

The next generation of cellular networks will see novel deployment architectures as a means of increasing coverage, reducing cost and also, controlling energy consumption. The key developments include the widespread deployment of cloud Radio Access Networks (cRAN) with Remote Radio Heads (RRH) [4]. This approach combines centralized baseband processing in a cloud, in conjunction with a dense network of RRHs, so as to create a flexible, functionally adaptive network. It is envisioned that the network nodes (RRHs) shall be deployed densely, in overlapping coverage with each other and the network will be able to dynamically map functions to individual nodes as per demand. Already, in some current networks, we see this kind of a deployment, where there is one macro-cell with several femto-cells in its coverage region whose primary job is to off-load local traffic from the macro. This is the kind of environment where inter-node coordination functions such as CoMP are readily applicable; by multiple network nodes cooperating with each other, we can ensure that all network holes and cell-edge points are adequately serviced.

However, in such a network, management of interference (especially co-cellular interference) is a big challenge. Due to the close proximity of the network nodes, tight restrictions on frequency re-use are both inefficient and complex. Rather, the focus has been on time-sharing techniques like ICIC. Such techniques are primarily based around scheduling and not directly on interference control.

A. Multi-user MIMO, massive MIMO and remote radio-heads

Another innovation in next generation networks is the advent of widespread MIMO. Starting from basic single user MIMO, we have progressed to multi-user MIMO and CoMP. It is a fact that it is easier to add transmission elements to a network node, as compared to a user-terminal, especially a hand-held. As of now, the practical limit of antenna on a user-terminal is 2-4. With the advent of RRHs this difference shall be further increased. However, studies have shown that additional antennae don't usually lead to significant changes in throughput, since the independence of the paths are limited. This creates the challenge of using the larger number of antennae on the network node; either through time-diversity schemes (which also suffers the path independence problem), joint transmission/reception schemes of MU-MIMO, etc. This is one of the features of ANF; that it uses these additional network elements for improvement of network conditions.

B. Previous work

The application of multiuser MIMO methods to the interference coordination problem in general has been introduced in [5] [6]. Both these papers highlight the possible co-existence between the semi-static optimization brought in by standard ICIC techniques and the dynamic, frame by frame optimization achievable by CoMP techniques such as Joint Transmission (JT). However, none of these works consider adaptation of CoMP specifically for the ICIC purpose.

In the field of transmitter/precoder based interference cancellation, the previous literature that we have seen on multiple transmitter MIMO is divided into two parts. First is joint encoding with with partial interference pre-substraction and the other is in zero-forcing with block diagonalization (ZF-BD). In interference pre-subtraction our principal reference derives from the decision feedback precoding approach given in [3]. Other related work in this area has been done using trellis precoding techniques [7]. Both of these use special joint pre-coding of the transmitted vectors so as to cancel out interference, taking into account the different channel matrices. Caire and Shamai [8] consider the problem in the context of a single transmitter and multiple single-antenna receivers with full knowledge of the entire channel matrix on both sides and show that for two users, the sum-rate approaches the optimal theoretical Dirty Paper Coding (DPC) output. While their work is based on single antenna receivers, the idea of ordering the two users such that the first user is interference free, but the second user has to deal with the first is introduced by them.

Techniques for ZF-BD for multi-user transmission is given in [9] [10] and others. The basic SVD technique for extracting precoding matrices orthogonal to other users are given in [9]. Zhang [11] describes a cooperative algorithm for zero-forcing transmission with per network node power constraints. Zukang Shen and his co-authors [12] extend this to show that a significant part of the Marton's upper bound can be achieved using the analytically feasible BD approach.

ZF-BD is part of a more generic problem in optimal MIMO MAC precoding matrix design introduced in [13] and further discussed in, for example, [14] and others. These are global cooperative methods that require network nodes to jointly compute the precoding matrices for all nodes simultaneously (typically they involve solutions that require the manipulation of the term $\sum_{k,k\neq i}^{K} \log(H_k Q_k H_k^*)$. In [15], the authors provide a framework for comparing the relative capacities of the Multiple Access Channel with cooperative precoding and the interference presubtraction approach and conclude that the two cover each other. In more recent work [16] describes a method of optimal linear precoding called 'Soft Interference Nulling' (we found the paper after we had already coined our own term, so any similarity is coincidence), which is also a global technique. In SIN, clusters of base-stations transmit a data stream to a single UE using a jointly constructed set of linear precoding matrices.

C. Our contribution

In this paper, we propose a new method for multi-user MIMO operation, which we call Active Null Forming. Our solution is designed for the multi-transmitter, multiple receiver MuMIMO case; specifically where the number of antennae per transmitter is larger than the number of antennae per receiver. In this sense, it is different from existing algorithms.

The crucial difference in our approach is the use of additional network elements; we propose to use them *explicitly* for modifying the transmitted signal so as to actively cancel interference (as opposed to the passive means suggested in ICIC). As far as we are aware, this approach in general has not been addressed in pre-existing work. Our algorithm is particularly suited to use in next generation mobile networks that are expected to use distributed antenna systems (DAS) [17] [18] liberally to improve signal penetration and diversity, since there will be likely a large number of elements available to each network node.

Technically, our approach is derived from broadcast MIMO; however, by the very nature of our method, it is easy to scale it a number of transmitters. We will show our algorithm achieves results close to cooperative precoding without requiring a global optimization, due to the very nature of the approach; each node can independently compute their own precoding matrices. A second issue that we consider is the power diversion problem; when we do optimal precoding for interference mitigation, we are, to an extent sacrificing the immediate needs of the network node for some global objectives. In this case, this comes to power; in a power constrained network node, we need to decide how much power should be diverted for the purpose of interference mitigation at the cost of SINR for the primary signal. Both these issues are addressed in our paper, as we shall see.

Our algorithm is hence an alternative to the ZFBD algorithm and its variants. In general, ZFBD requires the target UEs to have orthogonal channel matrices [19], i.e., $H_i Q_j H_i^* \equiv \delta_{ij}$ and scheduling algorithms have to take this into account. Our algorithm is not dependent on this condition, which gives it additional flexibility, especially when the number of UEs is relative small, i.e., the $K \to \infty$ condition is not met.

III. Active Null-Forming - the general framework

A. Problem Context

The Figure 1a shows the deployment of the proposed approach. We see a small cluster of inter-connected and coordinated network nodes servicing a group of UEs. Each node is assumed to have full state information of the channel to all UEs (in TDD systems, this is easy, but in FDD systems this will require additional signaling and coordination between network nodes for pilot transmission). There is a central coordination and scheduling function, which, for each transmission time slot determines the subset of UEs $\mathfrak{S}$ to be transmitted to and the mapping from nodes to UEs, i.e., for a given UE u to be transmitted to, which node N_u is going to transmit to it. For a given node, the UE to which it has to transmit data to at a particular instant is called the *target UE*. The other active UEs (which are going to receive transmissions from any of the other network nodes) are called *co-resident UEs*. This is shown in Figure 1b.

Each node then computes a precoding matrix as per the ANF algorithm (Section IV). The objective of ANF is to simultaneously transmit the intended signal to the target UE, while minimizing the signal received by the co-resident UEs as much as possible. We achieve this by using the additional transmission elements and a specifically computed precoding matrix to create 'nulls' at the receiver, conceptually similar to the null-forming done in beamforming systems. The core of the algorithm is a specially selected structure for the precoding matrix as given in Sub-Section III-D. Due to this structure, the precoding matrix is guaranteed to make the transmission to the target UE completely free from the rest of the signal (as is achieved in interference subtracting broadcast MIMO). Figure 1b shows ANF in some detail, from the context of a single network node. Note that all the UEs don't need to have the same number of receive antenna and the sum of receive antennae for the UEs may be less than, equal to or greater than the sum of transmit antennae N_t for the network node; the only restriction is that the receive antennae for the target UE must be less than the number of transmit antenna N_t.

B. Conventions and naming

The terminology used in this paper is as per conventional norms. Lowercase variables z, w, etc. refer to vectors, whereas uppercase variables V, W are complex matrices. $\mathfrak{M}_{a\ x\ b}$ is the set of matrices with a rows and b columns, $a < b$ having a eigen-values. If w is a vector, w^* refers to its conjugate form, i.e., each element is replaced by its conjugate and w^T is its transpose. If X is a matrix, $X_{a,b}$ refers to the element in its ath row and bth column, X^* is its complex adjoint (Hermitian) form and $\|X\|_P$ refers to the Frobenius Norm $\|X\|_P = \sum_{i,j} X_{i,j} X^*_{i,j}$. The vector norm is the square norm $\|w\| = \langle w, w^* \rangle$, unless otherwise specified. A matrix may be partitioned columnwise into two matrices, in which case it is designated as $W = [W_i\ W_j]$.

C. Realization at each transmitter

In this section, we discuss the implementation at each network node. We consider a single OFDM network node, with N_t transmit antennae with several UEs in its immediate range. As mentioned above, at each time interval, each node receives channel state information implicitly (through uplink reference signals in TDD mode) or explicitly (feedback on a shared PUSCH in FDD mode). One of the UEs is selected as the target for transmitting data to by a centralized scheduler (which makes this selection for each network node jointly). The network node then uses the CSI of the other UEs to code the transmission in such a way so as to minimize interference for all the others. In our problem, the ith UE has an antenna count of $N_i < N_t$. We designate the number of antenna available to the target UE as N_r and the total number of antennae for all the other UEs as $N_u = \sum_i N_i - N_r$. The channel matrix between the network node and the ith UE is given as $H_i \in \mathfrak{M}_{N_i\ x\ N_t}$.

Each channel matrix H_i has a singular value decomposition $\mathbb{U}_i \Sigma_i \mathbb{V}_i^*$, where $\mathbb{U}_i, \mathbb{V}_i$ are orthonormal column matrices and Σ_i is a diagonal matrix. Since H_i is a matrix with more rows than columns, the SVD actually looks like

$$H_i = \mathbb{U}_i \begin{bmatrix} \Sigma_i & 0 \end{bmatrix} \begin{bmatrix} V_i & \tilde{V}_i \end{bmatrix}^* \tag{1}$$

D. Structure of the precoding matrix

The transmitting network node uses a precoding matrix of the form

$$\begin{aligned} \Phi F &= \begin{bmatrix} V_r & W \end{bmatrix} \begin{bmatrix} I & -D \\ 0 & I \end{bmatrix} \\ &= \begin{bmatrix} V_r & W - V_r D \end{bmatrix} \end{aligned} \tag{2}$$

Φ is a diagonal power loading matrix, which is used to scale the matrix F to meet the power constraint (see Section III-E). We note that V_r is the sub-matrix of $\mathbb{V}_i$ corresponding to the non-null eigenvalues. W is the 'null forming' matrix and is the key to interference minimization, as we shall show in Sub-Section III-F. The matrix D is given by $D = V_r^* W$; this is dictated by the target UE interference nulling requirement. The precoding matrix F is then applied on a transmit vector $\begin{bmatrix} z & \tilde{z} \end{bmatrix}^T$, where z is the vector

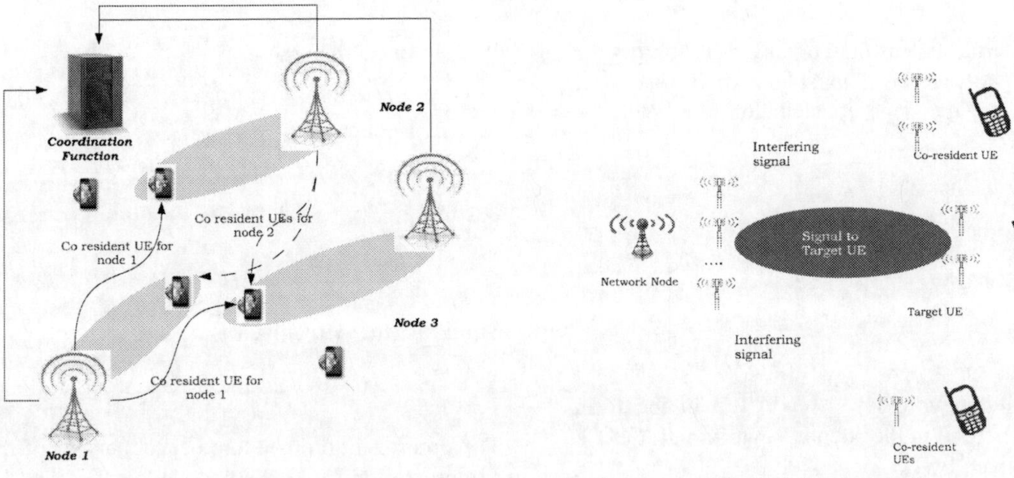

(a). ANF - deployment diagram (b). ANF: Single Node Case

Figure 1. ANF deployment in the network

of N_r symbols (post-modulation) to be transmitted to the target UE. The vector $\tilde{z}$ of size $N_t - N_r$ is also statistically independent and derived from z

We first show that the precoding matrix as shown in (2) will ensure that the signal received at the target UE is free of any effect of the precoding for the other UEs (specifically the interference minimization term W). The received vector on the target UE is given by (3). We ignore the power loading matrix Φ temporarily, since it only has an amplifying effect.

$$y_{tgt} = H_r F \begin{bmatrix} z & \tilde{z} \end{bmatrix}^T \tag{3}$$

$$= \mathbb{U}_r \begin{bmatrix} \Sigma_r & 0 \end{bmatrix} \begin{bmatrix} V_r^* \\ \tilde{V}_r^* \end{bmatrix} \begin{bmatrix} V_r & W \end{bmatrix} \begin{bmatrix} I & -D \\ 0 & I \end{bmatrix} \begin{bmatrix} z \\ \tilde{z} \end{bmatrix}$$

$$= \mathbb{U}_r \Sigma_r \begin{bmatrix} I & V_r^* W \end{bmatrix} [\begin{bmatrix} I & -D \\ 0 & I \end{bmatrix} \begin{bmatrix} z \\ \tilde{z} \end{bmatrix}$$

$$= \mathbb{U}_r \Sigma_r \begin{bmatrix} z & (V_r^* W - D) \tilde{z} \end{bmatrix} \tag{4}$$

By taking $D = V_r^* W$, we ensure that the signal received by the target UE is of the form $\mathbb{U}_i \Sigma_i z$, which can then be decoded using a standard MMSE equalizer [20]. We note that the vector $\tilde{z}$ has no impact on y_{tgt} whatsoever.

E. Obeying the power constraint

Given that the transmission vector $\begin{bmatrix} z & \tilde{z} \end{bmatrix}$ has a constant modulus, we have to designthe precoding matrix F given in (2) so as to obey the power constraint that $\mathrm{Tr}(FF^*) \leq P$. It is easy to see that the power term $\mathrm{Tr}(FF^*)$ can be written in a simplified form as in (5), using cyclic permutations

$$\mathrm{Tr}\left(\begin{bmatrix} V_r & W \end{bmatrix} \begin{bmatrix} I & -D \\ 0 & I \end{bmatrix} \begin{bmatrix} I & 0 \\ -D^* & I \end{bmatrix} \begin{bmatrix} V_r^* \\ W^* \end{bmatrix} \right)$$

$$= \mathrm{Tr}\left(\begin{bmatrix} V_r^* \\ W^* \end{bmatrix} \begin{bmatrix} V_r & W \end{bmatrix} \begin{bmatrix} I & -D \\ 0 & I \end{bmatrix} \begin{bmatrix} I & 0 \\ -D^* & I \end{bmatrix} \right)$$

$$= \mathrm{Tr}(I + W^* W - D^* D) \tag{5}$$

We note that since W and V_r are not square matrices $W^* W - D^* D$ do not automatically cancel out.

In order to achieve equality with a given overall power constraint P, it is normal to add a diagonal power loading matrix $\Phi = \begin{bmatrix} \vec{\phi_1} & \vec{\phi_2} \end{bmatrix}$ consisting of real amplification factors so that $\mathrm{Tr}(\Phi F F^* \Phi^*) = \mathrm{tr}(\Phi^2 F F^*) = P$. Taking the expression from (5) and putting it into the form above, we get

$$\mathrm{Tr}(\Phi^2 F F^*) = \mathrm{Tr}\left(\vec{\phi_1}^2 + \vec{\phi_2}^2 (W^* W - D^* D) \right) = P \tag{6}$$

Clearly, the Signal strength as seen by the target UE is a function of $\vec{\phi_1}^2$, whereas $P - \mathrm{Tr}\left(\vec{\phi_2}^2 (WW^* - DD^*) \right)$ is the power diverted for the purpose of ANF. We would like to choose W so as to bring $\vec{\phi_1}^2$ as high as possible. This in turn means minimizing $\mathrm{Tr}(W^* W - D^* D) = \| (I - V_c) W \|_{FP}$.

F. Interference minimization

We now consider the interference to the co-resident UEs due to the combined effect of V_r and W. The task of the transmitter is to choose W of size $N_t * N_u$, so as to minimize the energy as received by the co-resident UEs, with channel matrices H_i. Since the transmitter is power constrained, we have to limit the overall energy expended in transmission. Let the combined matrix corresponding to the individual channel responses for all the antennae on be given as

$$X = \begin{bmatrix} H_1 & H_2 & \ldots & H_{r-1} & H_{r+1} & \ldots \end{bmatrix}^T \tag{7}$$

where, as previously mentioned H_r is the channel matrix for the targetted UE. We note that X is a $N_u \; x \; N_t$ sized matrix.

The interference vector ιreceived by a co-resident UE with a $N_u x N_t$ channel matrix X is given by (8). We note that the choice of $\tilde{z}$ is not particularly important, other than meeting the constant modulus approach. Rather, it must be selected based on other criteria, such as maintaining PAPR across the transmission sequence. Hence, $\tilde{z}$ must be a known vector of symbols chosen from the same constellation as z, with the same statistical properties.

$$\begin{aligned}\iota(W) &= X\Phi\left[\begin{array}{cc} V_r & W - V_r D \end{array}\right]\left[\begin{array}{c} z \\ \tilde{z} \end{array}\right] \\ &= X\left[\begin{array}{cc} V & W - V_r D \end{array}\right]\left[\begin{array}{c} \vec{\phi_1} z \\ \vec{\phi_2}\tilde{z} \end{array}\right] \\ &= XV_r\vec{\phi_1}z + X\left(W - V_r D\right)\vec{\phi_2}\tilde{z} \qquad (8)\end{aligned}$$

We can expand and rewrite $W - V_r(V^*W)$ in the form of $(I - V_c)W$, where I is the identity matrix and V_c is a $N_t \; x \; N_t$ matrix given by

$$V_c[i,j] = \sum_k V_r[i,k]V_r[j,k]^* \qquad (9)$$

We substitute this back into (8) to get

$$\iota(W,\tilde{z}) = XV_r\vec{\phi_1}z + X\left(I - V_c\right)W\vec{\phi_2}\tilde{z} \qquad (10)$$

IV. Constrained Interference Minimization

Minimizing the interference directly can be written as minimizing $\|I(W)\|$ where I is given in (10) The most direct way to do this is to make $\|\iota(W)\|$ is 0. From (10), this leads to selecting W, ϕ such that $W = (I - V_c)^{-1}V_r$ and adjusting ϕ_1, ϕ_2 suitably. However, it can easily be seen that $(I - V_c)$ is ill-conditioned, having $N_t - N_r$ eigenvalues near zero, so it cannot be directly inverted. This may also be true for X and $X(I - V_c)$. Also, as noted in Section III-E, we have to balance the interference with power constraints as well.

In the simplest approach, we jointly minimize both $\iota(w) = \|I(W)\|_2$ as well as $\|F\|_P$. Φ can then be scaled so as to maximize the transmit power of entire transmission, subject to the power constraint given in (6).

We note that the expression for $\iota(w)$ is equivalent to minimizing the norm of the vector sum $XV_r z + X\left(I - V_c\right)W\tilde{z}$. In general, we can solve equations of this nature iteratively by doing a linear search around the existing gradient. Since z will change for every sub-carrier, we need to eliminate the dependence on it. Hence, we choose an orthogonal transformation $\tilde{z} = Mz$, where M is an orthonormal matrix. As is usual in convex optimization problems, we replace the constraint by a log-barrier function with a multiplier μ, which can be iteratively adjusted for each optimization step to ensure that the power bound is met.

$$\begin{aligned}\text{Minimize} \quad & \|XV_r + X\left(I - V_c\right)WM\| \\ \text{subject to} \quad & \|(I - V_c)W\|_{FP} \le P_m \\ \equiv \text{Minimize} \quad & \|XV_r + X\left(I - V_c\right)WM\| \\ - \quad & \mu \log\left(P_m - \|(I - V_c)W\|_{FP}\right) \qquad (11)\end{aligned}$$

The gradient of an expression of the nature $\|Y + H.W.M\|$ where Y, W, H, M are matrices of the appropriate dimensions can be computed by noting that

$$\frac{\partial \mathrm{Tr}\left[AX^*B\right]}{\partial X} = BA, \quad \frac{\partial \mathrm{Tr}\left[AXB\right]}{\partial X} = A^*B^*$$

We can expand Y as

$$\begin{aligned}\|Y \quad + \quad & HWM\| = \mathrm{Tr}\left(Y + HWM\right)\left(Y + HWM\right)^* \\ = \quad & \mathrm{Tr}(YY^*) + \mathrm{Tr}\left(Y(HWM)^*\right) \\ + \quad & \mathrm{Tr}\left(Y^*HWM\right) + \mathrm{Tr}\left(HWM(HWM)^*\right)\end{aligned}$$

Substituting, we get

$$\Rightarrow \frac{\partial\|Y + HWM\|}{\partial W} = 2H^*YM^* + 2H^*MM^*W^*H^*$$

Similarly, the derivative of the log-barrier term becomes

$$dW_2 = -\frac{\left(W^*(I - V_c)^*(I - V_c)\right)}{P_m - \|(I - V_c)W\|_{FP}}$$

The optimization procedure hence consists of the following steps. We start with the knowledge of X and V_r. For W we do the following steps

1) Start with $W = 0$, which is a feasible starting point.
2) Compute the corresponding matrix $D = V_r^*W$ and the interference vector $\iota(W)$
3) Compute the gradient matrix $dW = \frac{\partial|\iota(W)|}{\partial W} + \mu dW_2$
4) Find the maximal linear step size γ, such that $W \leftarrow W + \gamma dW$ improves the interference without violating the power constraint.
5) if $\gamma >$ minimum step size, go to 2, else terminate
6) Set ϕ accordingingly.

It is clear that the outcome of this operation depends on the relative orthogonality of X^*V_r. We define the normalized metric

$$\gamma = \frac{\mathrm{Tr}(X^*V_r)}{\mathrm{Tr}\left(X^*X\right)}$$

If $\gamma \longrightarrow 0$, the effectiveness of interference cancellation will correspondingly go up.

V. Network wide performance - theoretical analysis

We now consider the performance of the ANF in a network wide environment and present the simulation results.

We simulate a single network node transmitting to one target UE with 2 receive antennae $N_r = 2$. The transmitter has 4 antennae $N_t = 4$, with the remaining two antennae dedicated to ANF. The overall maximum power available to be diverted to the cause of ANF is an optimization variable η. Each co-resident UE is modelled as a single antenna receiver with statistically independent channel matrix, known to the network node. The output metric γ is the ratio of the interference energy received at the coresident UEs divided by the interference energy if there had been no ANF, i.e., $W = 0$.

$$\eta = \frac{P_m}{P_t} \qquad (12)$$

$$\gamma = \frac{\|\iota(W^{opt})\|}{\|\iota(0)\|} \qquad (13)$$

The results for $\eta = 2dB$ and $\eta = 3dB$ are given in Figure 2a and 2b, respectively. It can be seen that for a single coresident UE, 80% of the cases the interference suppression

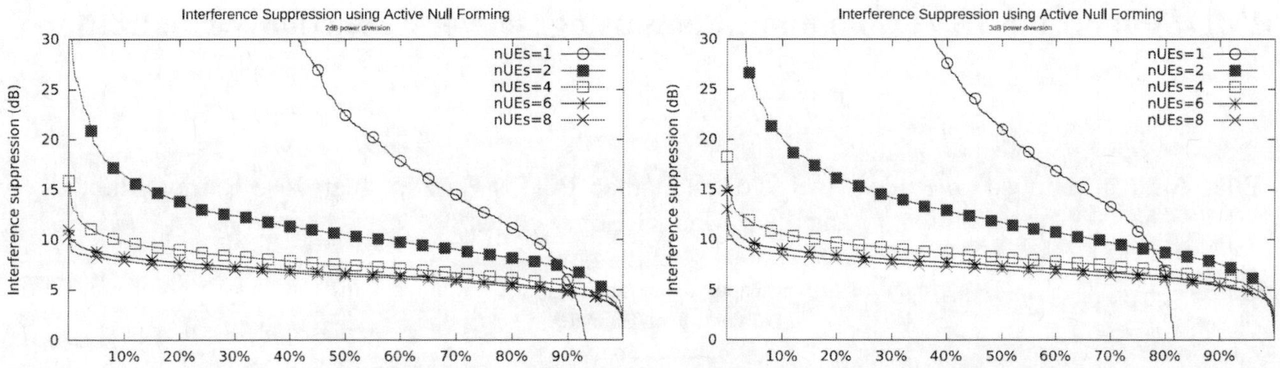

(a). Case 1: 2dB pwr diversion (b). Case 2: 3dB pwr diversion

Figure 2. Simulation Results

is better than 10dB and in the top 50% it is better than 20dB. The cases where a single coresident UE cannot be improved is where its channel matrix is very close that of the target UE As the number of UEs increase, the maximum improvement drops; however, as we can see, even in the case of 8 co-resident UEs, we get a 10dB interference suppression by diverting 2-3dB of power for the ANF purpose.

VI. Conclusion

In this paper, we have demonstrated a novel technique for utilization of multi-user and distributed antennae equipment in the network by directed interference cancellation. Our algorithm demonstrates large improvements in SINR and consequently resource utilization for 1,2 4 and 8 UEs. In the future, we shall explore more complicated network scenarios and feedback conditions

References

[1] Q. Spencer, C. Peel, A. Swindlehurst, and M. Haardt, "An introduction to the multi-user MIMO downlink," Communications Magazine, IEEE, vol. 42, no. 10, Oct 2004, pp. 60–67.

[2] A. Saha, "Active null forming," in Advanced Technology Conference 2015, Proceedings of the, October 2015.

[3] W. Yu and J. Cioffi, "Sum capacity of Gaussian vector broadcast channels," Information Theory, IEEE Transactions on, vol. 50, no. 9, Sept 2004, pp. 1875–1892.

[4] S. Zhou, T. Zhao, Z. Niu, and S. Zhou, "Software-defined hyper-cellular architecture for green and elastic wireless access," IEEE Communications Magazine, vol. 54, no. 1, Jan 2016, pp. 12–19.

[5] Y.-N. R. Li, J. Li, W. Li, Y. Xue, and H. Wu, "CoMP and interference coordination in heterogeneous network for lte-advanced," in Globecom Workshops (GC Wkshps), 2012 IEEE, Dec 2012, pp. 1107–1111.

[6] S. Sun, Q. Gao, Y. Peng, Y. Wang, and L. Song, "Interference management through CoMP in 3gpp lte-advanced networks," Wireless Communications, IEEE, vol. 20, no. 1, February 2013, pp. 59–66.

[7] W. Yu, D. Varodayan, and J. Cioffi, "Trellis and convolutional precoding for transmitter-based interference presubtraction," Communications, IEEE Transactions on, vol. 53, no. 7, July 2005, pp. 1220–1230.

[8] G. Caire and S. Shamai, "On the achievable throughput of a multiantenna Gaussian broadcast channel," Information Theory, IEEE Transactions on, vol. 49, no. 7, July 2003, pp. 1691–1706.

[9] Q. Spencer, A. Swindlehurst, and M. Haardt, "Zero-forcing methods for downlink spatial multiplexing in multiuser MIMO channels," Signal Processing, IEEE Transactions on, vol. 52, no. 2, Feb 2004, pp. 461–471.

[10] V. SStankovic and M. Haardt, "Generalized design of multi-user MIMO precoding matrices," Wireless Communications, IEEE Transactions on, vol. 7, no. 3, 2008, pp. 953–961.

[11] R. Zhang, "Cooperative multi-cell block diagonalization with per-base-station power constraints," Selected Areas of Communication, IEEE Journal on, vol. 28, no. 9, 2010, pp. 1435–1445.

[12] Z. Shen, R. Chen, J. Andrews, R. Heath, and B. Evans, "Sum capacity of multiuser MIMO broadcast channels with block diagonalization," Wireless Communications, IEEE Transactions on, June 2007.

[13] W. Yu, W. Rhee, S. Boyd, and J. Cioffi, "Iterative water-filling for Gaussian vector multiple access channels," Information Theory, IEEE Transactions on, vol. 50, no. 1, Jan 2004, pp. 145–152.

[14] S. Serbetli and A. Yener, "Transceiver optimization for multiuser MIMO systems," Signal Processing, IEEE Transactions on, vol. 52, no. 1, Jan 2004, pp. 214–226.

[15] S. Vishwanath, N. Jindal, and A. Goldsmith, "Duality, achievable rates, and sum-rate capacity of Gaussian MIMO broadcast channels," Information Theory, IEEE Transactions on, vol. 49, no. 10, Oct 2003, pp. 2658–2668.

[16] C. Ng and H. Huang, "Linear precoding in cooperative MIMO cellular networks with limited coordination clusters," Selected Areas in Communications, IEEE Journal on, vol. 28, no. 9, December 2010, pp. 1446–1454.

[17] A. Manolakos, Y. Noam, and A. Goldsmith, "Null space learning in cooperative MIMO cellular networks using interference feedback," Wireless Communications, IEEE Transactions on, vol. 14, no. 7, July 2015, pp. 3961–3977.

[18] W. Feng, Y. Li, S. Zhou, J. Wang, and M. Xia, "Downlink capacity of distributed antenna systems in a multi-cell environment," in Wireless Communications and Networking Conference, 2009. WCNC 2009. IEEE, April 2009, pp. 1–5.

[19] T. Yoo and A. Goldsmith, "On the optimality of multiantenna broadcast scheduling using zero-forcing beamforming," Selected Areas in Communications, IEEE Journal on, vol. 24, no. 3, March 2006, pp. 528–541.

[20] H. Sampath, P. Stoica, and A. Paulraj, "Generalized linear precoder and decoder design for MIMO channels using the weighted mmse criterion," Communications, IEEE Transactions on, vol. 49, no. 12, 2001, pp. 2198–2206.

MME Support for M2M Communications using Network Function Virtualization

Pilar Andres-Maldonado, Pablo Ameigeiras, Jonathan Prados-Garzon, Juan Jose Ramos-Munoz and Juan Manuel Lopez-Soler

Department of Signal Theory, Telematics, and Communications
University of Granada
Granada, Spain
Email: pam91@correo.ugr.es, {pameigeiras, jpg, jjramos, juanma}@ugr.es

***Abstract*—The use of massive Machine to Machine (M2M) communications on future mobile networks may lead to a signaling traffic explosion. Small Data Transmission (SDT) procedure appears as an efficient option for M2M small data transfer in Long Term Evolution (LTE). However, this procedure entails more processing load in the Mobility Management Entity (MME). Moreover, the fixed capacity in current LTE core hardware-based infrastructure can limit the scalability of this solution. To overcome this, we propose to: i) virtualize hardware dedicated MME (vMME) using Network Function Virtualization (NFV), ii) prioritize the vMME processing of Human to Human (H2H) signaling messages by means of priority queues, and iii) use the Differentiated Services Code Point (DSCP) field to identify priorities. The results show that, by increasing the number of NFV instances, the vMME capacity can be raised to manage the massive M2M SDT requests. Additionally, they show that the delay increase of H2H control plane procedures, caused by M2M communications, can be mitigated. Therefore, we conclude that our solution eases the deployment of massive M2M communications in future mobile networks.**

Keywords–NFV; 5G; LTE; Machine-to-Machine.

I. INTRODUCTION

The foreseen increase of Machine to Machine (M2M) communications brings a new signaling and data burden to mobile networks. In Long Term Evolution (LTE), the transmission of data from an idle User Equipment (UE) requires the use of the Service Request procedure to allocate UE's network resources. This procedure implies the download of the UE's context to the eNodeB (eNB) and bearer establishment. Unfortunately, most of M2M communications involve small and occasional data transmissions. This leads to numerous release and reallocation resource procedures which create an excessive increase of signaling load. In the present paper, we concentrate on massive and delay tolerant M2M communications that transmit infrequent and small data packets.

One efficient option to convey this type of data packets is Small Data Transmission (SDT), a dedicated procedure with an optimized sequence of LTE messages [1]. SDT uses the pre-established Non Access Stratum (NAS) security context to transfer one IP packet as NAS signaling without establishing Radio Resource Connection (RRC) security. At first, the UE and the eNB establish the RRC connection to send the small uplink data onto the initial NAS uplink message to the Mobility Management Entity (MME). Then, the MME uses the UE security context previously stored to authenticate and decrypt the message, and forms the GPRS Tunneling Protocol - User data (GTPU) packet with the information obtained, to send it to the Serving Gateway (S-GW), as shown in Figure 1.

The adoption of the SDT procedure to convey packet data transmissions from M2M communications would imply a massive increase of the signaling load processing. The Radio Access Network (RAN) will experiment a lack of radio resources due to the large number of simultaneous UEs trying to establish the RRC connection with the eNB [2]. In the core, where we focus on this paper, the MME's capacity will need to be increased to handle new functionalities imposed [1]. This, combined with the current high exposition of the MME to signaling in LTE [3], and the fixed capacity of current core LTE hardware-based infrastructure, can limit the scalability of the SDT solution.

To overcome this limitation, Network Function Virtualization (NFV) provides a novel framework to deploy network services onto virtualized servers. NFV benefits include, among others, reduced CAPEX and OPEX investments, openness of platforms, scalability and flexibility or shorter development cycles [4].

In this paper, we propose a new solution to mitigate the incurred signaling overload on the MME. The solution is composed of three points. The first point consists of replacing con-

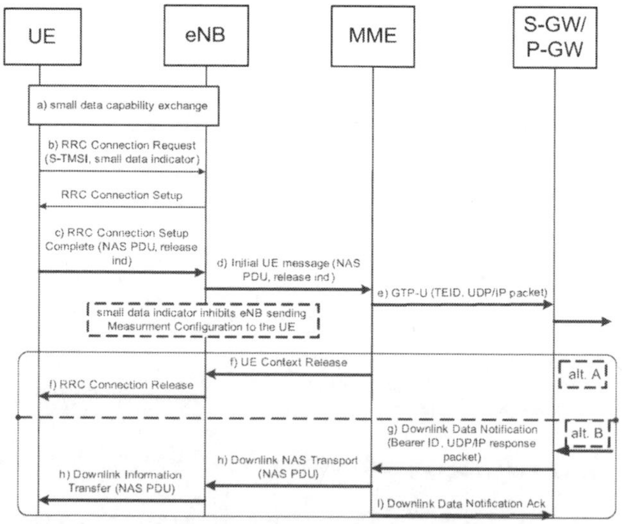

Figure 1. SDT procedure sequence [1].

ventional hardware dedicated MME entities by NFV instances, called virtualized MME (vMME). Our results show that, by increasing the number of NFV instances, the vMME capacity can be raised to manage the massive M2M SDT requests. However, our results also show that, as the signaling messages treatment of the vMME is equal for Human to Human (H2H) and M2M, the addition of more vMME NFV instances cannot always avoid the rise of the vMME response time for H2H procedures. The second point consists of prioritizing the vMME processing of H2H signaling messages over signaling messages of delay tolerant M2M communications by means of priority queues in the NFV instances. The third point consists of using the Differentiated Services Code Point (DSCP) classes to identify the priority of the signaling packets in the control plane. Our results show that the increase in delay experienced by H2H signaling traffic, when M2M communications are included, can be alleviated by adding priorities in the control plane, at the expense of decrease M2M signaling priority, which does not imply a critical penalty for the M2M delay tolerant applications considered here.

The paper is organized as follows. Section II presents the system model. Section III describes the proposed signaling management approach. In Section IV, we show the results of the simulations. Finally, Section V draws the main conclusions of the paper.

II. SYSTEM MODEL

We consider a LTE network, with a MME, which handles UEs control procedures requests. We assume two types of communications: H2H and M2M. The H2H UEs have sessions, which consist of activity periods separated by readings time periods. During activity periods, the H2H UE generates traffic, according to the UE's application running. For M2M communications, we consider low cost/low power consumption massive M2M communications, which we assume that send occasional and small data transmissions, and that are delay tolerant [5]. For simplicity, we consider only two types of M2M UEs: M2M high priority (HP) devices and M2M low priority (LP). This could be generalized for more types of M2M UE devices.

The H2H and M2M UEs data transmissions trigger control procedures in the network. Each control procedure involves several signaling messages between different control plane entities. From all control procedures of LTE, we focus on the ones which generate more signaling load on MME entities [6], see Table I. For each procedure and message, we model the processing tasks to be performed by the MME. We assume that M2M UEs small data transmissions are handled by SDT procedure, as shown in Figure 1. For simplicity, we focus on M2M uplink small data transmissions, since SDT procedure is similar in downlink transmissions. We assume H2H UEs move following a fluid-flow mobility model, while M2M UEs are stationary devices.

III. PROPOSAL

Our solution is composed by three main points, explained in the following subsections.

A. Virtualized MME

The first point of our proposal consists of replacing hardware dedicated MME entity by virtualized NFV instances of MME and scale the number of instances according to the MME load. Our solution is based on the 1:N architecture extracted from [7], represented in Figure 2. This mapping option is based on the web services paradigm and decomposes each LTE core entity into multiple elements, which combined form a virtual component pool. These elements are classified in three types: i) the *front end* (FE), which is responsible of the communication between entities, ii) a stateless virtual component (W), which implements the virtualized network functions, and iii) the *state database* (SDB), which stores all UE's session state and allows a stateless design. External entities will see the virtual component pool as a single node. This enables scale out/in of elements of the pool without impacting other nodes. However, synchronization issues appears due to the communication between the SDB and the different virtual elements inside the entity, which can be solved serializing the access to the SDB, or between different nodes of the core to perform the control procedure, which could increase processing delay [7].

TABLE I. CONSIDERED CONTROL PROCEDURES

Com. Type	Control procedure	MME pkts processed	Used to
H2H	UE Triggered Service request	3	Send new data from the idle UE to the network and the UE does not have available resources.
	eNB Triggered S1 Release	3	Release UE's resources due to its inactivity. UE's state changes from connected to idle.
	X2-Based Handover	2	Switch the bearers end point from the source to the target eNB due to UE's mobility.
M2M	SDT procedure	1	Send small data packets from the idle M2M UE to the network and the M2M UE does not have available resources.

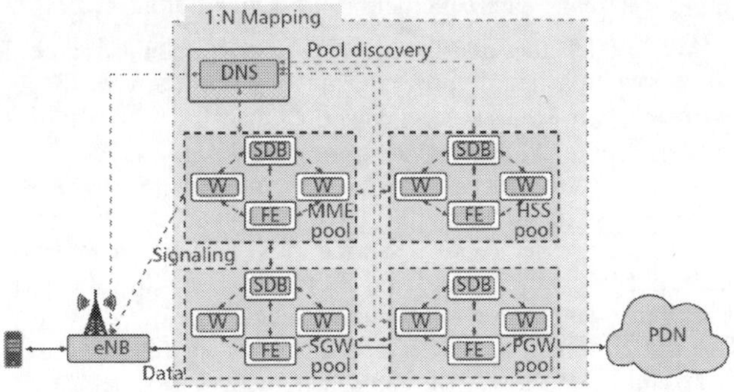

Figure 2. Architecture reference model for 1:N mapping [7].

We model the architecture of the virtualized MME as shown in Figure 3. This model is based on [8][9] and it is composed of the following entities:

- Arrival process of signaling messages: H2H or M2M devices which generate traffic that triggers control procedures requests in the network. The signaling messages needed to perform these procedures are processed by vMME NFV instances.
- Distributor: Acts as a load balancer between vMME NFV instances. It distributes signaling messages de-

pending on the average workload of each instance.

- Database: Shared database for vMME NFV instances which is accessed during each transaction. The database stores protocol and UE's state.
- vMME NFV instances: NFV instances which virtualize MME functionalities. We suppose that vMME NFV instances are identical. Each control procedure needs a different number of messages, which can involve other core entities not considered here to perform it. To improve NFV processing, the control procedures are splitted into request and response transactions. The protocol and UE's context is kept in the shared database. This allows the vMME NFV instances to retake the state of a procedure after the reception of a new signaling message and continue with it.
- Egress switch: Signaling messages output switch.

We model the distributor, the shared database and the egress switch as single processor queues, and the vMME NFV instances as a $M/G/m$ queueing systems.

We denote S the service time needed for each vMME NFV instance to process the signaling message. S is a random variable that depends on the transactions needed to process the message. The average service time for the messages of the procedures in Table I are extracted from [8]. For SDT procedure, we assume an average service time of $1.05 \cdot 10^{-4} s$. The shared database is accessed during each transaction with a probability p, as we consider every request processed by the MME will need an access to the shared database, $p = 1.0$.

Let us define the mean vMME response time $\overline{T}$ as the time required by the vMME to process a message and generate the corresponding reply. The mean vMME response time is composed of several factors: $\overline{T}_D$ denote the mean response time of the distributor node, $\overline{T}_{NFV}$ denote the mean response time of vMME NFV instances, $\overline{T}_{DB}$ denote the processing time of the shared database and $\overline{T}_{OS}$ denote the egress switch node processing time. So, $\overline{T}$ can be calculated as

$$\overline{T} = \overline{T}_D + \overline{T}_{NFV} + \overline{T}_{DB} + \overline{T}_{OS} \quad (1)$$

In order to scale the capacity of the vMME according to the load it has to process, we assume that the number of vMME NFV instances m, used as a dimensioning criterion in our results, is selected as expressed in (2), where $\overline{T}_{max}$ represents the maximum permitted mean vMME response time

$$m = \min\{M : \overline{T} \leq \overline{T}_{max}, M \in \mathbb{N}\} \quad (2)$$

An increase of signaling load on the MME caused by M2M traffic is to be compensated with an increase number of vMME NFV instances. However, $\overline{T}$ is equal for H2H and M2M, which implies that in certain situations, the addition of more vMME NFV instances cannot avoid the rise of $\overline{T}$ compared to scenarios without M2M traffic involved.

B. Priority Queue Discipline

We propose to prioritize H2H signaling messages over M2M signaling messages. The goal is mitigating the rise of the mean vMME response time suffered by H2H procedures due to the signaling overload generated by massive M2M communications. For this purpose, we propose to organize the signaling messages received by the vMME through non-preemptive priority queues inside vMME NFV instances. Messages belonging to same priority obey the first-come first-served discipline. Then, signaling messages with higher priority are served in the vMME NFV instance before others with low priority. The corresponding vMME model is represented in Figure 4.

C. Priority Management

In LTE, signaling messages between a UE and a MME are secured with NAS security context. To transfer these signaling messages over the radio interface, the RRC protocol is used between the UE and the eNB. When a UE wants to send a NAS signaling message to the MME, the message is delivered to the eNB as included in a RRC signaling message. Then, the eNB sends the NAS signaling message contained in a S1AP signaling message to the MME. Figure 5 shows the control plane protocol stacks for mentioned LTE entities. As the eNB cannot know the content of a NAS message, which holds useful information to sort signaling messages sent to the MME, we propose to use RRC Establishment cause in the eNB to discern signaling messages priorities.

Current signaling traffic over eNB-MME interface is marked as high strict priority [11]. Therefore, it is mapped to the Expedited Forwarding (EF) class in the DSCP field of the IP packet transporting the signaling message. As all signaling traffic is marked equally, the vMME cannot apply prioritized queuing of the signaling messages before being processed by the vMME NFV instances. We propose to use the DSCP field of the IP packet transporting the signaling message to discern

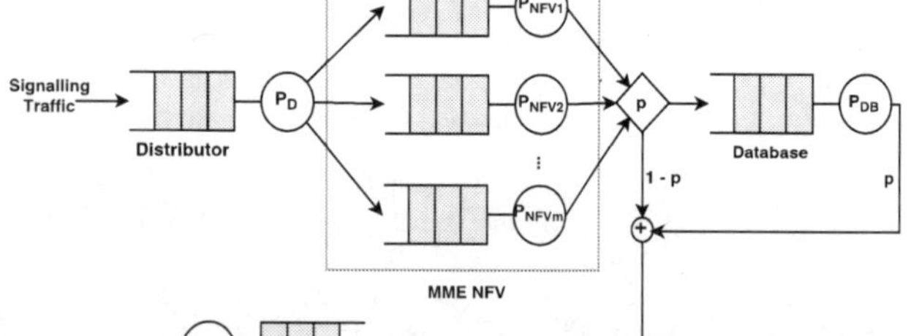

Figure 3. Virtualized MME model [8].

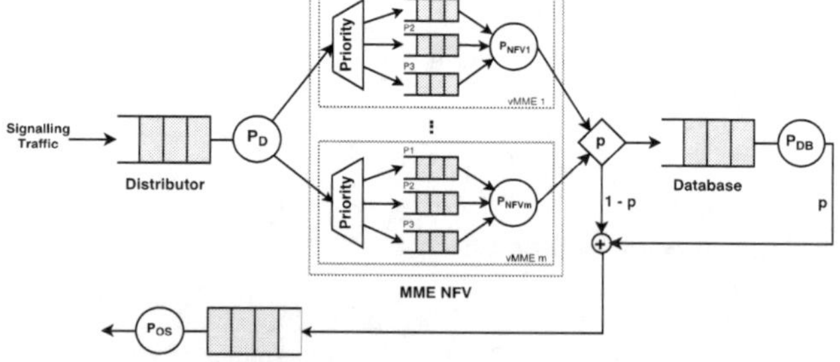

Figure 4. Proposed vMME system model.

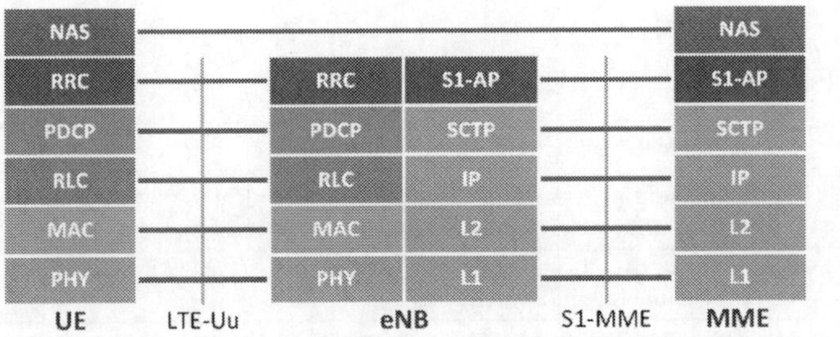

Figure 5. LTE control plane protocol stacks [10].

signaling traffic from different types of communications. This IP header field is easier to analyze by FE elements due to it is not required a deep packet inspection. By adding priorities to the signaling traffic, the vMME distributor can schedule the control messages taking into account their priority. The DSCP classes used in this paper are summarized in Table II.

Since the eNB is responsible for uplink packet marking, the eNB will mark the IP datagram of the signaling messages according to the UE's RRC Establishment cause. Specially for M2M communications, which use SDT procedure, the RRC Establishment cause reported by the M2M UE when the RRC connection is established in the SDT procedure will be analyzed by the eNB to determine the DSCP class for the M2M UE SDT signaling. For this, it will take advantage of the possible values "small data" or "low priority small data", as described in [1]. Other possible RRC Establishment cause value to differentiate priorities in the signaling messages can be "delay tolerant access", introduced within the release 10 version of the 3GPP specifications [12], and currently used if the UE has been configured for "low priority NAS signalling".

IV. Evaluation

In this section, we evaluate the impact of using the SDT procedure on the vMME mean response time. As authors of [8], we generate procedure requests using NS-3 simulator [13]. The queue model presented in Section III is simulated using the Matlab Simulink framework.

A. Experiment Setup

We evaluate three scenarios:

- Scenario 1: M2M data traffic is not conveyed by the SDT procedure. The vMME processes signaling messages generated only by H2H UEs.
- Scenario 2: M2M data traffic is conveyed by the SDT procedure with no priorities. The vMME processes signaling messages generated by H2H UEs and by M2M UEs.
- Scenario 3: Similar to Scenario 2 but with priorities. The vMME applies the prioritization scheme presented in Section III.

TABLE II. PRIORITY TREATMENT

Type of signaling traffic	RRC Establishment Cause	DSCP class	Priority
H2H	Mo-signaling	EF	1
M2M HP devices	Small data	AF41	2
M2M LP devices	Low priority small data	AF31	3

1) H2H traffic models: H2H communications use three possible applications along their sessions: web browsing [14], HTTP progressive video [15] and video calling [16]. At the beginning of the session, one of these applications is selected. Web browsing application download time of a session depends on the web page size, the link data rate, and the time needed for the web browser to parse the embedded objects of the web page. HTTP progressive video application follows the Youtube traffic model, in which the download rate ranges from a initial period of high downloading rate, to a constant limited rate after this initial period. The number of downloaded video clips per session is set to follow a geometric distribution [17]. Video calling application generates a constant bit rate traffic at 1.5 Mbps during the activity period duration.

2) M2M traffic models: The M2M HP devices follow a traffic model extracted from [18], which is modeled as a Markov Modulated Poisson Process, but without taking into consideration the coordinated behavior for M2M devices. The M2M LP devices follow a traffic model based on [19], which sends infrequent report transmissions.

Scenarios 2 and 3 have three M2M devices per each H2H UE. We assume $\overline{T}_{max} = 3\ ms$. The main vMME characteristics, and details of the traffic models shown in Table III, are extracted from [8].

B. Experimental Results

To show the impact of the inclusion of M2M communications, Figure 6 depicts the mean vMME response time versus the number of H2H UEs for Scenarios 1 and 2. According to Figure 6, the mean vMME response time increases exponentially with the number of H2H UEs. When $\overline{T} = \overline{T}_{max}$, a new vMME NFV instance is added to the system, represented as a new curve. The results for Scenario 2 show that, by increasing m, the vMME's capacity rises to manage the massive M2M SDT requests. However, as $\overline{T}$ is equal for H2H and M2M UEs, there are some ranges where the addition of more vMME NFV instances cannot avoid the rise of $\overline{T}$ compared to Scenario 1 in which the M2M traffic is not involved.

Figure 7 depicts the mean vMME response time versus the number of H2H UEs for Scenarios 1 and 3. For almost the entire considered range of the number of H2H UEs, the mean vMME response time of H2H signaling messages in Scenario 3 is lower than in Scenario 1. That is, for almost the entire considered range of the number of H2H UEs, the proposed prioritized treatment of the signaling messages manages to prevent the increase of the mean vMME response time in H2H signaling traffic caused by the processing of the M2M traffic. Furthermore, this prioritized treatment allows H2H UEs and M2M HP devices signaling traffic to reduce their exponential signaling delay growth, at the expense of increase M2M LP devices signaling traffic delay, which reach a mean value of 9.65 ms. For delay tolerant M2M applications, this assumed increase of the mean vMME response time for M2M LP devices signaling traffic does not imply a critical penalty.

V. Conclusion and Future Work

In this paper we propose a new approach to handle the foreseen increase of signaling traffic in MME entities due to massive M2M communications deployment, with no

TABLE III. TRAFFIC MODELS CHARACTERIZATION

Com. Type	Traffic Type	Parameters	Statistical Characterization
H2H ($IAST$ = 1200 s [20])	Web browsing (HTTP) $P_{app} = 0.74$	Main Object Size	Truncated Lognormal Distribution: μ=15.098 σ=4.390E-5 min=100Bytes max=6MBytes
		Embedded Object Size	Truncated Lognormal Distribution: μ=6.17 σ=2.36 min=50Bytes max=2MBytes
		Number of Embedded Objects per Page	Truncated Pareto Distribution: mean=22 shape=1.1
		Parsing Time	Exponential Distribution: mean=0.13seconds
		Reading Time	Exponential Distribution: mean=30seconds
		Number of pageviews per session	Geometric Distribution: p=0.893 mean=9.312
	HTTP progressive video $P_{app} = 0.03$	Video Encoding Rate	Uniform distribution with ranges: (2.5, 3.0)Mbps / (4.0,4.5)Mbps / (12.5, 16.0)Mbps / (20.0, 25.0)Mbps, for equiprobable itags: 137 / 264 / 266 / 315 respectively.
		Video Duration	Distribution extracted from [15]
		Reading Time	Exponential Distribution: mean=30seconds
		Number of videoviews per session	Geometric Distribution: p=0.6 mean=2.5
	Video calling $P_{app} = 0.23$	Call Holding Time	Pareto Distribution: k=-0.39 s=69.33 m=0
		Number of calls per session	Constant = 1
M2M	M2M HP	Discretization time interval	Δ_T = 1 sec
		Markov chain state transition matrix	$P = \begin{pmatrix} 1-p & q \\ p & 1-q \end{pmatrix}$ where $p = 6.75 \times 10^{-5}$ and $q = 1.47 \times 10^{-4}$
		Markov chain state rates	λ_1 = 0.0015 packets/s; λ_2 = 0.065 packets/s
		Packet Size	100 b
	M2M LP	Mean arrival rate	Poisson Distribution: λ = 0.0167 packets/s
		Packet Size	8 b

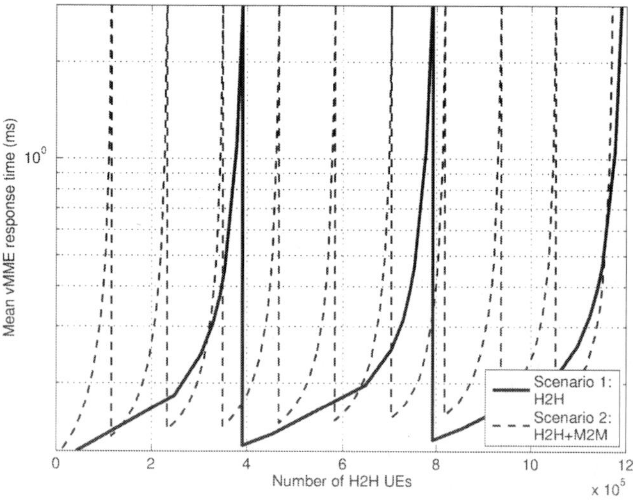

Figure 6. vMME response time in Scenarios 1 and 2 (three M2M devices per each H2H UE).

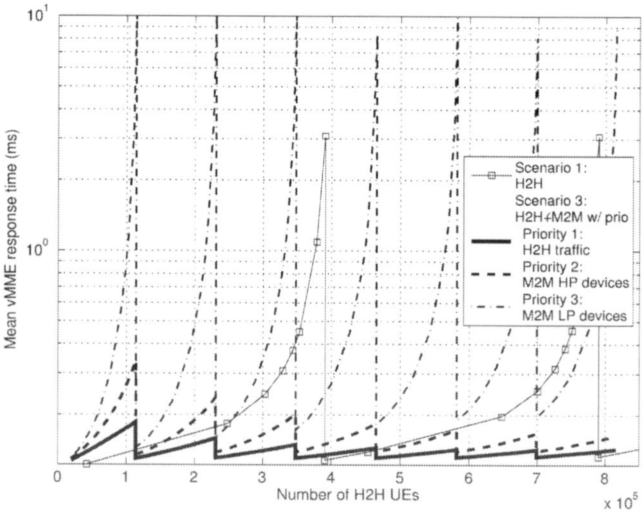

Figure 7. vMME response time in Scenarios 1 and 3 (three M2M devices per each H2H UE).

significant penalty in H2H. Particularly, we propose to replace conventional hardware dedicated MME entities by NFV (vMME) instances, as well as to prioritize the control plane signaling traffic with different DSCP classes. The reported results have shown that giving priority to H2H traffic can mitigate the increase in delay experienced by H2H signaling traffic in H2H and M2M scenarios when delay tolerant M2M communications are included. Therefore, we can conclude that the proposed solution facilitates the massive deployment of M2M communications in future mobile networks.

For the future work, we intend to incorporate further LTE entities to the model. Apart from that, it could be interesting to analyze priorities with bound queues, or possible NFV overheads in the vMME instances proposed.

Acknowledgment

This work is partially supported by the Spanish Ministry of Economy and Competitiveness and the European Regional Development Fund (project TIN2013-46223-P), and the Spanish Ministry of Education, Culture and Sport (FPU grant 13/04833).

References

[1] Study on Machine-Type Communications (MTC) and other mobile data applications communications enhancements, 3GPP TR 23.887 Rel 12 v12.0.0, 2013.

[2] P. Andres-Maldonado, P. Ameigeiras, J. Prados-Garzon, J. J. Ramos-Munoz, and J. M. Lopez-Soler, "Reduced M2M Signaling Communications in 3GPP LTE and Future 5G Cellular Networks," Wireless Days Conference (WD), March 2016.

[3] Nokia Siemens Networks, "Signaling is growing 50% faster than data traffic," White Paper, 2012, URL: http://networks.nokia.com/system/files%20/document/signaling_whitepaper_online_version_final.pdf [Retrieved: 2016-04-04].

[4] ETSI, "Network Function Virtualization: An Introduction, Benefits, Enablers, Challenges, & Call for Action," 2012, URL: portal.etsi.org/NFV/NFV_White_Paper.pdf [Retrieved: 2016-04-04].

[5] Service requirements for Machine-Type Communications (MTC), 3GPP TS 22.368 Rel 13 v13.1.0, 2014.

[6] Alcatel-Lucent, "Managing the signaling traffic in packet core," Application note, 2012, URL: http://resources.alcatel-lucent.com/asset/155160 [Retrieved: 2016-04-04].

[7] T. Taleb et al., "EASE: EPC as a service to ease mobile core network deployment over cloud," Network, IEEE, vol. 29, no. 2, 2015, pp. 78–88.

[8] J. Prados-Garzon, J. J. Ramos-Munoz, P. Ameigeiras, P. Andres-Maldonado, and J. M. Lopez-Soler, "Latency Evaluation of a Virtualized MME," Wireless Days Conference (WD), March 2016.

[9] J. Vilaplana et al., "A queuing theory model for cloud computing," The Journal of Supercomputing, vol. 69, no. 1, July 2014, pp. 492–507.

[10] NMC Consulting Group, "LTE Network Architecture: Basic," Netmanias Technical Document, July 2013, URL: http://www.netmanias.com/en/post/techdocs/5904/architecture-lte/lte-network-architecture-basic [Retrieved: 2016-04-04].

[11] E. M. Metsala and J. Salmelin, Eds., LTE Backhaul: Planning and Optimization. Wiley, 2015.

[12] Evolved Universal Terrestrial Radio Access (E-UTRA); Radio Resource Control (RRC); Protocol specification, 3GPP TS 36.331 Rel 12, 2015.

[13] G. Riley and T. Henderson, The ns-3 Network Simulator. Springer Berlin Heidelberg, 2010, pp. 15–34.

[14] NGMN, "NGMN Radio Access Performance Evaluation Methodology," NGMN Alliance, Tech. Rep., 2008.

[15] P. Ameigeiras, J. J. Ramos-Munoz, J. Navarro-Ortiz, and J. M. Lopez-Soler, "Analysis and modelling of youtube traffic," Transactions on Emerging Telecommunications Technologies, vol. 23, June 2012, pp. 360–377.

[16] T. D. Dang, B. Sonkoly, and S. Molnar, "Fractal analysis and modeling of voip traffic," in 11th International Telecommunications Network Strategy and Planning Symposium. NETWORKS 2004. IEEE, June 2004, pp. 123–130.

[17] P. Gill, M. Arlitt, Z. Li, and A. Mahanti, "Characterizing user sessions on Youtube," SPIE 6818, IEEE Multimedia Computing and Networking, vol. 6818.

[18] C. Anton-Haro and M. Dohler, Machine-to-Machine (M2M) Communications: Architecture, Performance and Applications. Woodhead Publishing, 2015.

[19] Machine-to-Machine (M2M) Evaluation Methodology Document (EMD), IEEE 802.16p-11/0014, May 2011.

[20] I. Tsompanidis, A. H. Zahran, and C. J. Sreenan, "Mobile network traffic: a user behaviour model," in 7th IFIP Wireless and Mobile Networking Conference (WMNC). IEEE, May 2014, pp. 1–8.

AUTHOR INDEX